COLUMBIA COLLEGE

3 2711 00027 2828

C0-DKN-136

JUL 15 2005

ANDRZEJ PANUFNIK'S MUSIC AND ITS RECEPTION

Acta Musicologica Universitatis Cracoviensis

XI

COLUMBIA COLLEGE LIBRARY
600 S. MICHIGAN AVENUE
CHICAGO, IL 60605

STUDIES EDITED BY
JADWIGA PAJA-STACH

ANDRZEJ PANUFNIK'S MUSIC
AND ITS RECEPTION

MUSICA IAGELLONICA
KRAKÓW 2003

Cover design
Alina Mokrzycka-Juruś

Text by Polish authors translated by
Beata Bolesławska with John Allison, Anna Kaspszyk, Anna Piotrowska, Christine Rickards-Rostworowska, Zbigniew Skowron, Cara Thornton

English tranlation by Polish authors revised by
Camilla Panufnik

Publikacja ukazała się dzięki dofinansowaniu Komitetu Badań Naukowych
Publication donated by State Committee for Scientific Research

© Copyright 2003 by Musica Iagellonica and the Authors

ISBN 83-7099-124-6

Musica Iagellonica
ul. Westerplatte 10
31-033 Kraków, Poland

We invite you to visit
our Internet bookstore
at http://en.mi.pl

Contents

Part III. Reception of the Composer's Work

Preface

The main artistic idea of Andrzej Panufnik—to achieve balance in a musical work between emotional wealth and intellectual content—accompanied him along his entire artistic path. While the composer's sound system crystallized only at the end of the 1960's, the seeds of this system, and his tendency to compose a clear form, can already be observed at the beginning of this path. The drawing of stylistic elements from the music of other composers, natural in the early period of artistic work, resulting from a fascination with the music of the masters and from learning the compositional craft, co-existed in the poetic language of Andrzej Panufnik's music with a search for new principles for the relationship between sounds, which would provide a work with a unique musical logic, but at the same time not remain a purely intellectual speculation in the world of sound. His soon-crystallized awareness of his artistic goal, and consistency in work on his individual sound system, permitted Andrzej Panufnik to compose music which, via sound structures shaped with the precision of an architect, expresses a broad spectrum of emotions and moods: lyricism and drama, joy and sadness, states of contemplation and uninhibited spontaneity.

We do not know many of the works from the youthful period of Andrzej Panufnik's *oeuvre*. All went up in flames or disappeared during the Warsaw Uprising in 1944. The composer reconstructed only three works after the war: *Piano Trio*, from 1934 (reconstruction 1945, revised version 1977), *Five Folk Songs* from 1940 (reconstruction, entitled *Five Polish Peasant Songs* 1945, revised version 1959) and the *Tragic Overture* from 1942 (reconstruction 1945, revised version 1955). In the *Trio*, one can discern influences of Ravel; and in the *Overture*, of a Romantic formal character. However, in both of these works, the seeds of Panufnik's individual style are already budding. These are manifested in a predilection for selected harmonic expressions; and in the *Overture*, also in a tendency to tie an entire work together with a common tone cell.

In the works composed at the end of the 1940's, we notice a combination of selected stylistic characteristics of Romantic and Neo-classical music with Panufnik's original compositional technique. Echoes of Chopin in the piano work *Circle of Fifths* (1947)[1], and classical formal models (sonata allegro, rondo, variations) in the *Sinfonia Rustica* (1948), co-exist with a symmetry of tone structure characteristic of the composer's mature legacy.

The end of the 1940's and beginning of the 1950's brought hard times for Polish culture. During that time, intensified control of socialist-realist ideology over science, literature and all forms of art inhibited the development of individual creative thought. The political authorities, usurping the right to direct citizens' style of life and thought, enforced obligatory canons of art—which was to be understandable to the masses and, at the same time, proclaim socialist ideas. In the music field, the artistic work promoted was that which was based on extremely simple compositional means, and whose subject matter was associated with life in a socialist country. Thus, financial support—as well as the opportunity to publish and perform their works—was obtained by artists whose music met the expectations of authorities not having any discernment either of contemporary trends in music, or of the values contained in the works of distinguished artists. The political pressure placed on the music community caused the concert repertoire of the time to be filled mainly with so-called 'songs of the masses' and cantatas whose texts were associated with the ideological program in force; and the sound plane was based on the basic functions of the major-minor system, march or waltz rhythms, and melodic expressions patterned on popular music, or else on Polish folk songs. Such a situation gave small-time composers a chance at popularity and success, while depriving composers having ambitions to express themselves in an original, novel musical language of the opportunity to develop an artistic career. In conditions of terror—well-known to those who lived during that time in the socialist-bloc countries, but difficult to imagine for those who have not experienced life in a totalitarian system—many composers gave in to political pressure and wrote works stylistically consistent with the postulates of socialist realism. To escape from

---

[1] Work published later in Great Britain, by Boosey & Hawkes, entitled *Twelve Miniature Studies*.

politically-active artistic work, they wrote pedagogical pieces, or compositions based on Polish early music, which also gained the authorities' approval.

The times of socialist realism cast their shadow on Andrzej Panufnik as well. Though he was a privileged figure in the music community by virtue of his position as conductor of the Kraków (1945/46) and Warsaw (1946/47) Philharmonics—as well as vice-president of the Polish Composers' Union (1948–54)[2]—as a composer, he enjoyed no greater freedom than others. At that time, he did not write much. He arranged early works, and his attempt to compose a work in simplified style—such as, for example, the *Peace Symphony* (1951)—satisfied neither the decision-makers, nor the composer himself, who as a result deleted the piece from the list of his works.[3] The tendency toward enslavement of minds in Poland, unbearable for an artist, dictated to him the thought of emigration.[4]

Panufnik left Poland in 1954 and settled in Great Britain. His illegal departure from the country was understood as an act of political enmity, which meant that the state authorities ordered Panufnik to be deleted from Polish culture via a ban on publication and performance of his works, as well as writing about the composer. Sometimes it was possible to get around the ban and present one of his works at a concert, but these were sporadic cases. Practically, for music-lovers and musicians in the country, Panufnik's art did not exist. The situation changed little after 1977, when the Polish Composers' Union caused the ban on performance of the composer's works to be repealed. Twenty-odd some years of absence from Polish culture had just this effect. The real return of Andrzej Panufnik's music to concert halls in Poland dates only from the political turning-point in 1989. At the Warsaw Autumn International Festival of Contemporary Music in 1990, performances of 11 of the composer's works were prepared—several of them conducted by the composer himself, who after 36 years abroad had visited his home town. Also contributing to the popularization of his works in the country are the Days of Music of Andrzej Panufnik, as well as the Composition

---

[2] Andrzej Panufnik left the Board of the Polish Composers' Union, at his own request, for the period from January to September 1951.

[3] Panufnik prepared a new version of the symphony in 1957—without the vocal-instrumental 3rd movement (to words by Jarosław Iwaszkiewicz)—giving it the title *Sinfonia elegiaca*.

[4] Cf. composer's autobiography *Composing Myself* (London: Methuen, 1987), Polish edition entitled *Panufnik o sobie*, transl. by Marta Glińska (Warszawa: NOWA, 1990).

Competition named after him (international since 2001), which has
been taking place in Kraków since 1999.

Panufnik's artistic career in Great Britain stumbled initially upon
various obstacles. The first years of the composer's life in exile did
not favor the development of his compositional craft. The stress
associated with leaving his home country, the attempt to find his
place in a new environment, a family crisis and the normal difficulties
of life inhibited his artistic development. His work as music director
and conductor of the City of Birmingham Symphony Orchestra
(1957/58 and 1958/59) turned out to be very absorbing and distracting
from composition. Thus, Panufnik decided to give up all jobs that
would take him away from writing music. His compositional style,
however, was not accepted or appreciated in London's avant-garde
music circles, because he did not present compositional techniques
fashionable at that time.

The works composed in exile, from the *Rhapsody* for orchestra
(1956) to the *Katyń Epitaph* (1967), display the further development
of the composer's main musical ideas, known from his earlier works.
Panufnik concentrated on perfecting his own compositional craft,
remaining independent from the novel musical trends of the 20th
century. Dodecaphony and serialism, he had already rejected during
his studies in Vienna, when he became acquainted in detail with the
scores of Schoenberg, Berg and Webern. He also did not assimilate
later, avant-garde compositional techniques associated with electronic
music, open form, collage or any type of musical experiments into
his musical style. In his works, he still utilized traditional instruments in
a manner consonant with their natural sound, developed his harmonic
language, invented rhythmic models governing the principles of time
organization, presented symmetrical structures of pitch and instrumental color, striving to create a work orderly in its every aspect.

The *Autumn Music* for orchestra, a work from 1962 (2nd version
from 1965), possesses an enchantingly ingenious and at the same time
clear construction. Panufnik's beloved symmetry found application in
the scoring, in the formation of microstructures and in the general
architectonic plan of the work. Precisely-ordered tone structures served
the composer here in creating the dramatic and lyrical expression of
the work. The *Sinfonia sacra* from 1963—one of Panufnik's most
popular works—also is characterized by precise rules of construction,
which remain here at the service of a rich, spirited musical action.

From 1968 onwards, there follows, on the one hand, a continuation
of formal principles known from earlier works—such as, for example,
tone-cell manipulation and utilization of the principle of symmetry; and

on the other hand, new ways of organizing pitch and rhythm appear, as well as new architectonic plans of works. An essential change in the character of Panufnik's music took place by virtue of utilizing the tone cell F-B-E, as well as inversions and transpositions thereof. In so doing, Panufnik's works became dominated by tritone-fourth, fourth-minor second and minor second-tritone sounds. The F-B-E cell, in becoming the basis for organization of horizontal and vertical structures, changed the composer's sound system in a decisive manner.

The first works written in this system were *Reflections* for piano (1968) and the cantata *Universal Prayer* for solo voices, choir, 3 harps and organ (1969). Rigorous utilization of this system, in combination with the principle of tone structure symmetry known from earlier works, resulted in works of unusually plastic architecture and precise construction, in which the occurrence of each pitch finds its logical justification. In Panufnik's compositions, he developed his system, introducing other 3-tone cells as well: minor third-major second, diminished triad and augmented triad. An example of a work in which all of these cells found application is *String Quartet no. 1* (1976, 2nd version 1977). Further metamorphoses of the system consisted of including in it other scales (e.g. pentatonic), or elements of the tonal system. Always, however, the structural foundation remained the cell F-B-E and its metamorphoses. This cell also permeates the sound fabric of the composer's last works—*Symphony no. 10* (1988, 2nd version 1990) and the 'Cello Concerto (1991).

The pitch system is not the only strictly-ordered aspect of Panufnik's compositions. He also invented a set of rules concerning rhythm. He manipulated rhythmic models, repeated and subjected to various transformations; he used, among others, retrograde and additive rhythms. His vision for the form of an entire work also took on regular shapes; it was patterned predominantly on geometrical figures. Famous examples of such forms are the spiral in the *Metasinfonia* for organ, tympani and strings (1978), and the triangle in *Triangles* for 3 flutes and 3 'cellos (1972). The form of a work is emphasized by appropriate scoring, articulation, tempo and dynamic markings, and though it is not possible to recognize the entire subtle organization of pitch and rhythm through hearing alone, without doubt each of the composer's works reveals itself to us, already upon the first hearing, as a coherent whole of clear, ordered construction.

The music of Andrzej Panufnik, despite its undeniable values and recognition in the world, has not found, thus far, synthetic, holistic discussion in the academic literature. The works devoted to it have been mainly popular or otherwise aimed at a general audience. Among books published before 2001, there are two items of particular value: Bernard Jacobson's *Polish Renaissance*[5] and Tadeusz Kaczyński's *Andrzej Panufnik i jego muzyka*.[6] Jacobson devoted his book not only to Panufnik, but also to Lutosławski, Penderecki and Górecki, showing silhouettes of the most distinguished Polish composers of two generations against the background of historic events. Kaczyński drew his portrait of Panufnik as a composer and conductor, a person co-creating the world of music and at the same time entangled in the world of politics, an artist appreciated in musical circles and, at the same time, a person struggling with everyday difficulties. He showed the composer's life and art, including his own studies, as well as an interview with the composer and statements by Nigel Osborne and Jan Krenz.

Academic publications include Krzysztof Stasiak's doctoral dissertation,[7] as well as a few articles devoted to selected works by the composer.[8] The significance of Stasiak's dissertation cannot be overestimated. The author has thoroughly analyzed (for the first time in the world literature) the pitch organization, as well as rhythmic procedures in Panufnik's instrumental and vocal-instrumental works composed up to the mid-1980's, showing the stylistic transformations in the composer's art, and the most important characteristics of his compositional technique.

The last two years have brought two interesting books of differing character: a monograph by Beata Bolesławska and Ewa Siemdaj's doctoral dissertation.[9]

Beata Bolesławska[10] emphasizes the artist's biography, describes in detail the history of his life, acquaints us with the artist's personality traits, as well as giving a general character profile of his *oeuvre*. She subjects only one aspect of Andrzej Panufnik's music to

---

[5] Bernard Jacobson, *A Polish Renaissance* (London: Phaidon Press, 1996).

[6] Tadeusz Kaczyński, *Andrzej Panufnik i jego muzyka* (Andrzej Panufnik and his Music) (Warszawa: PWN, 1994).

[7] Krzysztof Stasiak, *An Analytical Study of the Music of Andrzej Panufnik*, doctoral dissertation, Queen's University, Belfast, 1990 (unpublished).

[8] It is worth mentioning the ancillary significance of Krystyna Jaraczewska-Mockałło's *Andrzej Panufnik. Katalog dzieł i bibliografia* (Andrzej Panufnik. Catalog of Works and Bibliography) (Warszawa, 1997).

[9] Ewa Siemdaj, *Poetyka muzyczna twórczości symfonicznej Andrzeja Panufnika* (Musical Poetics in the Symphonic Oeuvre of Andrzej Panufnik), doctoral dissertation, Kraków 2002, Academy of Music in Kraków, published as: *Andrzej Panufnik. Twórczość symfoniczna* (Andrzej Panufnik. The Symphonic Oeuvre), Kraków: Academy of Music, 2003).

[10] Beata Bolesławska, *Panufnik* (Kraków: PWM, 2001).

detailed analysis, namely the symmetry, which she presents giving examples from the composer's symphonic works.

Ewa Siemdaj's book contains analyses of all of Panufnik's symphonic works (including those for solo instruments and orchestra as well), in chronological order. The author characterizes Panufnik's stylistic syndrome, describing a set of essential fundamental and complementary traits of the composer's music. Among the fundamental properties, she mentions, among others: 'rootedness in tradition [...], accentuation of ethnic identity [...], pursuit of precision and logic in development of the musical process,' as well as 'tendency toward programmaticism—that is, treating a work as a bearer of senses and meanings.'

Also of particular, inestimable value are the writings of Andrzej Panufnik himself, as a source of knowledge about the artist's views, and about the technical secrets which he was so kind as to divulge to us, to those who listen to his music.[11]

The aforementioned general-audience and academic publications still do not fill in all of the gaps in musicological knowledge concerning the composer and his music.

The International Musicological Conference entitled *Andrzej Panufnik's Music and its Reception*, which took place in Kraków (23–25 November 2001) to mark the composer's 10th anniversary of death, permitted us to present the results of research conducted on Andrzej Panufnik's artistic activity by musicologists from several countries in Europe (Great Britain, Germany, Poland) and the USA.[12] The aim of the conference was to present Panufnik's artistic attitude, the characteristics of his compositional technique, to show the originality of the composer's style, as well as the significance of Andrzej Panufnik's *oeuvre* in the history of 20th-century music.

The present collection of studies, as gleanings from this conference, expands musicological knowledge in 3 subject areas: 1. the genre of instrumental music, which represented the broadest field for Andrzej Panufnik's artistic expansion, 2. reception of the composer's music, 3. aesthetic language and artistic attitude of Andrzej Panufnik.

The first subject has appeared many times in previous writings about Panufnik's music, and in their reflections, authors have concentrated on the composer's symphonic works, thanks to which he gained

---

[11] Andrzej Panufnik, *Impulse and Design in my Music* (London: Boosey and Hawkes, 1974) (commentary on his own works); Andrzej Panufnik, *Composing Myself* (*op. cit.*).

[12] See program of conference and accompanying concert on pp. 273–274.

a reputation as one of the foremost symphonic composers of the 20th century. The subject of Panufnik's symphonies has also been under-taken as one of the leading topics in this collection of articles, with the aim of showing this genre from various points of view. Thanks to this, light has been shed on various aspects of his symphonic *oeuvre*, of general and detailed nature—among others, dramaturgy of form, rules concerning tone structure (types of chords and tone cells), as well as the specific characteristics of Panufnik's symphonic style against the background of the symphonic *oeuvre* of the 20th century. Beyond this, also touched upon were problems associated with his chamber music and piano *oeuvre*, about which, up until now, no thorough or complex academic studies have been undertaken.

The subject of the reception of Panufnik's music in the USA, Great Britain and Poland, discussed in several papers, on the one hand, reveals unknown facts; and on the other, makes us aware how many issues have not yet been worked on, as well as clearly showing which of them should be presented in a broader historical context.

Andrzej Panufnik's artistic attitude has been characterized by interpretation of his published statements, as well as by direct report of his wife Lady Camilla Jessel Panufnik, thanks to which we become acquainted with the composer's personality, character traits, interests, lifestyle, creative process, as well as relationship to the music of other composers.

The problem of Panufnik's national identity winds recurs in many texts, and it seems not unreasonable to cite a statement of the artist himself: 'All the time during my stay in exile, I composed music inspired by events in Poland. My absence from the country was only of physical character; I lived in England for 36 years, but my music was always closely connected to Poland and considered as Polish. I was inspired by events from the early and more modern history of our people. [...] Despite my British passport and gratitude to Great Britain for accepting me and making my artistic work possible, I feel myself a Polish composer.'[13]

In preparing the present book for printing, we have received invaluable help from Lady Camilla Panufnik, who kindly made stylistic adjustments in the texts. We hereby extend to her our warm gratitude.

Jadwiga Paja-Stach
Translated by Cara Thornton

---

[13] Statement of A. Panufnik, in: Tadeusz Kaczyński, *Panufnik i jego muzyka* (*op. cit.*), pp. 85–86.

Part I
The Composer's Personality

Andrzej Panufnik's Ethos of Life and Work

Camilla Panufnik

Andrzej Panufnik had one interest above all others. He wanted to compose. But for almost his first half century the agonies of war, political suffocation and a series of personal tragedies prevented him from fulfilling the true extent of his creative ambitions. When I met him, he had no surviving family except for his beloved niece,[1] out of his reach for years because of his exile from Poland. He still mourned the baby daughter[2] of his first marriage, his parents[3] and his heroic brother.[4] He had suppressed his memories of the wartime destruction of all the music that he had composed up to the age of 30: his two incinerated symphonies, his "Psalm" for chorus and orchestra, the piano duos which he composed for Lutosławski and himself, and all his other works destroyed in the conflagrations of 1944. Till the end of his life he grieved over the years lost to him for serious composition, especially the period in which socialist realism was imposed, when, as Poland's leading composer, he was subjected even more severely than his contemporaries to destructive political and psychological pressures. The depression he suffered as a result almost totally extinguished his creative powers.

In exile in Britain, he had hoped to be able to write freely once more, but, distracted by lack of money and his collapsing marriage, he was still unable to rediscover his creative individuality. As Chief Conductor and Music Director of the City of Birmingham Symphony Orchestra, he had to conduct the whole year round, study an extensive new repertoire, attend committee meetings, auditions, and fulfil other

---

[1] Ewa Panufnik-Dworska.

[2] Oonagh Panufnik.

[3] Tomasz Panufnik, Matylda Thonnes-Panufnik.

[4] Mirosław Panufnik.

duties. By 1960, he had decided to escape from all worldly considerations, to live very simply and inexpensively in a tiny country cottage.
He closed himself off, contacted no one, did not even open all his
letters, and started to try to make up for lost time. It was in the
following year that I was asked by mutual friends to be a bridge
between him and the world. It had begun to concern him that he'd
heard nothing about performances or future commissions, though this
was hardly surprising: when I started helping him with contacts, I
found he was ignoring a bundle of dusty letters, many containing
significant professional approaches.

In the early 60s at last he was beginning to compose seriously
again, producing some outstanding works: the *Concerto for Piano &
Orchestra* and *Autumn Music* (his elegy for his dying friend[5]). Although
artistically these were successful, he was unsatisfied with the results
and became convinced that he must develop his musical language,
must search for new ground again as he had in the 1940s. First,
though, he had to complete another important commission, *Sinfonia
Sacra*, his tribute to the Millennium of Polish Christianity and
Statehood, which was also a political gesture against the Communist
system. Another work of that period was *Landscape*, inspired by one
of our many peaceful visits to the English county of Suffolk with its the
flat and wide open landscapes which reminded him strongly of Poland.

After the completion of *Sinfonia Sacra*, Panufnik was free from
urgent commissions and was longing to begin the regeneration of his
experiments in musical language, but he was still having to struggle
with the trivialities of survival. It was clear to me, quite apart from
my own deep feelings for him, that he needed someone to look after
him, to remove all pressures of daily living from him. It took time
however to revive his faith that a love affair could end in anything
other than misery.

When at last we married in 1963, my generous parents helped
us to lease our beautiful house by the River Thames. At that time
the house was a wreck, with leaks everywhere, rising damp and dry
rot. Before even repairing the roof, the kitchen or our bedroom, first
I directed the builders to prepare his studio, and there he composed
for the rest of his life.

He went to this studio six or seven days a week. Attached to the
old stables at the end of our garden, it was an ascetically furnished
room with a piano, a desk and a leather trunk for his manuscripts.

---

[5] Winsome Ward.

We put in three high windows with a view only of the sky so that he would not be distracted by any activity from the outside world. Calm routine was essential for his work: four hours in the morning, an afternoon walk, then another four hours till supper time. He maintained that inspiration did not come unless one called for it, so that he stuck to his daily pattern even in the early planning stages of a new work, before he was ready to write one note.

Now at last he could experiment and compose as he truly wished. I shall never forget the day in 1968 when he rushed into the house waving some manuscript paper, and, like Archimedes shouting "Eureka!", announced that at last he had found the key to his new musical language.

Searching for the core of each new work was a long and painful process for Andrzej, taking weeks, sometimes even months. He was often steeped in depression as his first attempts dissatisfied him. Even then each successive work had to be individual in form and content. "The emotional impulse must come first," he said (in a written reply[6] to questions prepared for a radio interview with Antony Hopkins in 1986). "Once I have decided on the poetic or spiritual message, the structural element follows almost immediately; because for me – the musical content (the content which lies behind the notes) and the form of the composition—have to develop together as a single undivided inspiration." He also said, in the same interview, "My symphonies certainly have no programmatic element. The title only indicates the character, the climate of the work."

Eventually, once this "emotional impulse" and the shape of the new idea crystallised, he began to make sketches (which, to the sorrow of musicologists, he mostly destroyed, describing them as his "private kitchen").

Not for Panufnik the writing of a main theme, then afterwards the orchestration. He would pass week after week dreaming about content, context, deciding on the new work's unique geometric skeleton and its specific triadic intervals with their resultant reflections and transpositions. These were the happiest creative moments for him. The abstract thinking continued as he wove all his ideas into his own musical language and spiritual stratosphere, and he would hold the whole work in his memory, even Symphony No. 9 (*Sinfonia della Speranza*) 40 minutes long for a large orchestra. Not until an entire work was fully conceived in his mind, note for note, harmonically,

---

[6] Panufnik Archive, Twickenham, A2805.

rhythmically, dynamically, would he start to fill the enormous expanse of waiting empty staves. Then he would work at vast speed. He would come into supper each night, his wrist aching, but he would not let up until the manuscript was complete.

His insistence that each new work should have its own "architecture" reflected his inner need to free himself from any previous concept or rule. He felt that the individual geometric outlines on which he built each work gave unity as well as a structure through which he could direct all his contemplative, poetic expression and emotional fire, without resorting to historical conventions in form. His use of geometry was esoteric and personal, not directly mathematical, rather an architectural frame on to which he could build the musical harmonies and the onward flow of each musical creation.

Sometimes he took his outlines from mysticism or nature, as in his *Arbor Cosmica* with its branches in the ground and its roots in the heavens. Sometimes he was inspired by sequences of circles, as in *Sinfonia Mistica*, and in *Sinfonia di Sfere* where even the main (percussion) instruments are circular and where the sound circles the orchestra. The golden ellipse inspired his Tenth Symphony and one of his works was based entirely on triangles.

Often the key to a new work would come to him when he was out for his daily walk beside his beloved River Thames. The river is never the same from day to day: the tide may be higher, lower, sluggish or fast-running. The reflected trees along the banks are skeletons in winter, heavily cloaked in summer. The light may be shimmery silver or spring green, dank grey in winter, golden under a summer sky. For a composer who took visual inspiration from geometry, nature and trees, the ever-changing reflections and eddies of the river must have subconsciously shaped soundscapes almost without his awareness.

The philosophies of different religions were also a source of constant fascination, and painting exhibitions of all periods excited him. He read quantities of books, loved the theatre (especially Shakespeare), enjoyed brilliant or subtle comedians, and enthusiastically studied new architecture. He considered the creation of good food and serious wines to rank amongst the high arts. Indeed he appreciated all the arts – except musical performances! He liked to go to friends' concerts, but otherwise, especially with his adored Mozart whom he described as his "God No. 1", he preferred to read the scores and hear the music in his imagination exactly as he wanted it. At a concert, if a performer sang out of tune, he stuck his elbow painfully in *my* ribs! His ear was so good, that he could hear one wrong note at the back of the second violins, which I considered amazing, but unfortunate too, because he was bound to enjoy concerts less than I did. Of course there were several conductors whom he admired greatly. However he remained profoundly influenced by his experiences as a favourite pupil of Weingartner at the Vienna Academy before World War II, and by great conductors such as Furtwängler, whose awe-inspiring interpretations helped to form the musical tastes of the eager young student from Warsaw.

Andrzej enjoyed conducting from time to time, because he liked to have the "orchestra in his hands", and found his compositional processes stimulated by "live contact" with musicians. He had a continuing, warm relationship with the London Symphony Orchestra who commissioned three new works from him and recorded most of his major works. Conducting the Chicago Symphony was a happy experience, and, at the end of his life, he developed great rapport with the Scottish Chamber Orchestra and the New York Chamber Symphony. As he grew older, he preferred to perform only premières of his own works, or Mozart, or Schubert or Brahms. Sometimes he agreed to conduct new works to help other contemporary composers, or accepted concerts in interesting places like South America, which satisfied his love of foreign travel. But his *raison d'être* remained composition.

He needed a lot of sleep and did not like late nights. He refused almost all social invitations, except for events connected directly with his concerts, or conversations with his closest friends – musicians, artists and writers. He also declined all invitations to lecture at Universities, and he refused to hold workshops, teach at music colleges or appear on television. This was not only because of his innate shyness: he could not get used to the contemporary trend, still extant, which forces composers to become speakers extolling their own compositions. He felt that the public's demand for explanation had given rise to a false intellectualism. He was never unkind to anyone he met, but amongst friends he was wickedly funny about composers who had allowed themselves to be over-dominated by 1960s and 70s musical gimmickry, colleagues who all too often put their "concoctions of acrobatic or tortured notes" on to manuscript paper only after they had written their "verbally glittering" lectures.

Immersed as he was in his own world of sound, Andrzej never lost his dislike of publicly discussing his personal approach to his composition. "Music is my language, not words," he insisted. To his dismay, however, by the mid-70s, the demand for composers' programme notes had become universal. He sacrificed a month of precious composition time, and we prepared programme notes for each of his works, with the hope that no one would ever ask him to speak or write about them again. These notes *Impulse and Design in my Music*, were published as a booklet by Boosey & Hawkes in 1976. Thereafter, each time he completed a new work, he would bring it to my office and would demand instant help to anglicise his musical ideas. He would then put the programme note into the manuscript, close its pages, send it off for the writing of orchestral parts. Later, after performances, he often made revisions to his scores. But with newly completed works, he wanted to forget every aspect until the première. He needed to clear his head so that recent ideas would not influence whatever he was going to compose next. Though his compositions are always recognisably his, it was his intention that each should start from a fresh musical viewpoint, and not owe anything to its predecessor.

As he spent half his life in Poland and half in England, I am often asked how English he became by the end of his life. There was much he loved about England, not least the respect of the British for the privacy of others. He had suffered in Warsaw, in the difficult post-war period, from gossip, pulp-fiction-style invention and then later, after his escape, from ugly propaganda. In England it was possible to live and work without any interference: ("You can even starve privately in England!" he once said to me with ironic but genuine appreciation, talking about the early 1960s when this almost happened.)

Inevitably he eventually became part of the English musical scene, despite his retiring nature. He himself respected English composers such as Vaughan Williams and Elgar, but he did not want to be influenced by them or anyone else. His music was naturally atonal, and he ignored fashions whether the impetus came from the 2nd Viennese School or any other of the mid-twentieth century trends.

His interest in Polish political developments never waned. Daily he anxiously scanned the newspapers and every shade of Polish political change was of significance. Until the last year of his life, he did not believe that the Soviet grip on Poland could ever slip, in which fortunately he was mistaken. His music was banned for 23 years in Poland, but even after it was reinstated in 1977, it was against his principles (having left Poland as a protest against the political system) to return his beloved native land until elections were declared and democracy was in sight. His only return to Poland in 1990 was deeply moving.

He warmly appreciated that the British people eventually took him to their hearts, and he found their sense of honour and responsibility close to the ethos of his Polish upbringing. He had distant English ancestors[7] on his mother's side; if it were not for his rolling accent, his slanting Slavonic cheekbones and hypnotic brown eyes, he could have been mistaken in his stance for an Englishman. He remained however deeply Polish in his warmth, his natural good manners, and his profound sense of family duty, which made him a wonderful husband, father, and son-in-law to my ageing parents.

His Polishness was most evident in his music, and it never left him. From about 1968, after he found for himself an abstract musical language all his own, the unmistakable Polish characteristics came surging back into even his most abstract music.

Andrzej Panufnik looked on politics as a curse, and music as the great blessing of life. Recently I listened again to his ten surviving post-war symphonies in numerical order, passing from the naïveté and charm of his innocent 1948 *Sinfonia Rustica* through the evolving stages of his innate Polishness onwards to the development of his abstract power. In Andrzej's music, alongside the peaceful contemplation, the charm and delicacy, the high spirits and spirituality, one sometimes encounters a terrifying violence—a strange manifestation to emerge from such a gentle and humorous man – but understandable when one realises the tortured realities of his early life. The horrors of the Second World War and the Stalinist period never quite left him. His nightmares made him shout in his sleep, and always they were about Warsaw, always the 1950s. Meeting him, however, no one would have known how much he had suffered in his past life. He was never bitter, and rarely complained of the considerable injustices in his lifetime to himself and to his music.

Andrzej Panufnik remained true until the end to his *credo*, his continuous search to try to discover, like his hero Mozart, *"the perfect balance between heart and mind, intellect and emotion"*, a balance he eventually came close to achieving both in his life and in his *oeuvre*. Through the notes of his lovingly crafted, intellectual musical structures I hear his humanity, poetry, serenity, passion, despair, energy and wit, all intrinsic aspects of his personality as well as his response to his own dramatic life.

---

[7] A genealogical search is currently in progress.

Andrzej Panufnik's Artistic Attitude and his Aesthetics

Zbigniew Skowron

> Beauty, harmony, strength and order are the aesthetic qualities which seem to me dictated by the form and the life of trees: but they also communicate to me something much more than sheer physical presence. Beyond the aesthetic pleasure and sensual delights of appearance, touch or smell, trees seem to me to exude some mysterious power through their moods, and through their souls.[1]

The aim of this paper is to present a broad retrospective of the output of Andrzej Panufnik, one of the famous composers of 20th century Polish music, whose music, paradoxically in the most prolific period of his life was banned in his native land, where he had grown up both as a man and an artist. He rightfully regained recognition in Poland only in his late phase, at first through the performances of his works at the 'Warsaw Autumn' Festival from 1977 onwards when his *Universal Prayer* was performed, then when he was welcomed in person in 1990, after 36 years' absence: as it turned out, only one year before his death.

The issue of Panufnik's artistic attitude and his aesthetics impels us to reflect on the many spheres of his creative existence, not only in its artistic, but also purely human sense. It was Tadeusz Kaczyński who had already pointed out these different dimensions in his monograph, when he wrote:

> 'Most of Panufnik's works are connected ... with events in which he participated; also with his deeply personal experience, reflections and

---

[1] Andrzej Panufnik, *Composing Myself* (London: Methuen, 1987), p. 342.

observations on the natural acoustic phenomena which he translated into the language of music. Panufnik's work cannot be fully understood without knowledge of the place on the map or of the environment from which he came."[2]

The composer's individual musical characteristics had been formed through his personal experience in childhood, then during his youth and student years; also through the extension of his musical education before the Second World War. This individual perspective was further extended by his contact with a broader spectrum of new music from the West as well as from within Poland. The other crucial factor strongly influencing Panufnik's future was the historical and political post-war situation, which prompted him to make not only aesthetic choices, but also personal decisions, which, from 1954, were dramatically to determine the direction of his life and his creative path. All these crucial factors need to be taken into account if we are to describe accurately the maturation and development of Panufnik's aesthetic views. In looking back on them, I would like to present them as a dynamic process in various phases; then, within each phase, to point out the ideas which attracted his attention and which found more or less direct expression in his works. This method tends to combine both the diachronic and synchronic approach. It attempts to reconcile viewing the continuity of Panufnik's creative path and the significance of its separate elements. In this connection one question needs to be answered: to what extent did Panufnik's artistic attitude changed over time and to what extent was it based on self-imposed norms? His attitude seem to reveal a certain number of deeper beliefs, which were shaped in his youth, perhaps even in his childhood, as more or less *constant* ideas. One might say that these personal aesthetics became a kind of internal mirror in which he reflected different impulses emanating from the surrounding musical world. Certainly these stylistic and technical models were experienced by Panufnik not only as a composer, but also as an attentive listener. It was through this constant and *critical* confrontation of his own *credo* with the musical stimuli reaching him from all sides that he shaped his artistic attitude and manifested it in his works. Yet the filter of his consciousness appears to be impenetrable by certain elements such as twelve-tone technique or post-Webernism; it simply rejects them in spite of peer pressure and their omnipresence. Such

---

[2] Tadeusz Kaczyński, *Andrzej Panufnik i jego muzyka* (Andrzej Panufnik and his Music) (Warszawa: PWN, 1994), p. 19.

an aesthetic and psychological mechanism seems to point towards the essence of Panufnik's artistic personality, making him a composer, who remained faithful to his own aesthetics throughout his life.

The composer's autobiography, *Composing Myself* (1987) is particularly valuable as a direct source in reconstructing Panufnik's standpoint as a composer. In it one finds many aesthetic issues which remain constant throughout the chronological course of the book. These beliefs are clearly fixed elements, they constitute what Władysław Tatarkiewicz called 'formulated' aesthetics and which are in fact, the composer's ideological *credo*.

It should be pointed out that Panufnik was one of those 20th-century composers who did not find it particularly important to express their reflections on paper. On the contrary, he stated frankly that he found this problematical. Thus, in the preface to his *Impulse and Design in my Music* he wrote: 'I have prepared these brief descriptions of my works at the invitation of my publishers, though I found writing them most difficult. Not only because notes rather than words are my true métier, but also because I find my creative work a most personal and intimate matter.'[3] This laconic statement reveals another symptomatic aspect of Panufnik's artistic attitude. What we have here is a testimony to the deeply *personal* character of his own work. This kind of declaration seems to be relatively rare among 20th-century, especially among the post-war avant-gardists who ardently wanted to expose their ideas about their output. This attitude (of personal reserve) remains constant throughout Panufnik's life.

Although the main source of this reconstruction of the composer's views will be his 'formulated' aesthetics, I would also like to consider their direct parallel, in other words the 'immanent' aesthetics implicit in his works. This task is made easier by Panufnik himself, who pointed out in his *Impulse and Design in my Music* many aesthetic aspects of his works composed between 1942 and 1972.

One of the main keys which allows us to reconstruct Panufnik's artistic attitude must be the understanding of his formative years as a composer: his studies at the Warsaw Conservatory and, later on, his education abroad in Vienna and Paris. There is no doubt that during his student years Panufnik was disillusioned by the situation of new music in Warsaw. Nevertheless, he was constantly absorbing

---

[3] Andrzej Panufnik, *Impulse and Design in my Music*, Foreword (London: Boosey and Hawkes, 1974).

every aspect of modern tendencies, which, in spite of disapproval, were filtering through to the Warsaw Philharmonic. Panufnik's opinion of the status of new music in the Philharmonic's repertoire policy was severe:

> The Polish conductor Fitelberg occasionally conducted the more acclaimed avant-garde works of the time; for example, *The Iron Foundry* by the Russian, Mosolov, *Pacific 231* by Honegger and a dazzling piano concerto by Prokofiev. These performances were major events for me, and I remember my even greater excitement the first time I heard some Stravinsky when Klemperer conducted *Petrushka*. ... These tantalising visions of the world of new music, however, were excruciatingly rare. Warsaw must have been the only important European capital where there was no pre-war performance of *The Rite of Spring*. Stravinsky was hardly heard; Bartók, Schoenberg and Webern were not played at all.[4]

Panufnik owed his early development as a composer to Kazimierz Sikorski, the greatly respected professor at Warsaw Conservatory. What attracted him to this teacher, was, as it seemed then to Panufnik, his openness towards the new music, especially the fact that Sikorski held Szymanowski in high esteem. However, it soon became apparent that the relationship between student and master was not free of friction or controversy. When Panufnik declared himself an admirer of modern music, Sikorski immediately would dampen the enthusiasm of his student, by reminding him of the first necessity, a good command of a compositional technique, which was in his view a tonal *métier*.

> 'Consciously setting out to be somewhat avant-garde', wrote Panufnik, 'I began my Symphonic Variations writing in four keys simultaneously, to be free from conventional harmonies. However, when I rather proudly showed him the first few pages, to my dismay, instead of admiring my boldness, his face contracted into deep disapproval. He curtly ordered me to abandon my polytonal technique and to begin again, strictly in the traditional tonal language. I felt as if my wings had been clipped. But he was my teacher: I had to obey him.'[5]

Sikorski's attitude, although it might provoke an inner protest by his student, had in fact a positive impact on Panufnik's future career. Apart from mere proficiency and compositional skill, it strengthened his sense of the integrity of a musical work and his responsibility for its form, while consolidating his respect for classical musical values.

---

[4] Andrzej Panufnik, *Composing Myself*, p. 41.
[5] *Ibid.*, p. 48.

'Sikorski', Panufnik admitted in retrospect, 'was right to force me first to master the craftsmanship of conventional tonality before letting me fly off in an exciting whirlwind of exploration: in this way he helped to instil into me the necessity for unity of style and discipline, which was to stand me in good stead in my future searches for my own musical language and rules.'[6]

Like many of his Polish colleagues, Panufnik decided to broaden his musical knowledge after he graduated from the Warsaw Conservatory. However, unlike the numerous members of the Association of Young Polish Musicians in Paris, instead of making his way to the famous classes of Nadia Boulanger, he went to Vienna. He was attracted to this city not only through his admiration for the Viennese classics and Schubert, but also because it was 'the birthplace of exciting new developments in contemporary music'[7], epitomized by the ideas and works of Schoenberg, Berg, and Webern.

The first vivid contact with the Second Viennese School became one of the most important moments in maturing Panufnik's artistic consciousness and in searching for his own identity as a composer.[8] His previous lack of contact with the music of these three Viennese may be viewed as typical of the way they were perceived by the younger generation of Polish composers who during their studies were not only cut off from the music of the Second Viennese School, but were even made antagonistic towards it by their teachers and the conservative Warsaw critics. However, this prejudice was not strong enough to subdue Panufnik's interests. In his autobiography there is a long passage which shows that he familiarised himself with the unknown system of twelve-tone technique, followed by his own attempts to experiment with it because of the challenge it presented:

> 'It was an exciting experience to come to grips at last with this strange and fascinating development in musical language. With passion and enthusiasm I read virtually all the printed scores, played them on the piano, analysed them in detail and contemplated them long and deeply. The

---

[6] *Ibid.*, p. 48.

[7] *Ibid.*, p. 54.

[8] It is worth noting that these contacts consisted mostly in analysing scores at the Academy of Music, since the music of the three Viennese was then—on the eve of the *Anschluss*—almost absent in the concert repertoire. Of Schoenberg's pupils only Webern was then active in Vienna. Schoenberg himself emigrated to the USA in the autumn of 1933, whereas Berg died in 1935, three years before Panufnik's visit to the Austrian capital.

composer to whom I felt closest was Webern. He seemed to me most original of the three, and I was attracted towards the exquisite crystal-like structures he built with such precision. I saw his music as puzzling, mystical shorthand sketches; as if he were offering an intriguing outline plan without mapping the inner pathways to his musical thought and language; he must also be expressing some profound and poetic human feelings, but in esoteric form, as though they were so secret that he could not bring himself to share them.

Berg's music came through to me as more direct, more communicative, partly because his language was more readily accessible than the pointillism of Webern, and partly because his compositions were strongly imbued with a dramatic element, even a romantic one in such works as his *Lyric Suite* for string quartet.

The nut which I found hardest to crack was Schoenberg. Being myself a so-called progressive composer, I came to his music with a wide-open mind and an eagerness to assimilate even his most difficult and complex scores. However, for all my enthusiasm and determination to come to terms with his ideas, I could not overcome my instinctive reservations. ...

Someone once perceptively observed that the notes in Mozart's music love one another. I had the impression that Schoenberg's notes hated each other. Listening to Mozart seemed to me like drinking the dew from an exquisite geometric pattern of leaves and flowers—or tasting the pure transparent water of a mountain stream. But with Schoenberg I felt as if I were sipping the stagnant contents of an artificial lake made by a speculative human hand rather than by nature.

Nevertheless I remained intrigued by the intellectual challenge of Schoenberg's theory; and considered studying with Webern. ... Meanwhile, I tried out the serial method on my own: at first I thoroughly enjoyed these mental gymnastics, but soon recognised that for me its limitations outweighed its advantages. I could see what Schoenberg was attempting. I agreed with the principle of a self-imposed discipline, a limitation to achieve unity. However, judged from the standpoint of my own purposes, his method seemed to achieve unity only at the cost of the equally desirable goal of variety. The "democratization" of the twelve notes of the chromatic scale seemed to block the way to essential expressive elements. ...

I threw my dodecaphonic sketches into my waste paper basket, and concluded that I should never again try to borrow methods from other composers. My instinct told me, however ambitious or pretentious it might seem in those early student days, that I must search unremittingly for my very own new means of expression, my own new language, at any cost, to remain independent and true to myself. I knew that I would require some discipline, some framework within which to build my own works, but it would have to be constructed by myself. It would have to meet my need for emotional content as well as structural cohesion. I realised even then that my life would be one of ceaseless search: that I would be taking great risks—that I might never reach my goal."[9]

---

[9] *Ibid.*, pp. 73–4.

I decided to quote this long passage because it gives detailed evidence of how Panufnik was maturing as a composer; it proves that he was fully aware of the necessity of creating his own artistic means. This statement also shows that from the very beginning Panufnik understood the significance of both the content and structure of a musical work. The fact that this conviction emerged from an opposition to the twelve-tone technique gives this an extra meaning.

The second area of broadening experience for Panufnik was the Parisian musical life in the late 1930s. Unlike his Polish colleagues, who were attracted to Paris by the master classes of Nadia Boulanger, he did not study composition, but rather French contemporary music, and he did so under the guidance of Philippe Gaubert (1879–1941), a conductor and famous interpreter of Debussy and Ravel. Apart from his analyses of their works, Panufnik became acquainted with a vast contemporary repertoire, such as music of Stravinsky, Poulenc, Honegger and Milhaud as well as the Second Viennese School in whose works and ideas he was interested much earlier. Meanwhile it seems that French neo-classicism seemingly did not arouse great enthusiasm in Panufnik nor captivate him by its poetics. One composer, however, did become for him a true revelation, as is shown in the autobiography:

> 'The work which impressed me most was Béla Bartók's Sonata for Two Pianos and Percussion. Hearing this masterpiece supremely performed by the composer, with his wife at the second piano, I found myself placing him in my score chart as the greatest living composer. I found his music uniquely satisfying spiritually, emotionally and aesthetically. Unlike so much new music, his compositions were rich with rhythmical vitality, harmonic ingenuity and a stunning feeling for tone colour.'[10]

The fascination of Bartók's music must have been fully absorbed by the young Polish composer. His keen sense of musical construction, of the structural role of rhythm, such as in the *Tragic Overture*, as well as his concept of tone-colour can certainly be related to the Bartókian models.

Panufnik's first compositional attempts bring to mind the similar beginnings of his one-year older colleague, Witold Lutosławski. They graduated together from Warsaw Conservatory and both found their attention drawn towards the phenomenon of new music, which caused them to act in defiance of the views of their teachers.

---

[10] *Ibid.*, p. 86.

'[Sikorski]', wrote Panufnik, 'would react against my pieces because, from my earliest years, I favoured clarity and economy of means of expression, making it my aim never to write a single superfluous note. Recognising that we differed in matters of taste, I settled to learn all the craftsmanship I could from him, but determined meanwhile quietly to go my own way.'[11]

Lutosławski similarly remembered his beginnings as Maliszewski's student of composition: 'I was sure that I was on the right path. After all, Maliszewski's opinion [on the Symphonic Variations of 1938] came as no surprise. I had long been aware of his aesthetic views and knew that if I adhered to them, I would be lost.'[12]

The fortunes of the two young musicians became interlocked during the Second World War in occupied Warsaw. At that time they initiated the only permitted kind of music-making: they performed in the city's cafés as a piano duo playing their own numerous transcriptions of the classical repertoire, from Bach and Mozart up to Stravinsky and Szymanowski, including also the banned composers Mendelssohn and Chopin, and— which may seem surprising—their own jazz creations, according to precisely drawn diagrams.[13] Panufnik would later admit that they both were 'obsessive perfectionists'[14] in solving various problems of piano technique.

The years of the war and occupation caused a painful gap in the development of the Polish composers who finished their studies in the second half of the 1930s and stayed throughout the hostilities in their homeland. We can therefore talk about their delayed débuts, which eventually took place in a totally new political situation. These circumstances, together with the falling of the 'iron curtain' were soon not only to cut the musicians of the Eastern Europe off from Western avant-garde innovations, but above all to put them under pressure to compose according to the dictates of socialist realism. However, if we first look at the period of a relative freedom between

---

[11] *Ibid.*, p. 49.

[12] Bálint András Varga, *Lutosławski Profile* (London, 1976), p. 5.

[13] In *Composing Myself* Panufnik recalls meticulous preparations for those jazz improvisations, which bring to mind both the diagrams of his own subsequent works and the precise sketches of Lutosławski: 'Before starting we would draw a diagram indicating tempo and harmonic progression in a given number of bars. From this tiny scrap of paper, we would spontaneously invent melodies, counterpoints and rhythmic patterns, taking staggering risks, terrifying each other by tearing away in flights of wild imagination, yet never giving away the secret to our audiences that we were improvising rather than performing carefully written and rehearsed music.' Ibid., p. 113.

[14] *Ibid.*, p. 112.

1945 and 1948[15], then Panufnik's profile shows in sharp outline against the output of his contemporaries. This could be explained by his pre-war experiences, especially regarding his attitude towards the Viennese and Parisian schools, which, far from any euphoric imitation of existing models, gave him an artistic personality with completely individual traits. This is clearly seen in his two works of 1947: *Nocturne* for orchestra and *Lullaby* for 29 string instruments and 2 harps, both works clear examples of Panufnik's 'searching', indeed his experimentation at that period. A similar attitude may be observed in the music of Lutosławski, although he displayed it in a larger scale work, his Symphony No. 1, also completed in 1947.[16]

It is a telling fact that Panufnik was compared with Lutosławski in the opinions of such a sensitive critic as Zygmunt Mycielski. In his *Diary* of 1950–59 we can find three symptomatic comments. 'Panufnik hears all, Lutosławski is a master of form and hears, too'[17], notes Mycielski briefly in 1951, and he puts it in this way in 1956:

> 'What does it matter ... if our colleagues [of the Polish Composers Union – Z.S.] know how to write a score, if they do not have anything to say? ... In my opinion, Panufnik at least had something to say, but can he manage to find his feet again in London? I think about him and about his music

---

[15] Zofia Helman in her book *Neoklasycyzm w muzyce polskiej XX wieku* (Neo-Classicism in Polish Twentieth-Century Music) (Kraków: PWM, 1985) points to the significance of that period for postwar Polish music. The author writes: 'I draw here special attention to the period between 1945 and 1948, since, apart from war damage and economic difficulties, which had a bearing on the state of musical culture, it is in this period when authentic problems emerge which engage composers, polarize their artistic positions, and mark their search for their own creative ways. This authenticity and individuality is seen particularly in the works of Palester, Lutosławski, Panufnik, Malawski, and Bacewicz' (p. 73).

[16] This comparison may seem not totally adequate, firstly because both Panufnik's works do not refer to any model from the past, whereas Lutosławski's symphony brings to mind the classical pattern and secondly, because Panufnik's originality of material and structure seems to be more far-reaching. Nevertheless, what makes this comparison plausible is the strong structure which permeates Lutosławski's work, and the fact that he was against associating his *métier* with the neo-classical style (see the composer's statements in 'I Have Never been a Neo-Classicist', conversation with Mieczysław Kominek, *Studio*, 2 (1992), pp. 4–6). It seems that only in *Musique funèbre* (1954–8) did Lutosławski reach the same level of originality which distinguishes Panufnik's *Lullaby* and *Nocturne*. These works should indeed have been acknowledged in their time as the forerunners of the Polish avant-garde, but they were not given this recognition because of the doctrine of socialist realism.

[17] Zygmunt Mycielski, *Dziennik 1950–1959* (Diary 1950–1959) (Warszawa: Iskry, 1999), 21 Jan. 1951, p. 39.

with extraordinary, intense affection. He is only one here, whose works moved me deeply. Lutosławski writes *well*, but his work tells me little, except for a few very well-phrased miniatures. Moreover his freedom seems to me very frigid.'[18]

Later on, in 1958, Mycielski notes: 'Krenz conducted yesterday Lutosławski's *Musique funèbre*. This reminded me of Panufnik's system of writing, especially his *Lullaby* and *5 Folk Songs*, but without Panufnik's poetry.'[19]

We could ask here, what impelled this doyen of Polish criticism to draw a parallel between Panufnik and Lutosławski. This comparison, even if it appears as a momentary thought, points both to a subtle difference and yet the similarity of their attitudes. Mycielski perceives clearly the common elements of both composers: their sensitivity to sound-colour, the sensual value of their sound-structures, and the perfection of their technique. Moreover, in Panufnik he discerns also, if not at first, a poetic atmosphere, an internal warmth which, in his mind, is lacking in Lutosławski's music. Thus, led by his intuition, that of a consummate critic, Mycielski perceives the most important of Panufnik's artistic attitude, which is the particular fusion of his sense of musical *construction* and the *poetic* message of his musical works. This opinion is fully confirmed from present perspective, since this characteristic, in spite of being created in a variety of ways, becomes the dominant aesthetic of the whole of Panufnik's *oeuvre*.

Let us come back, however, to the Polish composer's creative path and to the process of shaping his artistic attitude. An important question which should be answered in this context concerns Panufnik's approach to the two creative options inherited, one might say, from the period between the wars, then later, after 1949, considered the only possible (indeed, only permitted) styles: neo-classical and folkloristic. It seems that Panufnik did not join the enthusiastic adherents of the former, as could be seen from his earlier-mentioned Parisian preferences. It is also significant that, in his autobiography, he did not give any opinion, or make any specific comments regarding this style. On the other hand, his first postwar attempts show that, as long as access to the neo-classical poetics was a matter of free choice, Panufnik followed his own way with his typical, strong sense of musical structure and sensitivity to texture and sonority. One could

---

[18] *Ibid.*, 12 Jan. 1956, p. 178.
[19] *Ibid.*, 24–5 May 1958, p. 328.

therefore risk a hypothesis that, before 1949, both Panufnik and Lutosławski, at variance with their colleagues of the Association of Young Polish Musicians in Paris, rejected typical neo-classicism, and developed their own styles. Needless to say, to be a neo-classicist in Poland after 1949 was not so much a matter of a free choice, rather of hard necessity.

As for all Polish composers, for Panufnik too the year 1949 became a kind of boundary-date, the beginning of the five-year period of searching for ways of survival in the reality of, as he stated, 'socialist surrealism'[20] of the Stalinist-era. In this period, which ended with the composer's dramatic escape from Warsaw via Zurich to London in summer 1954, Panufnik started a game with the political establishment. He tried first of all to protect his individuality, but was ever conscious that he had to act within the imposed framework of the norms of socialist realism.

> 'I would think', he remembered, 'that I had found a way to walk the tight-rope of honesty above the chasm of conflicting pressures, but whenever I put myself in front of the beckoning sheets of manuscript, my mind kept returning involuntarily to the slogans and events of the previous two years. ... They had all left their mark.'[21]

The price for this tangled situation must have been an internal dilemma, which was growing in proportion to the signs of approval from the part of the communist regime, for which Panufnik's talent and his European fame was seen as a tool to legitimise the regime's cultural policy. Panufnik tried to come to grips with the imposed rules, the outcome of which is his *Symphony of Peace* (1951).[22] Yet the real creative 'niche' became for him the stylization of Polish old music:

> 'After lengthy thought, at last I worked out a way to avoid either confrontation or capitulation. Following the example of our architects who at that time were most inspiringly reconstructing whole sections of Warsaw, I decided to get myself to work as a restorer of sixteenth- and seventeenth-century Polish music. ... My *Old Polish Suite* for strings seemed unexceptionable to the stewards of the new order. ... Even the most accomplished experts in dialectic sloganry had difficulty in finding any derogatory labels to apply.'[23]

---

[20] Andrzej Panufnik, *Composing Myself*, p. 224.

[21] *Ibid.*, p. 203.

[22] Later on the composer withdrew the *Symphony of Peace* from the list of his works, using its first two movements in his *Sinfonia Elegiaca* (1957).

[23] Andrzej Panufnik, *Composing Myself*, p. 191.

The year 1954 marks the period in Panufnik's biography in which he not only begins his musical activity in exile, but also starts his independent, mature phase. In view of the new, sometimes even unexpected conditions and circumstances which he encountered in England, it was indeed a specific phase. To be sure, the author of the *Concerto in modo antico* left Poland as a composer with a well formed personality, but musical fashions were evolving to the point where he had to survive in a foreign artistic environment which was promoting mostly avant-garde ideas under the banner of post-Webernism, which he could not accept. Moreover, as an émigré, Panufnik was out of touch with the radical changes introduced by the youngest composers in Poland on the wave of the October 'thaw' of 1956. Would Panufnik's fortune have proceeded in a similar way to Lutosławski's, if—in spite of all—he had decided to stay in his homeland? The reference made in the early 1950s by Mycielski, based on the common traits in the attitudes of the two composers seems to justify asking such a question. The combination of Panufnik's talent and aesthetic views would lead us to expect that he could have encapsulated them in sounds comparable to the unconstrained explorations of other Poles at the end of the 1950s, so he would, most probably, have became just one more figure in the 'Polish School' of the 1960s.

However, his creative path took different direction, both in relation to the Western avant-garde and to the equally innovative tendencies in Polish music. As far as the latter is concerned, Panufnik distanced himself from the avant-garde wave which absorbed not only the younger Polish generation, but also older composers, like Bacewicz and Lutosławski. It is hard to avoid the impression that Panufnik, remembering the oppressive conditions in the country he left in 1954, remained haunted by political interference even when it did not affect him at all. He observed:

'This "difference" came as revelation to many composers, who were too excited to notice that they were jumping out of one stylistic straightjacket into another. Not only did the young Polish composers (most using the serial method as a springboard) plunge head first into the inviting experimental pool, but also the older ones – like Bolesław Szabelski, who, after fifty years of writing tonal music, became an atonalist overnight. ...

Of course the truly inspired amongst my fellow-countrymen managed brilliantly to transcend the restrictions of the fashionable idiom, and some extremely exciting music started to emerge. The fervent application of the Warsaw composers' high-spirited creativity and flair to an already slightly tired compositional convention filled the Western critics with awed delight. But in the eyes of many participants, this flowering of the Polish avant-garde

was a political demonstration as well as an artistic revelation, though no
one could risk letting Western visitors into the secret. ...

It was with mingled amusement and admiration, that I watched from
afar the dazzling avant-garde acrobatics of my colleagues.'[24]

Panufnik's critical appraisal of the eruption of creative ideas within
the 'Polish School' resembles the attitude of famous Polish critics,
such as Stefan Kisielewski and the previously-mentioned Zygmunt
Mycielski, who, with the principle intention of defending established
values, while also recognising the avant-garde wave, appealed to the
'angry young' Polish composers for reflection and for common-sense.

To observe Panufnik's opinions of Polish new music only in the
light of politics would be too great a limitation. What is always a
much more important issue in this context is his artistic attitude:
one can conclude that, after his departure from Poland, the turning
points in his development do not coincide with the sudden changes
in Polish music. Neither the year 1956, which marked a break from
the rules of socialist realism, nor the year 1975, which, in turn,
started a retreat from the avant-garde poetics (for instance in the
works of Penderecki, Górecki or Kilar), are significant dates in
Panufnik's music. This fact alone could point to the distinctive
character of his stylistic path and of the aesthetic views which
accompanied it. Everything shows that, by the end of the 1950s and
in the early 1960s, Panufnik was still searching (inasmuch as allowed
by his new situation in England) for his personal style, which search
he would continue steadfastly. After the series of works with a Polish
national character, such as *Polonia*, *Sinfonia Sacra* and *Katyń
Epitaph*, which were a kind of reaction to the oppressive situation
of the Stalinist years in Poland, Panufnik significantly changes his
orientation. He again starts searching for new structures which he
develops in the realm of absolute music with a universal message.
This need for a change of creative attitude contained some anxiety,
which was expressed in the following passage of the composer's
biography:

'I was searching ... for a new dimension in musical grammar and
language, because I felt that somewhere within my imagination lay something
different, undiscovered, a future source for fresh creative endeavours.

I resolved, however long it would take me, to persevere relentlessly until
I could discover a new way of expressing myself, influenced neither by my
native culture nor by the language of any other existing composer or musical
school of thought. ... I spent hour after hour ..., reflecting how to tackle my

---

[24] *Ibid.*, pp. 259–60.

new task. Sitting at my desk I would search on the staves of my manuscript paper, scribbling down endless different ideas, then trying them at the piano, until at last one day I realised that my ear, together with my intuition, was beginning to win over intellectual speculation: I suddenly found a group of three notes which, as I manipulated them within the stave and on the piano, I perceived had some evocative and strangely expandable qualities—even, it felt to me, some magical power. ...

I knew within minutes that this three-note cell would be the material out of which I could build small- and large-scale musical structures; that it had as much potential for poetic and human expression as it did for intellectual fastidiousness; that it was the ultimate basis from which all my future compositions could grow.'[25]

We could ask here how innovative was this discovery which so fascinated the composer. The idea of using sounds as the cells of a musical construction reaches back in his works as far as the early 1940s, for example the *Tragic Overture*. Remaining faithful to his early concept, Panufnik becomes aware in 1968 of its new, wider sense and structural potential: 'amazing new harmonies, new expressions, new sound colours'.[26] It is exactly in this *potential*, which opens the composer's new creative horizons, that we can see the novelty of this concept. The series of works in which it materializes starts with *Reflections* for piano (1968). Yet in order not to risk over-generalizing the characteristics of Panufnik's music since 1968, I would like to limit myself to pointing to its aesthetic aspects. It seems that *Reflections* initiates a group of works conceived both on a small and large scale in which Panufnik expressed his aesthetic principles to the full. Let us try to examine its main properties.

Starting with the *Tragic Overture*, already composed in 1942, Panufnik makes it his aesthetic aim to achieve a balance between form and feeling: 'the fusion', as he writes, 'of dramatic power with a strictly disciplined economy in musical material'.[27] In this overture he chooses as a device for obtaining this economy a four-note cell with a constant intervallic structure, subjected to various transformations.

'It was my intention' he writes, 'to explore this four-note cell to the very limit. It might be transposed, augmented, sometimes inverted, but I must strictly guard throughout the entire work the same intervals between the notes (minor third, major second and minor second), always within a framework of repeated rhythmic patterns.'[28]

---

[25] *Ibid.*, pp. 309–10.

[26] *Ibid.*, p. 310.

[27] *Ibid.*, p. 120.

[28] *Ibid.*, p. 119.

This statement foretells his concept of musical constructivism which he will then develop in many subsequent works. It should be stressed that Panufnik's constructivism, apart from its technical side, reveals original aesthetic aspects. One could infer that he made the idea of material framed in a perfect structure a condition of musical beauty. This idea did not have an abstract character; its purpose was not to serve, or to support, pure form. Moreover, it is only by answering the question of how the idea of musical construction fitted within Panufnik's aesthetic views that one can grasp their sense, specific character, and uniqueness.

Although the composer himself associated his concept of a sound-order with what we could call 'intervallic structuralism', his constructivist idea reached beyond mere organisation of pitch. It was not limited to the morphological level of a work, but rather it was to provide it with a coherence on a wider, syntactic level, and to integrate it as a whole. The main tool serving this purpose was Panufnik's *geometry* with its potential to provide coherence on both smaller and greater scale, and in consequence, to fulfil the idea of a complete structure, as could be described by the term *Gestalt*. In his autobiography Panufnik expressed clearly his fascination at the idea of geometry as the basis of a musical work:

> 'The idea of a musical work being contained and shaped by the perfect order of a geometric form was soon to emerge as a driving force which would permeate almost everything I wrote.'[29]

He also stated:

> 'I felt that geometric shapes could provide my compositions with an unseen skeleton within which my harmonic, melodic and rhythmic concepts could be bound together as a cohesive whole; an organised framework out of which both spiritual and poetic expression could freely flow.
>
> Accepting the definition of music as "unfrozen architecture", it seemed suddenly obvious to me that a composer, like an architect, might draw on the inspiration of geometric form. ... As I planned my next compositions, it became clear to me that each of them would have to grow organically out of its own individual geometric base.'[30]

---

[29] *Ibid.*, p. 325. In his autobiography Panufnik associates the origin of this idea with his *Triangles* commissioned in 1973 by the BBC Television. Yet the chances are that the idea of geometric patterns was used in his compositions as early as in the 1940s. It is worth mentioning here that geometric inspirations may be noted in some short films, which Panufnik made (to his and others' music) in Warsaw before and after the Second World War. Unfortunately, some of them have never been shown to the public.

[30] *Ibid.*, p. 327.

Since geometry in Panufnik's works will be a topic of a separate chapter, I would like to limit myself to a description of its aesthetic aspects. Thus, in his approach to geometry one can discern the whole network of relations or mediations. Thanks to them, his works do not produce an effect through form, but they reveal new extra-musical dimensions whose meaning becomes an important part of their general aesthetic message. This subtle connection between the geometry of sound-structures and their extra-musical meaning reveals a hierarchic character. At its top should be placed, first of all, the relationship to nature. This kind of mediation seems to be rooted more profoundly in the composer's consciousness. Shapes and patterns in the surrounding natural world fascinated Panufnik already in childhood.

> 'I preferred', he remembered, 'my own thoughts and images. I would sink on to the bench beside her [grandmother—Z.S.], and look up at the shapes of the leaves and the swinging movements of the branches overhead. The changing patterns fascinated me; they were like improvised choreography in a mysterious ritual dance.'[31] And he adds further: 'Often I sat dreaming on our balcony ... just watching the shapes of the clouds as they drifted by—they seemed to pile upon each other like moving sculptures in myriad variations of grey.'[32]

Similar reminiscences from childhood, this time conceived as a source of inspiration, re-emerge in Panufnik's commentary on his *Arbor Cosmica*:

> '*Arbor Cosmica* ... grew organically out of my passion for trees, dating back from my childhood expeditions to the Warsaw park with my beloved grand-mother. Still today I am entranced and comforted by the individual beauty of each tree; by the endless variety of shapes and colours. Always I find delight in watching the dance-like rocking branches in the wind, in listening to the song-like groaning and sighing, or the leaves rustling and whispering their mysterious secrets.'[33]

Geometric patterns borrowed from nature gave a shape to many of Panufnik's works. Apart from the tree-patterns which inspired the *Arbor Cosmica*, the composer drew inspiration from the subtle phenomenon of a rainbow, which, through the corresponding diagrams became the symbol for Symphony No. 9 (1986) and for its emotional trajectory. The extent of Panufnik's inspiration from nature is outlined in the following sentence in his autobiography:

---

[31] *Ibid.*, pp. 8–9.

[32] *Ibid.*, p. 14.

[33] *Ibid.*, p. 342.

'Equally important to me were the striking forms to be found in Nature, evolved without assistance from mankind: the perfect pentagon of the five-petalled rose, the logarithmic spiral in the centre of a sunflower, the arch of the rainbow, the parabola of a waterfall, hexagonal snow-crystals.'[34]

Apart from nature and the real world, the source of geometric inspiration for Panufnik pervades the realm of philosophy, religion, and the symbolic forms of archetypal character.

'Whether', he writes, 'in science, mysticism, religion or works of art of any period, geometric configurations, both coincidental and intentional, had always hypnotically appealed to my eyes.'[35]

Yet while all these natural influences endow his works with typically constructivist qualities, the second (i.e. cultural) realm of inspirations supplies their supplementary semantic traits. This may be seen in such works as *Sinfonia di Sfere*, *Sinfonia Mistica*, *Metasinfonia* or *Sinfonia Votiva*, whose geometric order, based on such patterns as ingenious combinations of circles or double spirals, contains a network of meanings of a metaphysical or even mystical character; or in *Triangles* or *Arbor Cosmica* where, in turn, the geometry refers to the mystic philosophy and art of Tantrism, and leads to the symbolic image of a cosmic tree.

Panufnik's vision of a musical order, based on the constructivist properties which are governed by geometry, would certainly not distinguish him much from other composers of the second half of the 20th century if it were not complemented by special poetic qualities encompassing both emotion and dreams. And although the composer always maintains a balance of both components of his aesthetics—the emotional content and the discipline of construction—it is hard to resist the feeling that it is the poetry embedded in his music, which appeals to the listener with redoubled strength. In contrast to those composers who try to hide their emotions under an objective and perfect structure, Panufnik exposes a poetic tone in his works, presenting them as objects of contemplation for the listeners. His standpoint, expressed in his autobiography, is clear and firm:

'I noted to myself that I should never, under any circumstance, allow the technical side of composition to become an end in itself, but that I should always humbly seek to find the truest possible balance between feeling and intellect, heart and brain.'[36]

---

[34] *Ibid.*, p. 327.

[35] *Ibid.*, p. 327.

[36] *Ibid.*, p. 330.

As with Panufnik's idea of musical construction, his poetic idea also penetrates his composition from the beginning of his creative development. The manner in which the poetry emerged within the sound structures is revealed in the composer's commentary to one of these works, the novelty of which at that time was very strong and spontaneous:

'Through ... my *Nocturne*, I was trying to detach myself, from the reality of the present as well as the painful memories of the war years. I was weaving for myself a kind of musical night vision, as in a dream; seeing at the beginning cloudy and mysterious images, which gradually were to emerge clearer and clearer, building very slowly and irrevocably up into an orgiastic climax, then transforming little by little back into the misty images of the opening.

While allowing the emotional content of the work fullest rein, I did not abandon my concept of strict discipline in designing the work. I hung my succession of dreamlike images onto a vast arch of sound, the end exactly mirroring the beginning. At the start, silence was broken by the faint rustle of a side drum; gradually more and more instruments were brought in, so that, at the centre, the full orchestra combined to create the maximum possible volume of sound. Then the arch of sound gradually descended again and the volume diminished as the images dissolved into cloud. Finally the side-drum again ... and silence.'[37]

A similar concept was behind the composition of *Autumn Music* in 1968, one of the most moving of Panufnik's works, in which the motif of dying nature intertwines with a reflection on human life passing away in suffering.

Everything seems to confirm the fact that Panufnik's music developed in a direction away from the main trends in the music of his time, especially those areas which were marked by the avant-garde principles, which he never accepted. However, if we tried to classify his music stylistically, our conclusion would be that it was part of the constructivist stream, which to a similar degree, but with all the rules kept, also included Lutosławski. Commenting on the essence of the constructivist art, a famous Polish expert on this subject writes:

'The constructivist revolution, as one of the "upheavals" in the 20th-century art ... was rubbing at its start against a new "morphology" of cubism while its roots were in fact embedded in a futuristic non-rational realism, in its slogan formulated by the poets: to substitute an expressive form by the form which shapes an idea. ... The autonomy of image was established once more in the realm of form; the essence of art became once more

---

[37] *Ibid.*, p. 165.

a language. The consequences of the futuristic "words on freedom" are to be seen in the constructivist painting.[38]

When we apply this comment to Panufnik's artistic attitude and to his aesthetics we should note that form, being an indispensable key to his art, never becomes a purpose in itself, a kind of 20th-century 'Art for Art's sake', while his sounds always maintain their capacity as a message of poetic expression. It is this that generates the strength of Panufnik's music and that makes him an artist of marked individuality.

Translated by Zbigniew Skowron

---

[38] Andrzej Turowski, *W kręgu konstruktywizmu* (All Around Constructivism) (Warszawa: Wydawnictwa Artystyczne i Filmowe, 1979), p. 242.

Andrzej Panufnik–National Identity of the Immigrant Composer

Anna G. Piotrowska

The question of nationality of immigrant composers is complicated in that the place of birth does not necessarily define a given composer's nationality. The country of residence can at times prove to be more relevant when discussing ties of national character found in musical works. The history of music offers many such examples: Beethoven is regarded as one of the three great Viennese Classical composers, while the German born Handel is often said to be more English than German, as is the Italian composer Clementi who is buried in Westminster Abbey. All three as mature adults chose countries other than those of their birth. Lully, however, brought to France as a young boy, was not given this choice: he is always considered a French composer. One of the most interesting examples, Chopin, not only spent half of his life in Poland and the other half in France, but also had a Polish mother and French father. A life divided between two countries would suggest empathy towards both; however Chopin considered himself to be Polish, as is evident in his music, his correspondence and his general approach. Emphasis should therefore be placed on the methods of determining a composer's nationality. The question is, by what criteria can audiences, musicologists and various researchers ascertain a composer's nationality?

Obviously music is composed in specific circumstances related in particular to place and time, hence it inevitably expresses (directly or indirectly) the composer's cultural background. Music may have local associations or it may reflect regional character. Generally speaking, though musical substance can mirror elements considered national, some compositions may be described as 'universal', a term culturally synonymous with European (or pan-European). Although

Hanslick strongly opposed the view that musical works are essentially representations of extra-musical phenomena, sociological research corroborates the conviction of many composers that music is never written in a vacuum.[1] It therefore follows that the national character of music is generated by a set of specific circumstances which may serve as a key to deciphering the nationality of a composer, which is concealed in his/her works. In his 'Nationality and its Musical Expression' Tomaszewski gives some examples of this style of music.[2]

Firstly, according to Tomaszewski the use of language is essential in order to establish the national character in music. Yet Panufnik composed relatively few pieces exploiting the Polish language; indeed English is rather more prevalent in his works, suggesting a closer identity with British nationality. Some other Polish musicologists share Tomaszewski's point of view; Lissa once wrote that language is crucial to a national style, although elsewhere she concluded that it has no bearing on the national character.[3] The truth is that music does not require the spoken word and Panufnik clearly preferred purely instrumental forms. We are reminded of his native language in only several compositions, for example: *Pięć polskich pieśni wiejskich* (Five Polish Peasant Songs), *Cztery pieśni walki podziemnej* (Four Songs of the Underground Struggle), *Modlitwa do Matki Boskiej Skępskiej* (Prayer to the Virgin of Skempe).

Following Tomaszewski's theories, the use of national dances provides further means of generating national character in music. Indeed, Panufnik readily used Polish dance motifs, among other in *Old Polish Suite*. The composer chose to revive old Polish dances like the *cenar, wyrwany* and *hajduk*.

---

[1] G. Hermeren, 'The Full Voiced Quire: Types of Interpretations of Music' in: M. Krausz (ed.), *The Interpretation of Music* (Oxford: Clarendon Press, 1995), pp. 9–31: "...music is not composed in vacuum. There are different kinds of contexts, not only personal but also historical and political [...] Sometimes music is composed in a nationalistic or patriotic favour, [...] sometimes it is used for such purposes whether or not intended by the composer".

[2] Mieczysław Tomaszewski, 'Kategoria narodowości i jej muzyczna ekspresja' (Nationality and its musical expression), in: L. Bielawski, J. K. Dadak-Kozicka, K. Lesień–Płachecka (eds.), *Oskar Kolberg prekursor antropologii kultury* (Warszawa: Akademia Muzyczna im. F. Chopina, 1995).

[3] Zofia Lissa, 'Problemy stylu narodowego w muzyce polskiej XIX wieku' (National style in Polish music of the 19th century), in: J. Wiśniewski, K. Pałubicki (eds.), *Z dziejów muzyki polskiej* (Bydgoszcz: Bydgoskie Towarzystwo Naukowe, 1965), p. 14.

A nation's history is mirrored in its art, which in time is labelled national. Poland's long and interesting history has always been a source of inspiration for Polish composers and, in analysing Panufnik's compositional output, one can find several works that reflect a Polish past. The composer himself remarked that: "I was inspired by the events of modern and old Polish history".[4] In 1970 Boosey & Hawes published Panufnik's *Concerto in modo antico, Jagiellonian Triptych* and *Old Polish Suite* in one volume entitled 'Old Polish Music'. It must be remembered that two out of three of these works: *Old Polish Suite* and *Concerto in modo antico* based on material from Jarzębski's *Tamburetta, Nativity Song* by Wacław of Szamotuły and *Cracovia civitas*, were composed while Panufnik was still in Poland. The *Jagiellonian Triptych* completed in 1966, ten years after his emigration to England surely indicates Panufnik's sentiments towards his country of origin. The "Jagellonian" of the title contains distinct references to Poland and the Polish royal dynasty as well as associations with Krakow and its university, which bears the same name. Although Panufnik exploited original Polish material in this work, it is the reference to Polish history in his choice of title that establishes his close links with Poland. With the exception of *Katyń Epitaph,* none of his other compositions makes such overt and direct reference to Polish history in the title. In 1949 Panufnik composed *Hommage à Chopin,* the title of which according to Kaczyński,[5] appears to give further indication of Panufnik's national character. While Chopin's nationality may be open to debate, to Poles he is undoubtedly a Polish composer. By the same token, Panufnik openly stated that despite problems concerning his citizenship, he saw himself as a Polish composer and, like Chopin, spent half his life in his native land and the other half in a country where he formed family ties.

Panufnik's identity can also be seen in *Katyń Epitaph,* the title of which provides more proof of the composer's 'Polishness' than the work's interesting concept of tonality and its varied compositional techniques. In this instance the title bears witness that the tragic war crimes perpetrated on Polish soldiers in Katyń during the Second World War was of deep significance to Panufnik. The crime of Katyń

---

[4] Tadeusz Kaczyński, *Andrzej Panufnik i jego muzyka* (Andrzej Panufnik and his Music) (Warszawa: Wydawnictwo Naukowe PWN, 1994), p. 85.

[5] *Ibid.*, p. 32.

though denied for decades was secretly remembered and has become a symbol of nationalism in the modern history of Poland. Panufnik used that symbol to emphasise his awareness of Polish history and to commemorate the suffering of his country. One could say he did this because of his national feelings as a Pole.

Considering that some of his works have direct or indirect associations with Polish history, it is surprising that Panufnik draws on Polish literature in so few of them. According to Tomaszewski,[6] literature is another key factor in the establishment of a national character in music. The absence of literary references in Panufnik's mature work is remarkable, particularly as many other composers have used literature as a source of inspiration. It is inconceivable that Panufnik was unfamiliar with or disliked Polish literature, or indeed that literature failed to impress him. So one may conclude that he deliberately chose not to use literary sources in his music, a fact closely related to the earlier mentioned absence of language.

In any discussion on national character in music folklore plays an important role, and Tomaszewski in his writings[7] acknowledges it as a contributing factor. Tracing folkloric melodies and rhythms in Panufnik's music is not a difficult task.[8]

Five Polish Songs, composed in 1940 clearly shows Panufnik's liking for Polish folk music. *Five Songs* is the first surviving composition conceived out of 'the love for Polish folk music'.[9] Each of the the five songs points precisely to its place of origin: *Od Zwolenia, Od Posuchy, Od Olkusza, Od Kazanowa, Od Janowca*. Seven years later in 1947, Panufnik composed his *Lullaby* in which he made use of a traditional melody from Małopolska that he probably heard while still living in Krakow (1945–46). The composer exploits folk rhythmic and melodic patterns in *Old Polish Suite*, and its simplicity and dance-like character serves to create a specific atmosphere. We can observe similar characteristics in *Sinfonia Rustica* where folk elements are exploited not only for their beauty but also fulfil an artistic

---

[6] Mieczysław Tomaszewski, *op. cit.*

[7] Mieczysław Tomaszewski, *op. cit.*

[8] Jadwiga Paja-Stach, 'The Hommage à Chopin of Andrzej Panufnik in the Context of his Works Based on Polish Folk Music', in: *Chopin and his Work in the Context of Culture*, Studies edited by Irena Poniatowska and others (Kraków: Musica Iagellonica, in print) (Ed.).

[9] Tadeusz Kaczyński, *op. cit.*

aim. In *Polonia* (1959) which contains three national dances the title speaks for itself and the music remains national in character throughout the work. Panufnik composed three out of four of the above works while still living in Poland. After moving to England, Panufnik's affirmation of his 'Polishness' became gradually apparent and one could almost say that the Polish folk element in his music became more veiled. Interestingly, Panufnik turned to another characteristic feature of Polish culture closely related to folklore, namely that of religion.

Tomaszewski makes no mention of religion in his article on national character in music, nor has music ever been a key factor of national character. However, the Polish example is somewhat diffe-rent, as religion is so much part of the 'Polish soul'. Even folklore is deeply rooted in Roman Catholic belief. In my opinion, Panufnik's use of religious chants is a further sign of his Polish identity. Polish religious traditions recalled from his time in Poland were to become one of his trademarks. Consequently there are many such quotations in his works written in England, as for example in *Concerto in modo antico,* where the opening phrase of the second movement is reminiscent of *Święty Boże* (Oh Holy God) or in *Prayer to the Virgin of Skempe*, which reflects the Polish cult of the Virgin Mary (which is equalled in intensity only by that of the Maltese). From among Panufnik's compositions inspired by the traditions of the Polish Church, attention must be drawn to *Sinfonia Sacra,* composed to commemorate 1000 years of Polish Christianity. It is based on the prayers of the *Canonical Hours* and on the *Bogurodzica* (Mother of God) which the composer would later exploit in *Sinfonia Votiva.*

It would seem that in order to counterbalance the use of Polish religious melodies in his works, Panufnik composed *Universal Prayer* in which he provokes controversy by stating that religion is universal in character. A marked display of Panufnik's affinity with Poland can be found in his instant and passionate reaction to political upheavals in his native country. His musical response to current events offers further evidence of his feelings for Poland—a country he never forgot or cut himself off from. Keeping abreast of events, he proved where his heart lay by composing Bassoon Concerto in memory of Father Jerzy Popiełuszko. By celebrating a Polish hero (for in the future the priest may well be considered a national hero) Panufnik emphasised his own identity, and, through linking together aspects of political and social concern, as in the previously mentioned *Katyń Epitaph,* he revealed his sensitivity to matters affecting Poland.

Having posed the question[10] of whether Panufnik was Polish or British, Kaczyński remains in no doubt that the composer was Polish. He was considered a 'Polish gentleman' and was regarded as a leading 'Polish composer'. What does being Polish mean? Particularly in the case of a composer who spent half his life in England but whose parents came from Poland? No suggested explanations seem to answer this question adequately. Sociologists trying to select characteristic features that would help to create an image of a typical Pole, emphasise that nationality can be perceived on two different levels: the first, seen in terms of local and regional associations and the second, viewed from a universal aspect. When discussing the influence of folklore on Panufnik's music, it is interesting to note that the folk melodies he exploited came from Mazowsze and Małopolska, regions where the composer used to live.

National background is an integral part of a wider unity—European culture. Seen from this point of view, it has often been described as universal or 'cosmopolitan'. The meaning of universal is 'not referring directly to any country', hence neither Poland nor England. Among Panufnik's 'nationally uncommitted compositions we find works that confirm his pan-Europeanism and his affinity with European tradition. It seems that for Panufnik, music itself was the greatest treasure and he saw no barriers between Polish, English or universal music. Panufnik's compositions are simply his music. Yet, even though some titles and sources of inspiration suggest European or English heritage, most of his works tend to gravitate towards Poland, which does not necessarily follow that Panufnik can or should be regarded as a Polish composer. Ultimately, a composer's nationality is dependent on his own attitude and intentions, often reflected in his music.

Although Panufnik declared himself to be Polish he did not keep in touch with many other Polish immigrants living in England. He felt they did not understand his music and never sought greater contact with them, and he was far more interested in Poles living in Poland. He chose to give his children a British upbringing, yet Kaczyński claims that his daughter feels Polish. Could it be that she became 'infected' with her father's Polishness? Panufnik was an immigrant composer, a status that carried certain consequences. Immigrants living and working in their 'second' homelands are often

---

[10] *Ibid.*, p. 16.

excluded from the musical culture of their adopted country. In his book dedicated to the music of the USA, Nicholls fails to mention the names of Stravinsky or Schoenberg, thus tacitly implying they are Russian and Austrian respectively.[11] This tendency of assigning composers to the country of their birth is arbitrary and unjust, as their intended nationality should be of greater importance, though sometimes difficult to determine if their wish is unclear. Fortunately, judging by his music and his remarks, it is evident that Panufnik was Polish.

Translated by Anna G. Piotrowska

---

[11] David Nicholls (ed.), *The Cambridge History of American Music* (Cambridge: Cambridge University Press, 1998).

Part II
Musical Style

Panufnik's Music in the Context of 20th-Century Music

Bernard Jacobson

My thesis will be that Panufnik was one of the supreme symphonists of the century we used to call our own. Is that, you may be inclined to ask—is that not a rather empty claim, given that the 20th century was a time when the death of the symphony was frequently proclaimed, and even celebrated? If "in the country of the blind," according to H. G. Wells's fable, "the one-eyed man is king," the eminence I am ascribing to Poland's greatest modern composer might look like nothing more than the most imposing tomb in the cemetery. But just as Mark Twain pointed out that a press report of his death was an exaggeration, it seems to me that a field cultivated by such masters as Nielsen in Denmark, Sibelius in Finland, Shostakovich in Russia, Elgar and Vaughan Williams in England, Henze in Italy, and William Schuman in America can hardly be dismissed as a graveyard.

That list of symphonic practitioners is far from being an exhaustive one. You will certainly notice that I have left out the name of Mahler, and this particular omission is not accidental. The last seven of Mahler's symphonies (if you include *Das Lied von der Erde* and the unfinished Tenth) qualify in terms of date. But my own view, unfashionable though it may be, is that what Mahler achieved in the field falls far short of what Nielsen, Sibelius, and Elgar were doing at the same time. We love the Mahler symphonies for their embodiment of all the angst, introverted self-dramatization, and Brechtian alienation of a psychoanalytical age—not for quality of musical inspiration, or for mastery of the symphonic principle.

What that principle is, and how Panufnik fulfilled it, must be the central concern of my remarks today. It would be arrogant to imagine that, within the limits of one short lecture, I could comprehensively define the essence of a genre so various in its manifestations and so profound and subtle in its resonance. But for our present purposes I should like to postulate that the fundamental characteristic of the symphony lies in its reconciliation of the conflicting demands of musical unity and musical variety, and to suggest further that the form presupposes a certain range of methods of getting from one musical point to another. That other great vehicle of musical thought for composers alike of the classical, romantic, and modern periods, the concerto, is also concerned with the reconciling of unity and variety. But it has another element—the interplay and balance of contrasted performing forces—at its heart, and it is this that distinguishes it from the symphony. Smaller forms, meanwhile, tend naturally enough to exalt unity over variety, as the merest glance at Panufnik's own *Tragic Overture* suffices to illustrate.

It is, then, the challenge of blending unity and variety in satisfying proportions, and the associated task of moving musically from point A to point B, that I want to consider in relation to Panufnik's symphonic achievement. It is his radically original way of reconciling unity with variety, combined with his equally personal sense of musical movement, that gives his work at once its strength and its subtlety—though the irresistible poetic and emotional appeal of his finest music is another issue, about which I want also to say something.

Those basic questions of musical form cannot be addressed without a word on the encompassing topic of musical language. The central problem of music in our time has been the problem of finding a language. If, as is widely supposed, a gulf has opened between contemporary composers and listeners, this is not because composers have run out of interesting things to say to their public. It is rather because a universally understandable way of saying them no longer exists. In addition to looking inside themselves and finding out what they need to express, composers have been forced to invent, as it were out of nothing, a new idiom for its expression. Their solutions have tended in an artistically rootless era to change radically from one work to the next, confronting audiences in turn with the task of beginning all over again each time they try to respond to a new composition. The Austro-British critic Hans Keller described this predicament well when he observed: "The typical 'bad' music of Mozart's time is all background and no foreground, and hence insignificant; while the typical 'bad' music of our age is all foreground and no background, and hence meaningless."

The crisis of language that came to a head in the music of the 20th century was not unprecedented, but its intensity had not been paralleled in several hundred years. The last comparably far-reaching change came in the 17th century, when the modal polyphony of the high renaissance gave place to the tonal harmony and counterpoint of the early baroque. Fundamental musical values were then called so radically in question that Monteverdi, for example, cultivated two entirely different styles through much of his composing life—the so-called *prima prattica* and *seconda prattica*—passing deliberately from one to the other as each fresh creative challenge dictated. The transition from baroque to classical style 150 years later was less disorienting to musicians and public, because this time the essential basis of the tonal language was not undermined, even though its resources and functions were greatly expanded.

By the beginning of the 20th century, the vast extension of chromaticism—of the use of notes "foreign" to a given key—in the music of Wagner and his late-romantic followers had indeed put tonality itself in jeopardy. This development was reinforced by the peculiar nature of Arnold Schoenberg's musical gifts, and drew added force from a questionable belief in historical inevitability. At the same time the spread of Freud's psychological theories was fostering a climate of thought that encouraged acceptance of pain, self-doubt, self-denial, and even neurosis as indispensable elements in artistic experience. For several decades composers, dazzled by this combination of historical factors and dominated by the strength of Schoenberg's saturnine personality, embraced the darker side of human experience as if it were the only fit material for art: pleasure, as an artistic principle, came to be seen as cause not for joy but for guilt. Except in the work of a few exceptional individuals, beauty itself became a suspect word and an all-but-forbidden concept.

Around the end of the 1960s, signs that this phase had run its course began to appear. In one of those paradoxes that make the arts and their enjoyment so endlessly fascinating, it is now the word "modern" that has itself come under suspicion. It tends now to denote a kind of music that is really rather old-fashioned, written in styles that I like to describe as "avant-derrière-garde." Senior composers formerly uncompromising in their rejection of tonal methods, like Peter Schat in the Netherlands, Kurt Schwertsik in Austria, Peter Maxwell Davies in England, and George Rochberg in the United States, have been among the many to readopt tonality in their recent works—while, for this audience, I scarcely need to mention the names of Krzysztof Penderecki and Henryk Mikołaj Górecki.

The relation to tonality is not the only index to a composer's stance vis-à-vis modernism and tradition, but it tends to be a very informative one, and it is through Panufnik's and Lutosławski's differing responses to the tonal/atonal/12-tone question that we can most clearly apprehend the individuality of each of these two men. If we start from their view of the supposed breakdown of tonality and of Schoenberg's reaction to that problem, the initial difference seems obvious and wide enough. Panufnik went to study in Vienna partly because he wanted to extend his knowledge of Schoenberg and his disciples, and hoped to study with Webern. Lutosławski saw his own line of descent in a quite other light.

> "There's practically no trace of twelve-tone doctrine in my music," he said; "Even if I use some rows containing twelve different notes, I think the very idea of the twelve-tone row doesn't belong to Schoenberg exclusively. It was in the air. It's quite natural that total chromaticism is something which is a question of our time. It is a natural step in the development of music in our time. But I think the other source from the past is the Debussy tradition. Debussy-early Stravinsky-Bartók-Varèse, that's a sort of line to which I clearly belong."

This is all very well, but the matter is not so simple. Like Peer Gynt's onion, the reality begins to look different as we strip the outer layers off. Rather like the great Swiss-born, Dutch-domiciled composer Frank Martin, Lutosławski may be said to have juxtaposed 12-tone elements with others that sound tonal (though he rejected the "tonal" label for his own music). But in contrast to Martin's case (and much more in line with that of Schoenberg himself), the idea of total chromaticism—of consistently using all twelve notes of the chromatic scale as the foundation of his harmonic language—remained cardinal in Lutosławski's stylistic evolution.

Panufnik, for his part, soon saw that he had to turn in a different direction. While still a student, he related in his autobiography, *Composing Myself,*

> "I could see what Schoenberg was attempting. I agreed with the principle of a self-imposed discipline, a limitation to achieve unity. However, judged from the standpoint of my own purposes, his method seemed to achieve unity only at the cost of the equally desirable goal of variety. The 'democratization' of the twelve notes of the chromatic scale seemed to block the way to essential expressive elements: the prohibition against note-repetition meant that, even if the composer succeeded momentarily in creating a certain expressive character by emphasising particular notes, he was immediately compelled to neutralize it by letting the others have their say.... I threw my dodecaphonic sketches into my waste paper basket, and concluded that I should never again try to borrow methods from other composers."

Lutosławski, we must remember, was as firmly determined as Panufnik on arriving at a language of his own. I am not suggesting that his fundamentally chromatic idiom was "borrowed" from anybody. The point is rather that he was not troubled in the same way by the problem that sent Panufnik off on another route: the element of sameness—of colorlessness—that music risks when it allots strictly equal time to all the colors (or "chromata"). In the 1990s, when "political correctness" was as hot a general topic as chromatic serialism had been on the musical scene in the 1930s, Janet Daley observed in *The Times* of London that, "carried to its inevitable conclusion, cultural relativism produces not tolerance but nihilism. If everyone is right, then no one is." *Mutatis mutandis,* that is exactly what Panufnik perceived about "democratizing" the notes out of which alone music can derive its character.

It was this perception that was to lead him to his own stylistic solution. More and more rigorously from the *Tragic Overture* on, his works came to rely for all their thematic material on one or two basic three-note configurations—"triads" in a non-technical sense of the word—articulated in every possible way and transposed to a wide range of pitches. The method produces a formidable, and entirely modern, sense of organic unity. Thus far, you may detect an apparent parallel with Schoenbergian serialism. What transforms the effect is, quite simply, the small number of the notes that make up Panufnik's thematic cells. By eliminating from each of these cells more notes than he included, he was able to create highly specific atmospheres, and to blend them at will in a wide variety of mixtures and proportions. The result can occupy any position whatever along the chromatic-diatonic axis, and the consequent breadth of expression is of a different order from anything within the range of orthodox 12-note serialism.

So we are faced, again, with a paradox: through a procedure that is in essence serial—the systematic deployment of specific thematic units—Panufnik was able to achieve the quite unsystematic goal of free poetic expression. The procedure itself reflects what remained irreducibly Polish about him through the 37 years he lived in England. Both within and outside "artistic" circles, the English mind tends to be suspicious of anything that smacks of system, or theory, or abstraction. It may well have been not so much fear of rabies as the threat of creeping metaphysics that inspired much of the English opposition to the Channel Tunnel. For metaphysics is seen as the way those intellectualist French people across the Channel do their philosophy, whereas "English empiricism" has become so endemic a manner of thought that the very phrase is tantamount to a tautology. Panufnik's mind, in contrast, was formed by a clearly Catholic intellectual tradition: it positively reveled in system—and the more formal, ambitious, and all-embracing the system, the better.

The results, in music like *Reflections, Universal Prayer,* and *Metasinfonia,* are much easier to appreciate if we rid our minds of certain confusions on this subject. The crucial confusion is the idea that "system" and "feeling" are in some way mutually opposed. For years, English partisans of Schoenbergian serialism proscribed the term "12-note system" and insisted on "12-note method" instead. The idea, apparently, was that a method was compatible with inspiration and a system wasn't. In truth, not unlike tonal composition, dodecaphony is—or rather, let us hope, was—a *method* that has its basis in a *system;* no one, after all, has any problem with the notion of a "tonal system." In the end, the emotional or artistic character of a piece of music depends on the composer's qualities of heart and mind, not on the technique he employs.

"For me personally," Panufnik insisted, "music is an expression of deep human feeling ...I never regard the technical side of a musical work as an end in itself," and no one who knew him could ever be distracted from this fundamental preoccupation by questions of method, or technique, or system. I worked with him for twelve years, as a staff member at his publishers, Boosey & Hawkes, and I can declare without hesitation that I have never known a musician who consecrated himself with more selfless integrity to that deeply personal end. This was a composer passionately involved in humanity's travails, refracting them with fierce quietude through the prism of his own soul; a composer utterly dedicated to poetic expression, but repelled by any kind of sentimental excess or rhetorical self-indulgence, bending a remorseless concentration of thought to the end of liberating his—and his listener's—imagination; a composer who used the discriminating outward ear of an accomplished and highly trained conductor in the service of a veritably mystical inner ear. There are conductor-composers whose music always "sounds." There are tone-poets whose music usually means something. To enshrine deep spiritual meanings and fresh, incalculable poetic inspirations in sound-structures of unfailing clarity and compelling resonance may be accounted Panufnik's distinctive achievement.

To a rare degree, a Panufnik work is "all of a piece"; you cannot distinguish in his music between surface and what lies beneath. There is, for one thing, no surface in his music at all, but rather a sense of absolute homogeneity fusing invention and treatment, line and texture, content and form. If anything, you may occasionally feel that a given piece insists *too* schematically on its monolithic one-ness of character. *Sinfonia Mistica,* for example, or *Metasinfonia,* or even that pivotal work in Panufnik's stylistic evolution, *Universal Prayer,* can in their granitic Parmenidean unity risk being heard as doctrinaire.

Still, it was the sheer single-mindedness of the man, as of his music, that most immediately and insistently captivated me. A proverb propagated by Isaiah Berlin after Tolstoy, who in his turn took it from the Greek fabulist Archilochus, has it that the fox knows many small things, but the hedgehog knows one big thing. On the basis of that formulation—which, I should emphasize, is in no simple way a value-judgement—Lutosławski, like Stravinsky, must surely be counted as a fox, and Panufnik (in common with Skryabin, a composer I don't even much like) as a hedgehog.

How, you may be wondering, does this picture square with Panufnik's stated reservations about a method that could achieve unity "only at the cost of the equally desirable goal of variety"? Wouldn't he (if my application of Archilochus is right) be the one to risk excessive uniformity in his music? No, for it was precisely because he perceived this danger that Panufnik devised his three- or four-note, instead of 12-note, thematic cells. Within a technique that systematically rotates and transposes and inverts and permutates a stringently limited thematic vocabulary, these cells function rather like the elements of traditional tonality: shifting the "triads" to new pitch levels has an effect comparable to that of modulation, and combining them simultaneously at several pitches parallels the use of heightened dissonance in a tonal context. And the resulting definiteness of character in turn facilitates variety, for it is vagueness, not definiteness, that inherently resists variation.

It is time now to consider the question I have already proposed about how music gets from point A to point B. Just as it is in performance, the secret of movement is one of the crucial aspects of the craft of composition. Anyone, more or less, can come up with a tune. It takes a real composer to transport us deftly and inevitably from one tune to another (which is, I suppose, why we don't call the creation of folk songs "composition"). More than almost any of his 20th-century colleagues, Panufnik possessed this faculty. There is about his music at once a seamlessness and a sense of purposeful progress that are alike subtle and cogent. For all the two composers' differences of ethos and language, it is such cogency that links Panufnik's style with that of Brahms. In neither man's textures is there any room for "spare parts": every line is organic, every note essential in driving the music on its forward course.

At this point, I should like you to listen for a moment to part of the second movement of *Sinfonia Rustica,* the first of Panufnik's ten symphonies—or the first, rather, to have survived, for two earlier essays in the genre were, like everything else he composed before 1944, lost in the aftermath of the Warsaw Uprising. (see Example 1)

An early work in Panufnikian terms, the symphony still partakes in its outer movements of what the composer calls "quasi sonata" form, and it breathes a beguiling atmosphere deeply rooted in Polish folk art. At several points, you may detect a spiritual affinity with the calm spaciousness of another folk-related, originally unnumbered, "country" symphony: Vaughan Williams's *Pastoral* Symphony of 1921. *Rustica* is also an early example of Panufnik's practice of taking visual and other images and symbols as a framework for his compositions: the symmetrical paper-cuts made by peasants in north Poland played a part in the formal organization of works as widely separated in time as this symphony of 1948 and the Third String Quartet, written 42 years later. In overall design, moreover, *Rustica* is prophetically symmetrical, both formally and in physical layout— the two string orchestras are disposed "stereophonically" at the sides of a small wind group—and the gentle dance movement you have just been listening to exemplifies the highly individual sense of movement that already marked Panufnik's music.

We should bear in mind at this juncture that, though the symphonic genre has traditionally been associated with sonata form, there is nothing inevitable about that connection. Provided the two tasks I have spoken of are fulfilled—reconciliation of the conflicting demands of unity and variety, and convincing movement from one musical point to another—there is nothing to prevent a composer from devising other means than expositions, developments, and recapitulations, or first- and second-subject thematic groups, for the organization of his symphonic form. In *Sinfonia di Sfere*—the sixth of his symphonies, dating from 1974/75—Panufnik achieved one of his most challenging and ingenious structures. Not beholden in any significant degree to the methods of sonata form, this is nevertheless a work of formidable seriousness and substance—at around 33 minutes, the second longest among the ten symphonies—and its unpredictable yet ultimately cogent twists of thought, articulated through skittering string and drum figurations, incisive piano chords, tense woodwind ejaculations, and some weirdly expressive solos for the brass principals, deserve more frequent hearings. (see Example 2)

Ex. 1: *Sinfonia Rustica*, II, beginning
© Copyright 1957 by Hawkes & Son (London) Ltd.
Reproduced by permission of Boosey & Hawkes Music Publishers Ltd.

Ex. 2: *Sinfonia di Sfere*, p. 80
© Copyright 1976 by Boosey & Hawkes Music Publishers Ltd.
Reproduced by permission of Boosey & Hawkes Music Publishers Ltd.

Sinfonia di Sfere raises a number of topics important for an understanding of Panufnik's music. To begin with, there is—as we have seen with *Sinfonia Rustica*—his inveterate use of geometrical, numerical, or other conceptual and visual models as a kind of scaffolding for his form. Spheres and circles, in *Sinfonia di Sfere* (1974/75) and *Sinfonia Mistica* (1977) respectively, gave place to the "golden ellipse" that in 1988 generated the form of Symphony No. 10, and to the mandorla of ancient religious art—the palindromic almond shape that results when two equal circles overlap—in the last work of all, the Cello Concerto written three years later. For *Metasinfonia,* in 1978, the presiding image was the spiral. A more abstractly conceptual image, the fundamental dualism of Tantric philosophy, gave rise in 1972 to *Triangles,* and the 1983 *Arbor Cosmica* sought to represent in sound the traditional artistic symbol of the cosmic tree.

Such pointers do not necessarily help an individual listener's comprehension of the piece in question, and Panufnik in his last years came to accept, if hesitantly, that it might in some cases be better to omit them from program notes as a potential distraction. On the other hand, it is worth emphasizing that each such image functions consistently as a pattern for the articulation of material throughout the work it is used in. For this reason, the practice is not open to the criticism that may be leveled at Lutosławski's interleaved *ad libitum* passages—namely, that they inject an alien static element into forms that are by intention dynamic and mobile.

Then there is the question of melody, which may very naturally come to mind as we listen to *Sinfonia di Sfere.* Are there any melodies in Panufnik? The answer, I think, is that there are no specific, formally organized, separable melodies of the kind to be found in most composers' symphonies, but there is indeed a wealth of melody in an overarching sense that often stretches from beginning to end of an entire work. This, too, helps to explain his preference for single-movement form. Roughly half of his symphonies are continuous structures—and continuous structures, furthermore, that cannot in any convincing way be broken down into constituent movements. I should like to suggest that the distinction between melodies, as conventionally conceived, and melody in Panufnik's sense is rather like the distinction in language between cultures and culture. Cultures, like melodies, are too often taken as tools for separation, whether of musical thoughts or of peoples. Culture and melody, by contrast, are concepts that help to articulate the notion of interconnection, of universality.

On the sheer distinctiveness of Panufnik's music it may be useful here to lay some stress. Other composers may occasionally come to

mind, when you are considering this or that aspect of his style. Just
as his way of building pieces out of narrowly restricted sets of notes
superficially recalls the serialism of Schoenberg and his school, his
scientific and mathematical affinities have something in common with
Xenakis. The delight in the fundamental materials of music that
informs page after page of his work is suggestive of composers as
widely different as Bartók and Nielsen. His manner of scoring for
clearly separated "families" of instruments (the woodwinds, for
instance, set in balanced opposition to the strings) recalls Bruckner;
his frequent use of *cantus firmus* as a foundation for proliferating
polyphonic lines likewise evokes the methods of Maxwell Davies. Yet
Panufnik's music never sounds remotely like that of any of those
forerunners or colleagues, for each of these resources and methods
is used in an entirely individual way, and in the furtherance of an
entirely personal artistic vision. I cannot resist letting a further
excerpt from *Sinfonia di Sfere* underline this point for you.

Ex. 3: *Sinfonia di Sfere*, p. 29
© Copyright 1976 by Boosey & Hawkes Music Publishers Ltd.
Reproduced by permission of Boosey & Hawkes Music Publishers Ltd.

For all the skill and craftsmanship of their treatment, you might think at first hearing that nothing could be simpler than Panufnik's musical materials. Yet simplicity is itself a deceptively over-simplified concept, for the none-too-simple reason, to start with, that it has two quite different and unrelated opposites: complication and complexity. Textures in Panufnik, and the melodies and rhythms that go into their making, are rarely complicated but unfailingly and richly complex.

The distinction is one of means and ends. Decadent music (and the sort of composer I mean is too obvious to need naming today) has progressive recourse to a more and more complicated apparatus in pursuit of ever punier artistic results. Panufnik's is the opposite way. Take the "simplest" of elements, but shape them artfully and put them together with skill, variety, and an audacious ear for nuance, and the consequence can be a true complexity out of all proportion to the apparent exiguity of the material. Described thus, the process could almost be said to sum up what minimalism sets out to do, but all too seldom achieves. Perhaps the aesthetic of minimalism has never been more masterfully realized than in this early example of the style:

Ex. 4: Pérotin, *Viderunt omnes,* beginning

(Well, a *very* early example of the style: that was the opening of Pérotin's *Viderunt omnes,* composed probably in 1198.) Read Panufnik's program notes on the carefully deployed "arcs" and "planes" of his Ninth Symphony, and even of the "palindromic form" and "lyrical geometry" of a relatively free-form piece like his Piano Concerto, and you may be led to expect a formalistic, not to say arid, sort of music. But pay attention to the profound humanistic sympathies hinted at in his words, and still more compellingly set forth in the music itself, and you will find that "emotional expression" no more conflicts, in Panufnik, with the "scientific laws" that articulate it than is the case with the even more rigorously formulated mathematical concepts of a composer like Xenakis. For both men, the underlying laws (and you must remember that we are not speaking of mere picayune "rules," such as those applied *ex post facto* by dusty 19th-century musicologists to the living creations of the classical masters) remain merely a structural scaffolding. The crucial expressive decisions are kept firmly within the purview of each composer's unfettered imagination. And the result, though never extended beyond the bounds of reasonable proportion, can attain a genuinely awesome grandeur of scale, as the gigantic opening paragraph of Panufnik's longest symphony, No. 9, shows at once. (see Example 5)

In that opening, an unbroken musical idea four minutes long (and already suggesting the 40-minute duration that its working-out will demand), the size and nobility of a Pérotin *organum* seems to reach across the intervening eight centuries in a mysterious foreshadowing of Panufnik's own fresh and unmistakably individual musical language. The seven symphonies Panufnik composed after *Sacra* vary in scale from the expansiveness of the *Sinfonia de Sfere* and Symphony No. 9 to the relative brevity of the 23-minute *Sinfonia Concertante* and the 25-minute *Sinfonia Votiva* (Nos. 4 and 8). The Tenth Symphony, written in 1988 and revised two years later, is the shortest of all at just over 17 minutes, but brevity here coexists with a breadth of inspiration that allows every idea to make its point without a hint of haste. There is no trace of the nervousness of manner that seems inseparable from Schoenbergian and other brands of total chromaticism. In its die-away closing pages, Panufnik's symphonic valediction breathes a tenderness perhaps foreshadowed in some passages of the *Sinfonia Sacra* 25 years earlier, which led Bernard Gavoty, the critic of *Le Figaro* in Paris, to salute the composer for "the gift of incantation, of sorcery, without which music is only artifice." That serene tenderness has perhaps never been so fully and breathtakingly realized as in this crowning conclusion. "The musical material of Symphony No. 10" (Panufnik wrote in his program

Ex. 5: Symphony No. 9, beginning
© Copyright 1987 by Boosey & Hawkes Music Publishers Ltd.
Reproduced by permission of Boosey & Hawkes Music Publishers Ltd.

note for the premiere, which he conducted in Chicago in 1990) "consists of tonal melodic lines with a simultaneous flow of reflected and transposed 3-note cells ... As in my previous symphonies, the beauty and mystic forces of geometry influenced me in the overall design. The invisible skeleton of this symphony is the 'golden ellipse'; its curving frame guided me in the ordering of the expressive contractions and expansions of musical texture. The music progresses along its elliptical course for one and a half orbits, until suddenly it straightens out into a new trajectory leading to the conclusion of the symphony ..."

All this might be decried as mere technique. On a deeper level, and more important in the end, is Panufnik's penchant for asking the ultimate questions. Even listeners not naturally given to mysticism are liable, under his spell, to be taken out of themselves, to be propelled beyond the normal mundane courses of thought and feeling. Wilhelm Furtwängler said that it was the performer's task to seek out the sense of the numinous in music. The task of the composer is to put it there, and it is a task that Panufnik fulfilled to perfection in one major piece after another. "Ecstasy" is a big word; but all it really means is "standing outside oneself." That, the secret of his stature as a 20th-century master, is where Panufnik's music leaves his audience, and where, with the conclusion of the Tenth Symphony, I shall let him leave you today. (see Example 6)

Ex. 6: Symphony No. 10, conclusion
© Copyright 1993 by Boosey & Hawkes Music Publishers Ltd.
Reproduced by permission of Boosey & Hawkes Music Publishers Ltd.

Feeling and Intellect, Heart and Brain: Technique and Content in Panufnik's Symphonies

Niall O'Loughlin

In much of Andrzej Panufnik's music, and especially in the symphonies, there is an apparent conflict between the techniques of
composition and the music's content and indeed its 'meaning'. This
feeling has arisen from numerous studies that have been published
over many years. Usually the point of departure has been shown in
the numerous charts and diagrams which have been presented by
the composer in connection with the understanding of these works.
These were clearly part of the composer's preparation and thinking
process and naturally formed part of his structural planning. These
consist of straightforward tables and, in the case of the later music,
geometric plans that are crystal clear in their conception but, if they
are taken literally, can give a somewhat simplistic idea of the
composition in question. It is sometimes possible to think that there
is little more to the music. Similarly, the short motifs that form such
an important part of the detailed working of Panufnik's music are
only a small part of this very fundamental creative process. The
translation of these basic ideas into the vital works that these
symphonies are is an amazing process.

Panufnik's music is so far removed from this potentially clinical
and detached world in its intensity, formal power and underlying
inspiration that one senses a rift between 'heart and brain'.[1] It was
perhaps inevitable that the composer's own writings focus on the
objective aspects of his music. His own view of himself as an architect
is particularly apt: 'I could liken myself to an architect, tackling each
work in three stages, always in the same order: first the purpose, or

---

[1] Andrzej Panufnik, *Composing Myself* (London: Methuen, 1987), p. 330.

reason for which the work is composed; then the architectural structure; then the material of which it is to be built'.[2] The composer's commentaries inevitably concentrate on these techniques. The details of mathematical structures and motivic groups do help to explain the rationale behind the music, but it is possible that they might in some way limit the intuitive response to the music. That Panufnik himself was very well aware of the possibility of this interpretation is clear in his writings. Three quotations clarify his views:

> I never regard the technical side of a musical work as an end in itself.[3]

> For me personally music is an expression of deep human feeling and true emotion.[4]

> I should humbly seek to find the truest possible balance between feeling and intellect, heart and brain.[5]

It is clear that Panufnik himself was fully aware of the possibility that there could be some conflict between the thinking processes on the one hand and the realisation of these ideas into music. It is the aim of the present paper to investigate the process by which the ideas are translated into musical form, the one in which we as listeners can receive these works. Taking the symphonies in chronological order shows how the process changed from a straightforward to a complex one, but also how the process was consistently effective. The symphonies form three natural groups: the first three inspired by Poland; the second group, dating from 1973–78 in which geometric plans were first presented; the third group, composed in the 1980s to important commissions.

The Polish symphonies

Two early symphonies were lost in the Warsaw uprising of 1944 so the first of the surviving series is the *Sinfonia Rustica*, composed in 1948 and revised in 1955, composed as a tribute to the rustic art of Poland. The two following works, the *Sinfonia Elegiaca* of 1957 and revised in 1966 (originally called *Symphony of Peace*) and the *Sinfonia Sacra* of 1963, move out in new directions. The *Sinfonia Elegiaca* was composed with the memory of the loss of many of the composer's

---

[2] Andrzej Panufnik, *Impulse and Design* (London: Boosey & Hawkes, 1974), p. 1.

[3] *Ibid.*, p. 1.

[4] *Ibid.*, p. 1.

[5] Andrzej Panufnik, *Composing Myself*, p. 330.

relatives during World War Two (the Polish dimension), but was intended to be a general protest against any human violence. The *Sinfonia Sacra* 'was composed as a tribute to Poland's Millennium of Christianity and Statehood'.[6] The strong Polish connection is with the Gregorian chant, the *Bogurodzica*, long associated with Poland, on which the work is based.

The *Sinfonia Rustica* is the most straightforward of Panufnik's symphonies. Based on Polish folk tunes, it presented a distinct challenge to the composer. Anyone who has tried to compose a piece using folk song will know of the difficulties of the extension of the statement of the single melody. The choice is whether to repeat the melody in full, repeat it with changes or treat it in an unfolk-like and more symphonic way by selecting parts of each melody for more detailed treatment. Panufnik does it in all ways. What is beguiling about his treatment is the imaginative way that each melody is presented and then varied. There is some similarity with the same type of melody in Janáček's *The Cunning Little Vixen* and the *Sinfonietta*. The formal chart (Fig. 1) that the composer published has certain symmetries, but these are of a traditional type and give little clue to what was to follow in the later works. The sonata construction of this movement and the finale is almost entirely denoted by different themes. The charming second movement *Con grazia* is given in a simple form which disguises the beautiful repeats of the main melody which begins to appear in a motivic way, while the yearning third movement *Con espressione* takes on the form of an expressive set of variations.

The *Sinfonia Elegiaca* takes over some of the features of the *Sinfonia Rustica*, but in a totally untraditional way and one that points to new formal developments. The idea of a sonata-type structure for the central section is of itself somewhat unorthodox, but the superimposition of a hybrid combination of rondo and variations on either side of it is amazingly new (Fig. 2). The written description barely begins to suggest what the work sounds like, although it provides a precise and clear statement of the form. It is in the content that the composer really shows his imagination. Divided cellos with basses and timpani rolls bring a poignancy that can scarcely be imagined just from reading the score. The simple four-bar phrases extended to five bars have a very unsettling feeling, while the freely elaborated cor anglais phrases are irregularly balanced in an unpre-

---

[6] Andrzej Panufnik, *Impulse and Design*, p. 5.

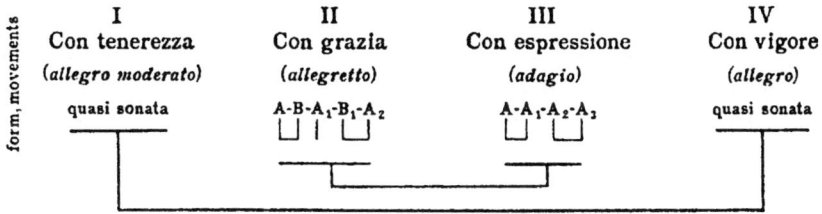

Fig. 1. *Sinfonia Rustica*

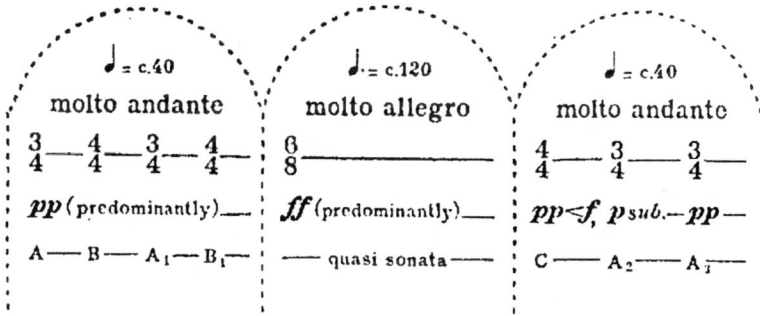

Fig. 2. *Sinfonia Elegiaca*

Fig. 3. *Sinfonia Sacra*

dictable way that was not found in the *Sinfonia Rustica*. We are now beginning to see the type of development of motives that was to play such an important part in later works. The central quasi-sonata section contrasts as violently as can be imagined with the sorrowful outer sections. The rhythmic vitality of this section has something of the rhythmic spring of the first movement of Beethoven's Seventh Symphony, but the constant change from two beats to three in the basic 6/8 time gives this section a completely new dimension from the earlier work. It is an example of Panufnik's fearless juxtaposition of extremes of tempo and dynamics, something which can also be found both in the *Sinfonia Mistica* and the *Sinfonia Votiva*.

For the *Sinfonia Sacra* the composer again used a chart to show the formal design, but he also now showed the way that his motivic material could be created. As a tribute to Poland, Panufnik used the Gregorian chant, the *Bogurodzica*, as the basis of the work (Fig. 3). By extracting the first three intervals from the melody, the composer used these for each of the three sections (here called 'Visions') that make up the first movement. The trumpet fanfares of the first vision are based on the fourth, the second vision on the major second and the third on the major second. The contrast between the visions is very large. The opening fanfares are powerful and immediate. The use of the perfect fourth for each instrument is simple yet effective; by building the sound of the four trumpets by inversion Panufnik was able to create a wide range of harmonic combinations to suit the intensity of the drama. In complete contrast the second vision which follows without a break is a very quiet interlude for strings, making very free use of the chosen interval. In the third vision the composer deliberately added the interval of the diminished fifth to create more 'contrast and heightened expression'.[7] The Hymn that constitutes the second movement prepares gently for the full appearance of the *Bogurodzica* and the dramatic return of the trumpet fanfares from the opening vision.

The *Sinfonia Sacra* is justifiably well known. It has a directness of expression that communicates its message effectively and a superb orchestral technique. It represents a watershed in the composer's music. The work also presents a number of the techniques and features that Panufnik followed in his later symphonies. Notable are the use of small melodic cells, sections strongly contrasted by dynamics, speed and orchestration, as well as a powerful emotional element barely suggested in the diagrams and charts.

---

[7] *Ibid.*, p. 5.

Geometric plans

The second group of symphonies, composed in the 1970s, takes as its foundation numerous geometric shapes and concepts as represented in various published diagrams. The symphonies also make considerable use of small motives in the symphonic tradition. All these works are unusual in their formal plans and, like all the previous symphonies, except for the *Sinfonia Rustica*, they are played without a break. While something of a traditional formal plan can be seen in the *Sinfonia Concertante* (Symphony No. 4), the formal plans of the next three symphonies (Nos. 5–7) show an imaginative originality that owes little to tradition. Indeed, they display enormous contrasts and conflicts of tempo, dynamics and instrumentation and they are informed by a brilliant transformation of geometry, symmetry, numerology and symbolism. That the listener is probably unaware of these ideas is not important in the first instance, because the works have an impact and intensity of emotion that is immediately obvious. The transformation of these ideas is the next focus of our attention.

The composer's plan for the *Sinfonia Concertante* looks abstract on paper (Fig. 4), with a five-part symmetrical first movement, a strongly rhythmic second movement called a development and consisting of twelve microstructures, and a very short third movement called *Postscriptum* which returns very remotely to some of the music of the first movement. The contrast between the first two movements could hardly be stronger: on the one hand, there is the first movement's gently lyrical flute melodies, the harp's subtle arpeggiations and the rich sounds of divided strings, and on the other hand, there is the second movement's opening *giocoso* bucolic double bass solo that is far removed from the restraint and dignity of the earlier music. The composer made no secret of this dichotomy, referring to:

> *cantabile—ritmico*; slow—fast; static—non-static; symmetry—asymmetry; flow—abruptness; lyrical elements—dance-like elements[8]

For the listener, this can be a disconcerting experience. Panufnik's way of bridging this gap was to base his music on a three-note motif in six different permutations plus transpositions in such a way that the music naturally arises from these small cells or triads. While some of these are not immediately obvious, with familiarity the

---

[8] *Ibid.*, p. 20.

I - Molto cantabile,   II - Molto ritmico,   Postscriptum

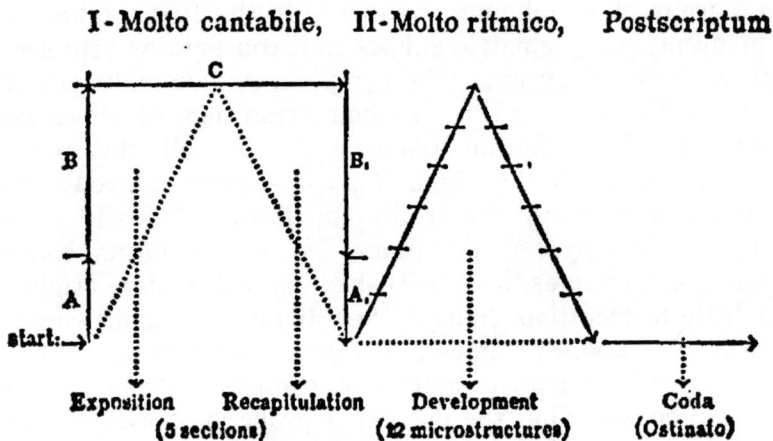

Fig. 4. *Sinfonia Concertante*

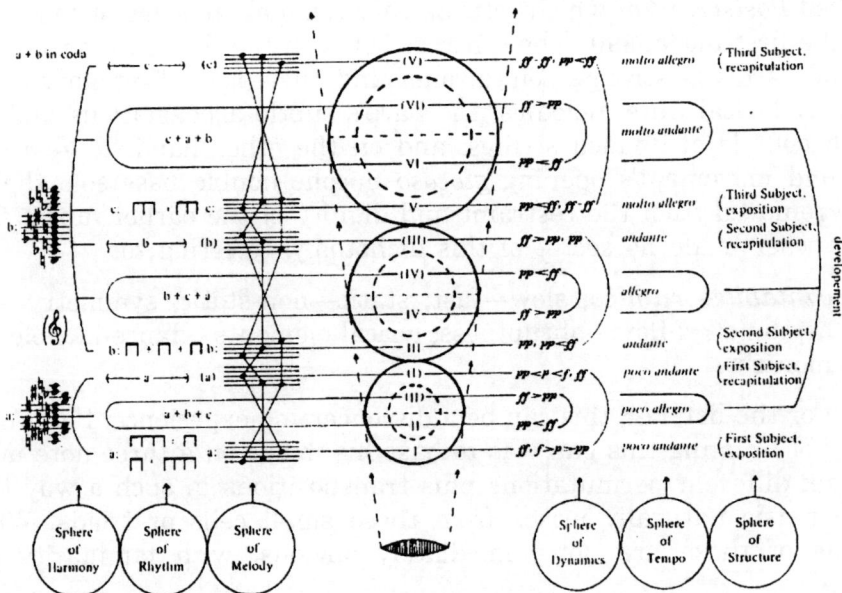

Fig. 5. *Sinfonia di Sfere*

connections become clear. Like much of Panufnik's music, the *Sinfonia Concertante* does not reveal its secrets in a great hurry.

Connections with numbers play an important part in the next three symphonies, but at the same time there is still a strong emphasis on very strong contrasts between sections, perhaps the most obvious initial feature. Both the *Sinfonia di Sfere* (Symphony No. 5) and the *Sinfonia Mistica* (Symphony No. 6) take the number 'six' as their starting point, while the *Metasinfonia* (Symphony No. 7) naturally takes the number 'seven'. These numbers influence the music at all levels.

In the *Sinfonia di Sfere* there are six spheres: harmony, rhythm, melody, dynamics tempo and structure (Fig. 5).[9] These are combined to create the six spheres which constitute the ground plan for the work. The diagram suggests a very contrived set of relationships in the work and one whose complexity seems impenetrably cerebral. The composer himself was obviously aware of this possibility when he said in the preface to the score that: 'readers, while hearing the work, might be too much preoccupied with technicalities, not allowing their perceptive powers to work inwardly and fully'.[10] The plan shows that the form falls naturally into three pairs of concentric spheres, which translates into a musical form of three consecutive ternary form sections, i.e. ABA-CDC-EFE. In actual practice the work is much subtler than this.

The composer calls the opening pair of spheres 'the first subject'. Sphere I (A) is slow, operating with a strong meandering melodic line derived from the three-note sphere of melody. Sphere II (B) by contrast is very fast and a scherzo of breathtaking delicacy which uses different subdivisions of rhythmic groups of six (4+2, 2+4, 3+3, 2+2+2) in a *tour-de-force* that derives all its pitches from the sphere of melody. The return to the opening section (Sphere I), played by the cellos, tuba, horn and trombone in succession, is again clearly audible, but now the spidery figures of Sphere II appear as counterpoints to the melody. In terms of traditional formal construction this is a straightforward ternary form with parts of the central section being combined with the opening music on its return.

The composer called the second pair of spheres, Sphere III and IV (C and D), 'the second subject'. Again the outer sections (Sphere III) are slow with a meandering melody or melodies passed around the

---

[9] This chart is given in the published score: Andrzej Panufnik, *Sinfonia di Sfere*, score (London: Boosey & Hawkes, 1976), p. ii.

[10] *Ibid.*, p. ii.

orchestra: violas, cellos, double basses, clarinet, oboe, violins/violas. The central section (Sphere IV) is again fast, using the rhythmic patterns of sphere II in a similarly contrasting section, but unlike the earlier section the rhythmic groups do not appear in rhythmic unison but with numerous parts independent of each other within the basic three quavers in a bar. The return to the music of Sphere III is again infiltrated by the fast-moving groups from Sphere IV, but they are progressively slowed down.

What Panufnik called the third subject is the last of the pairs of concentric spheres, Spheres V and VI (E and F). Here the tempos are reversed (quick, slow, quick), a brilliant move that allows the work to achieve a strong and powerful conclusion. Sphere V is strongly rhythmic with fast-moving percussion. The andante that follows (Sphere VI) is more melodic but with appearances in the texture of parts of the opening percussion. The final appearance of the molto allegro (third subject recapitulation) moves through the notes to a huge climax at the end.

The formal plan of the *Sinfonia Mistica* (Fig. 6) is much more straightforward than that of the *Sinfonia di Sfere*. Panufnik again took the number six as the basis for his form, melody, harmony and metre. The formal plan is the most immediate dimension for the listener. There are six sections which alternate between very slow and very fast (*molto andante* and *molto allegro*), with the slow sections being quiet and fast sections loud. Although the crotchet speed is only three times faster in the fast sections than the slow ones, the subdivision of the beat in the latter into multiples of three and six creates an impression of considerably increased speed and almost of frenetic activity. Like similar sections of the *Sinfonia di Sfere*, the rhythmic groupings and motivic activity are similarly obsessive and repetitive. Yet when one stops to study the rhythmic patterns in detail, one is aware of the enormous variety that Panufnik has achieved. The slow sections provide the material for the work but because it is so understated, it could easily be missed, for example in the *pianissimo* harmonics at the very beginning played by solo strings. The rapt intensity is much more apparent than symphonic connections. Even in the return of the slow music in the third section, the huge contrast between the slow and fast sections remains. The effective combination of these two materials only takes place near the end, the fast music on woodwind combined with slow string parts (score, fig. 40–42) followed by reversed roles (score, fig. 42–43). The final chorale that follows immediately draws out the slow motifs in a blaze of sound.

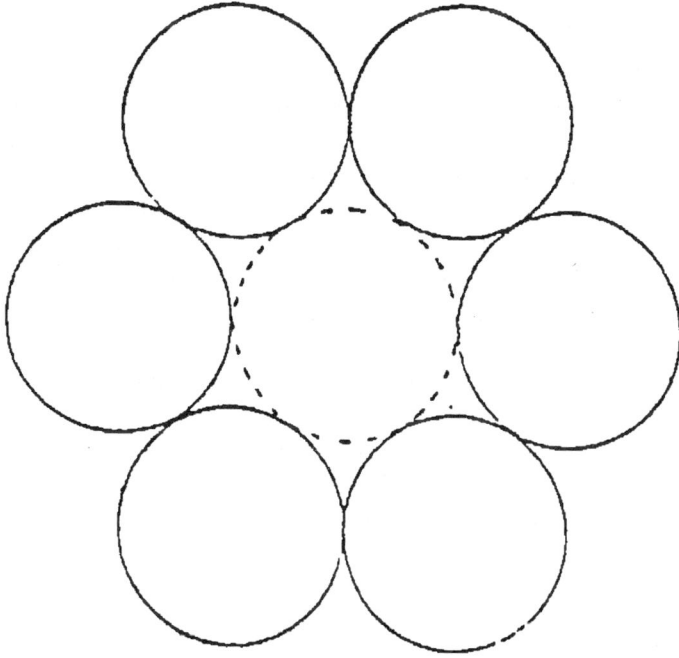

Fig. 6. *Sinfonia Mistica*

In the *Metasinfonia* for organ, timpani and strings of 1978, the overall plan is ingeniously worked around the number 'seven'. The opening bar-length of eight crotchets is incrementally reduced in each of the seven sections down to two crotchets in a bar, but keeping the speed of the crotchets steady (apart from an allargando at the end of each section). It is not surprising that the metrical significance of the changing bar length is not immediately obvious to the listener, although the different characters of the sections are. This situation is fundamentally changed at the halfway stage. At this point the composer reversed the process, starting at two crotchets to a bar and increasing it by one for each section until he reached eight again. What might appear to be a mechanical procedure is contradicted by three imaginative strokes, which tie together the disparate elements of the work.

The first is the entry of the pedal timpani (which had until now been silent) moving down and up in pitch over the full range of the instrument, taking fourteen crotchets for each traversal of the range (up or down). As the pitch is constantly changing, there are no fixed pitches at any one given moment. This then created a wave that descends in 14 (2 times 7) crotchets and ascends in 14 (2 times 7) crotchets whatever the basic barring for the organ and strings, creating a double layer for most of the second half. When the barring reaches seven crotchets the timpani are now synchronised with strings and organ for one section only, but are dislocated in the following section which has eight crotchets to a bar. The second masterstroke is the creation of a quasi-palindromic cadenza for organ which marks out the melodic shapes already found in the work in slow pedal notes while the manuals present a varied arpeggiated working of the motifs. This breaks the potentially automatic process suggested in the overall plan so far. The third feature that brings the music full circle is the coda that recalls the string melody from the very opening, now with timpani playing each of the notes of the melody at an exact and fixed pitch, with the organ also doubling the melodic and harmonic elements of the work. This provides the final unifying element in the work which presents so many apparently contradictory materials.

Commissioned symphonies

Panufnik's last three symphonies were written to commissions from major organisations: the *Sinfonia Votiva* for the Boston Symphony Orchestra, Symphony No. 9 (*Sinfonia della Speranza*) for the Royal Philharmonic Society in London and Symphony No. 10 for the Chicago Symphony Orchestra. There were hints that there would be some move towards orchestral virtuosity, but it was a temptation that the composer resisted. He said about his *Sinfonia Votiva* (No. 8): 'Although the work is symphonic in structure, it may also be regarded as a 'Concerto for Orchestra', allowing the players to show not only their technical skill, but also their expressive and poetic qualities'.[11] Similarly with the Symphony No. 10, Panufnik was tempted to write a showpiece for the Chicago Symphony Orchestra, but instead wrote 'a symphony which through various combinations of groups of instruments, would demonstrate their supreme sound quality, show off their collective musicianship and humanity, and their ability to convey their intense and profound feeling'.[12]

---

[11] Notes to the Hyperion recording on CDA66050, reissued on CDH55100.

[12] Composer's note to the score of Symphony No. 10 (London: Boosey & Hawkes, 1992).

The *Sinfonia Votiva,* a two-movement work from 1980–81, again makes stark contrasts between sections. The first movement, *con devozione—andante rubato,* is quiet and slow; the second movement is fast, strongly rhythmic and mostly loud. The structure is presented in a geometric figure (Fig. 7) that gives some clue to its overall shape. The progressive reduction of bar lengths from six crotchets to three over the two halves of the two movements is not immediately obvious. What is clear, though, is the beautifully built-up phrases of the solo instruments in the opening part of the first movement that are complemented by the vibraphone's mysterious sounds (or those of various other instruments in the composer's 1984 revision) and the

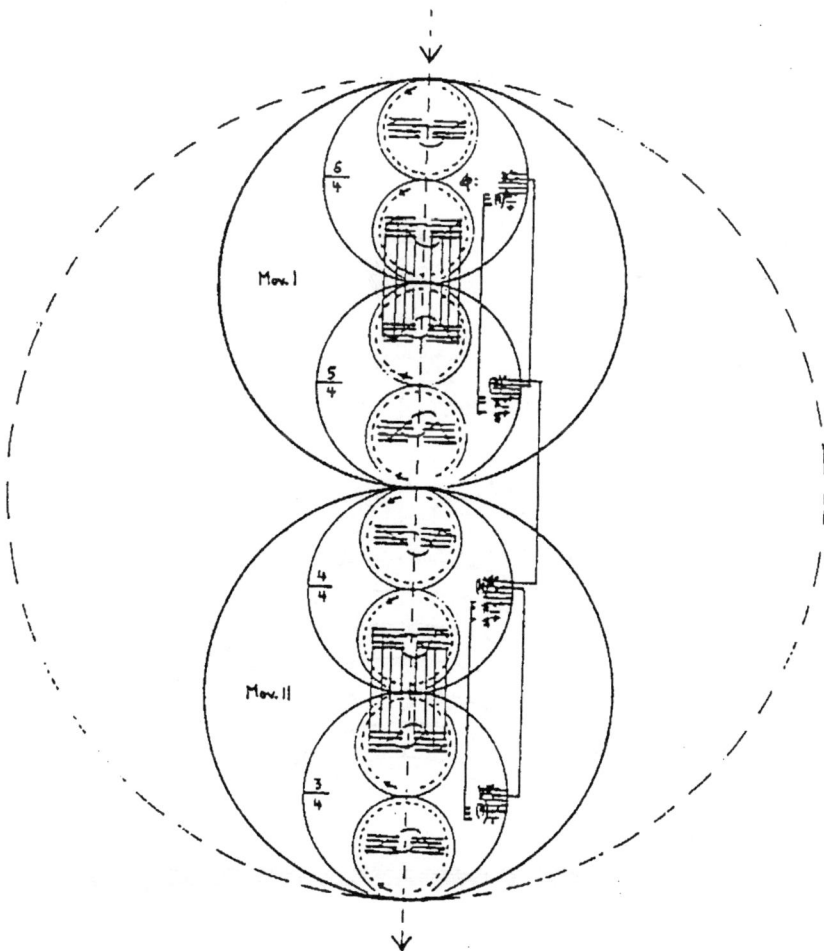

Fig. 7. *Sinfonia Votiva*

wide-spanning melodies in the second part of the first movement. The second movement provides a headlong rhythmic punctuation for another of Panufnik's slow moving and irregularly balanced melodies that are so much a feature of his style. When the metre contracts to three crotchets in a bar the music takes on a strong dance-like character which continues almost without a break until all is cut off for the bells to ring on at the end.

This of course is a very long way from the published diagram, although the connections can be followed easily enough. The same is true also of what is arguably the most powerful work in the whole series of ten, the Symphony No. 9, subtitled *Sinfonia della Speranza* ('Symphony of Hope'). The prismatic diagram (Fig. 8) that the composer presented with his notes for the work makes clear the arch-form or quasi-palindromic structure of the symphony. It also begins to show how the melodic cells are organised throughout. It

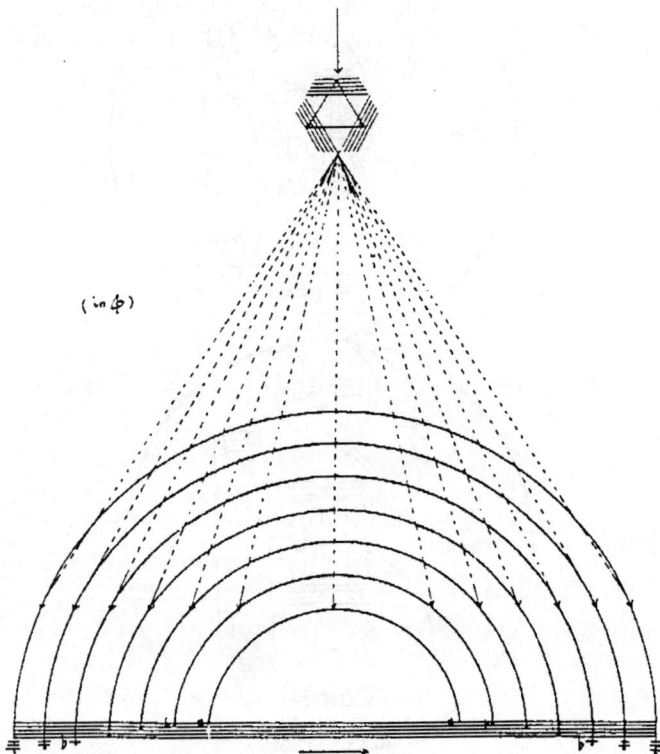

Fig. 8. Symphony No. 9

says nothing about the work's overwhelming power which is produced by going a long way beyond the diagram itself.

The opening melodic line which has some similarities with those in the *Sinfonia di Sfere* and *Sinfonia Votiva* provides a simple intensity of music like no other. The motivic transformations provide the basis for a faster central part of the symphony to counterbalance the mainly slower outer sections. Although the arch-form of the symphony appears to be symmetrical, it is modified in detail in line with the drama of the piece. The second half of the work does not feel in any way that there is an automatic reversal of the process of the first half. While in the *Metasinfonia*, Panufnik used various means to counteract that possibility—fixed-length timpani glissandi, organ cadenza, recapitulatory coda—here he used no such devices, but rather let the music speak for itself. At over forty minutes in duration, it is Panufnik's longest symphony and probably his greatest, as Harold Truscott said in 1987: 'It is his crowning achievement, so far'.[13]

One symphony followed, Symphony No. 10. It is half the length of the Ninth Symphony, and much more elliptical in expression. Its slow and powerful opening fanfares give way by stages to faster music until the opening slow tempo suddenly returns. No diagram is included with the published score, but it is not difficult to visualise a shape that could represent the form, with staged increases in tempo until the final return of the opening slow tempo.

Conclusion

Let us return to our opening question about whether there is an apparent conflict between the techniques of composition and the music's content. The published diagrams give some clues, but the way that they are transformed into music is not immediately obvious. In the case of the first two symphonies there is a clear connection with traditional forms. The second does include a notable symmetry. In the next symphony (*Sinfonia Sacra*) this is subtly transformed into something more unusual, with the symmetries and a layout that breaks away from traditional plans. What is clear is that the plans represent only a small part of the power of the work. The next four symphonies make considerable use of symmetrical plans and geometric diagrams. While the music of the *Sinfonia Concertante* is a little

---

[13] Harold Truscott, 'The Achievement of Andrzej Panufnik', *Tempo* 163 (December, 1987), p. 12.

difficult to relate to these symmetries, the next three symphonies
(*Sinfonia di Sfere, Sinfonia Mistica* and *Metasinfonia*) do this with
consummate ease and with a plan that is clearly part of the music
that affects the listener. In these three works the plan is fundamental
to understanding the work; it articulates the dramatic structure in
a completely convincing way. The contrast of loud and soft, fast and
slow, and the distribution of short motives are especially important
in this respect, arising completely from the composer's structural
plans. The plans of the last three symphonies, and particularly that
of the arch-form Symphony No. 9, form the basis of the works that
one hears. Rather than being abstractions with only a distant
connection with the musical sound of these symphonies, these plans
have been transformed by Panufnik from interesting ideas, shapes
and diagrams into bold and living music that gradually reveals its
secrets.

The Dramaturgic Development of Andrzej Panufnik's Symphonic Works*

Ewa Siemdaj

Throughout his life, Andrzej Panufnik was guided by the concept of "balance" between the emotional and rational elements in music. Now that his output is a closed chapter, Panufnik's compositional process, governed by this leading principle and achieved through consistently developed technical procedures, is easier to demonstrate.

From among the various principles of formal design that appear in Panufnik's work, three stand out with particular frequency, namely c o n s t r u c t i v i s m, the f i n a l - d i r e c t i o n a l musical process and the d i a l e c t i c s o f t w o c l a s h i n g e l e m e n t s. These principles can be found in almost every composition and thus have become *constant* features which represent Panufnik's creative identity, over and above the evolutionary process taking place in his own life. Though he uses these principles again and again his creative development is in no way hindered as each re-use is treated in a new and different manner.

Apart from a multiplicity of formal structures and genres, Panufnik's symphonic works all contain a powerful quality of logical development of dramatic expression. The final-directional process of concentrating the full force of emotional tension towards the main culmination has, from Chopin onwards, become a typical way of achieving dramatic expression in the work of Polish composers. This type of dramaturgic approach can be found in compositions by, among others, Witold Lutosławski, Tadeusz Baird, Henryk Mikołaj Górecki and Krzysztof Penderecki. According to Irina Nikolska, the extra-musical roots of the Polish imaginative mind-set which must have

* This article is based on Ewa Siemdaj's doctoral dissertation entitled *Poetyka muzyczna twórczości symfonicznej Andrzeja Panufnika* (Musical Poetics in the Symphonic Oeuvre of Andrzej Panufnik) (Kraków: Akademia Muzyczna, 2002), pp. 321–340.

influenced this type of dramatic expression in works of Polish composers, have their origins in traditions of Polish Romanticism. She writes: "The thought process of Polish romantics, influenced by specific historical circumstances, had an effect on contemporary musical creativity, in particular on the national trend in symphonic writings of dramatic character and has also determined individual qualities of emotional expression which have turned out to be amazingly enduring"[1]. This final-directional musical process has also become a distinguishing feature of Andrzej Panufnik's work.

Final-directional musical process

Mieczysław Tomaszewski calls the dramaturgic structure of a work its "inner structure"[2]. In composing the work, the dramaturgy takes over in creating the form and "itself determines the shape of the work". Accordingly, *a priori* forms are replaced by dramaturgic structures of individualised and different character, for example, in the final-directional process, creating a dramatic frame or a concentrated centre; an upward gradation or an echo structures, etc.[3]

Panufnik's compositions are especially characterised by a sense of final-directional dramaturgy[4]. Culmination becomes an objective of the developmental process, through which musical fulfilment is attained. In the composer's works this usually occurs in the final climax. This method of final-directional development can already be found in his early works where the composer imaginatively reconstituted classical designs, as well as in his later compositions in which he invented structural designs inspired by geometric shapes or shapes found in nature. He never strove to create a single ideal design, in each work he created a new structural solution, final-directional dramaturgy being an obligatory factor in his unified music-drama syntax, which always influenced the final design of each work[5].

---

[1] Irina Nikolska, 'Dramaturgia i forma u Chopina a polska muzyka XX wieku' (Dramaturgy and form in Chopin's music in view of Polish 20th-century music), *Rocznik Chopinowski* 19, 1990, p. 186.

[2] Mieczysław Tomaszewski, *Chopin. Człowiek, dzieło, rezonans* (Chopin. The man, the work, the resonance) (Poznań, 1998), p. 326.

[3] *Ibid.* Cf. Mieczysław Tomaszewski, 'Chopin', in: *Encyklopedia Muzyczna PWM*, ed. Elżbieta Dziębowska, vol. 2, pp. 162–163.

[4] Irina Nikolska differentiates between interrupted and final-directional dramaturgy. Cf. Irina Nikolska, *ibid.*, p. 186.

[5] Cf. Leonard B. Meyer, *Style and Music. Theory, History and Ideology*, (Philadelphia, 1998), p. 10. According to the author, strategies are a matter of individual style.

(1) A final-directional process is present in both the composer's cyclic and single-movements forms.

The overall design of each work has an unifying effect on the cycle, and in his later symphonies, Panufnik uses a single-movement structure. In his earlier symphonic works (from *Sinfonia Elegiaca* to *Sinfonia Concertante*) the unifying element can be seen in the "spontaneous" transitions between components of the cycle, while in the concerto genre *attacca* transitions become a normal part of the procedure[6].

The "naturalness" of the principle of final culmination is borne out by all cyclic designs seen in the composer's works: the two-movement design (introduced in *Sinfonia Sacra* and Cello Concerto), three-movements (in the Piano Concerto, Violin Concerto or *Concerto Festivo*) and five-movements (in *Concertino* and the Bassoon Concerto).

Final-directional dramaturgy is particularly clearly apparent in all his works of "conceptual" character and is to be found in the climactic syntheses in *Sinfonia Mistica* and *Sinfonia Votiva*, in the thematic finales of *Metasinfonia* and *Sinfonia della Speranza*, as well as in the thematic material of the synthesis in the finale of *Sinfonia Sacra*.

The perfectly proportioned geometric figures which influenced the formal structures of Panufnik's later symphonies did not alter the composer's principal intentions. However the final climaxes often disrupt these perfect proportions (this happens in *Sinfonia di Sfere, Sinfonia Mistica, Metasinfonia* and *Sinfonia Votiva*).

(2) Only a few compositions in Panufnik's entire symphonic output deviate from the principle of final culmination. These are: *Nocturne, Rhapsody, Autumn Music* and three symphonies: *Sinfonia Elegiaca, Sinfonia Concertante* and Symphony No. 10.

With the exception of Symphony No. 10 which has an elliptical form of structure requiring different culmination placement, all his work conform to an architectural arch design, reinforced by a combination with the principle of *enfiando*. Even though culmination of the above works is placed in the middle section or the middle component of the cycle, it still also contains similar final-directional dramaturgy.

---

[6] *Sinfonia Rustica*, an embodiment of the neoclassical formal model, is an exception here. As in all of his works of 'suite order', such as *Old Polish Suite, Polonia, Jagiellonian Triptych* and *Arbor Cosmica,* the composer refrained from smooth transitions between cycle parts.

The three-movement cyclic design exploited in *Sinfonia Elegiaca* and *Sinfonia Concertante*, while placing the climactic section in the middle movement, does not alter the place of culmination in the section itself. In the main cyclic movements of this architectural arch structure, the climax also appears in the finale. In his search for cyclic patterns the composers never deviated from his unwavering "inherent" principle of leading the complete musical process towards a final culmination. Further proof that this principle was an integral part of the composer's way of thinking is demonstrated by the fact that the main climax in the *Symphony of Peace* and *Sinfonia Elegiaca* was placed at the end of the cycle's final movement. In the case of *Sinfonia Concertante*, the third movement, *Postscriptum*, has the character of an extensively developed coda. The moderation of the climax at the close of the main movement, achieved through the return of opening musical motifs, can be ascribed to the work's dominant element of lyricism and its emotional expression. (Dedicated to his wife on their 10th anniversary, the work is an expression of the composer's deeply personal emotions.)

(3) Certain ubiquitous phases can be identified in single-movement forms and climactic sections of Panufnik's works. The most frequently used design includes three phases:

Table 1. Three-phase model of formal organisation
in symphonic works of Andrzej Panufnik

opening phase		middle phase	culmination phase			
i n t r o d u c t i o	E X P O S I T I O	PERTURBATIO / EVOLUTIO (transgressio)	C U L M I N A T I O	(ripresa / reversio / conclusio)	c l i m a x	+ coda

a) t h e   o p e n i n g   p h a s e   (*expositio*) which serves to set up the musical process by presenting the initial material of the work generally preceded by an *introduction*;
b) t h e   m i d d l e   p h a s e , which elaborates on the musical events through their transformation (*perturbatio*) or their develop-

ment (*evolutio*). Occasionally invasive (*transgressio*) new material is introduced, and at times the development of musical events in this phase undergoes division into two separate stages.

    c) t h e   c u l m i n a t i o n   p h a s e (*culminatio*) which closes the work. In this phase initial musical patterns often return (as *ripresa* or in reversed order: *reversio*), while new material generated by the organic development of the previous phases appears less frequently (*conclusio*). The development of musical dramaturgy is always concluded with a climax, often linked with or directly passing into a coda.

    In this typical Panufnik design, the climax plays a crucial role. The separate introduction of the opening phase also fulfils an equally vital function. Almost always the phases are separated by a general pause or an expressive *caesura*, while only rarely do transition or linkage patterns appear (*transitio* e.g. *Sinfonia della Speranza*).

    During his second creative period after 1968 Panufnik most frequently used as a means of expression, (a) division into two stages and (b) an evolutionary method of developing musical dramaturgy in the middle phase of his compositions.

    (4) In Panufnik's compositional technique, he always uses different structures to lead through each work's development up to the point of climax. Leonard B. Meyer's writings help us to identify the division of climaxes into those that are *syntactic*, occuring at a relative point of change between instability and stability, and those which are *statistical*, based on the secondary parameters of tempo, texture and dynamics[7]. Both of the above categories can be found in Panufnik's compositions[8] (table 2).

    A s y n t a c t i c climax appears in those works where the principle concept is symbolised within the thematic material as in the first bars of *Sinfonia della Speranza*. First seen in *Sinfonia Sacra*, it was to become a typical feature of the composer's later works (*Sinfonia Mistica, Metasinfonia, Sinfonia della Speranza* as well as Symphony No. 10). These works usually open with the "announcement" of a symbolic theme, which subsequently returns in the finale.

---

   [7] Leonard B. Meyer, *op. cit.*, pp. 205, 304.

   [8] Leonard B. Meyer's placement of a syntactic climax is at the point of change from an instable (development) to a stable relationship (recapitulation). In works by Andrzej Panufnik, syntactic is the return, in the climax, of thematic or motivic material from the introductory fragment; this return is treated as the entry into a stable relationship.

Table 2. Types of climax in Andrzej Panufnik's compositions

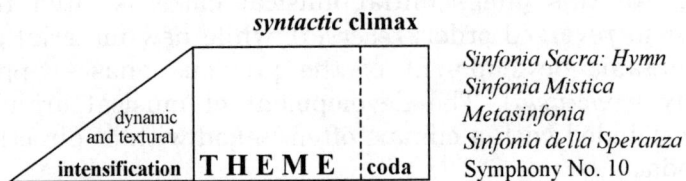

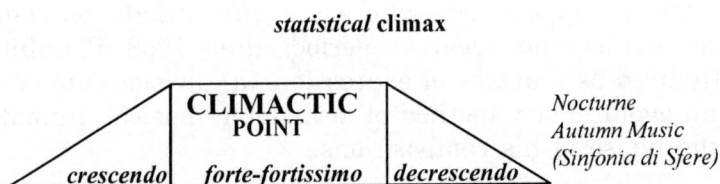

syntactic **climax**

Sinfonia Sacra: Hymn
Sinfonia Mistica
Metasinfonia
Sinfonia della Speranza
Symphony No. 10

statistical **climax**

Nocturne
Autumn Music
(Sinfonia di Sfere)

(1) agogic dynamics-related type

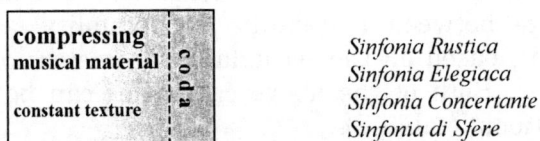

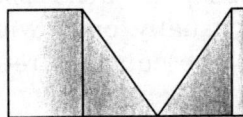

Sinfonia Rustica
Sinfonia Elegiaca
Sinfonia Concertante
Sinfonia di Sfere

(2) agogic chord-related type

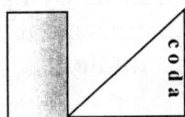

Sinfonia Sacra: Vision III   Sinfonia votiva

(3) agogic volume-related type

The climax is often emphasised through occasional repetition and rhythmical augmentation (*Sinfonia Mistica*, *Metasinfonia*, *Sinfonia della Speranza*). Sometimes, emotional expression is heightened by combining the theme with an individual characteristic element which, like the theme, has a symbolic function (in *Sinfonia Sacra* trumpets in the introduction and, in *Metasinfonia*, the timpani when, at the work, for the first time, it is used in a melodic manner).

A syntactic climax is usually developed in three stages: (1) dynamic and textural intensification leading to the *tutti*, (2) the introduction of the melodic theme in *tutti* together with, (3) a coda with the accompaniment in rich chordal harmony in *tutti*. Occasionally, when the coda becomes a longer section, the sonoristic elements start to dominate the melodic (*Sinfonia Mistica*, *Sinfonia della Speranza*).

Considering the individual properties of the Panufnik's works, the s t a t i s t i c a l climax falls into three categories: agogic in relation to dynamics, agogic in relation to chordal harmony and agogic in relation to volume. In Panufnik's compositions agogic accentuation is the crucial factor in all three categories of the statistical climax.

The a g o g i c d y n a m i c s - r e l a t e d climax only appears in the middle section of a composition and is present only in work of lyrical expression. It was first applied in *Nocturne* and later in *Autumn Music*, *Sinfonia di Sfere* and Cello Concerto. It consists of three stages where (1) dynamics are increased by means of *crescendo*, (2) the climactic point is intensified by a held chord in the dynamics in *forte-fortissimo*, and (3) dynamics are decreased by means of *decrescendo*. Textural contrast between the outer sections and the middle section plays an important role. In *Sinfonia di Sfere* a symmetrical mirror image of this design was used by the composer to construct a "negative" climax.

The most significant stage of this climax is its intensification, through a held chord, thus arresting the musical action at the point of culmination, characteristically brought about by agogic accentuation of the climactic elements, e.g. by constant repetition of the melodic motif (*Nocturne*), by the *vibrato* of a held chord (*Autumn Music*) or through a uniformity of rhythmic values (*Sinfonia di Sfere*).

This type of climax is most frequently seen in conjunction with palindromic symmetry, the axis of the palindromic structure occuring precisely at the point of culmination (*Autumn Music*, *Sinfonia di Sfere*, Cello Concerto).

The a g o g i c c h o r d - r e l a t e d climax is used conventionally throughout the musical repertoire. In Panufnik's works its point of departure initially is a rhythmic motif (in his later works he uses rhythmic cell) which forms the basis of rhythmic repetition in the *tutti* chords marked *fortissimo*. A motivic fragment is often repeated several times, its successive repetitions being submitted to a technique of compressing musical material that builds up the tension.

This type of climax consists of two stages: (1) agogic intensification (increased rhythmic density of chords by means of compression technique) and (2) a point of culmination which becomes a short chordal coda in *tutti* (rapid, identical rhythmic chords). This type of climax can be seen in many of the composer's works. Particularly expressive examples of its use are found in *Heroic Overture*, Piano Concerto and *Concerto Festivo*, as well as in the closing sections of the middle movements in *Sinfonia Elegiaca* and *Sinfonia Concertante*.

The a g o g i c   v o l u m e - r e l a t e d   climax is a compound culmination consisting of two parts: the first an agogic chord-related climax, the second, main part a reiteration of the first climax. It is primarily shaped through the gradual increase in the volume of sound. The compound structure of the agogic volume-related climax makes it a particularly dramatic form of expression. It is to be found in only two of Panufnik's compositions: *Sinfonia Sacra (Vision III)* and *Sinfonia Votiva*.

Postscriptum

In one of his conversations with Charles Bodman Rae, Witold Lutosławski referred to the Conservatoire lectures given by Witold Maliszewski. He recalled: "The course in musical forms that was given by my professor of composition, Maliszewski, has remained in my memory for my whole life. In his analyses of the sonatas of Beethoven, he explained the psychological factor in perceiving a form [...] So I think the psychological approach to form is absolutely essential in my work. All that I really learned then [...] I can give you the terminology he (Maliszewski) used. He used four different words of "character": Introductory, Narrative, Transitional and Concluding. In each large-scale form there is always the use of those four characters ...only in the Narrative is content the most important thing to be perceived, while in all the other three the role of the given section in the form of the music is more important than the content"[9].

---

[9] Charles Bodman Rae, *The Music of Lutosławski* (London: Faber and Faber, 1994), pp. 7–8, translated into Polish as *Muzyka Lutosławskiego* (Warszawa: PWN, 1996), p. 23.

One can imagine that these views could also made an impression on Maliszewski's other student, Andrzej Panufnik[10]. A psychological approach to musical form expressed through final-directional dramaturgy and roles assigned by Panufnik to specific sections (albeit fragments) of his compositions bears a considerable resemblance to Maliszewski's views. One can therefore surmise that these opinions had as resounding an effect on the composer's approach to form as they did on Lutosławski's. This also explains the existence of a certain organic similarity in relation to both composers' search and realisation of new compositional techniques.

Translated by Anna Kaspszyk

---

[10] Andrzej Panufnik never related to the theories of Witold Maliszewski as directly as did Witold Lutosławski.

Symmetry in the Symphonies of Andrzej Panufnik[*]

Beata Bolesławska

Many composers in the 20th century used some elements of symmetry in building the structure of their pieces (for instance, Bartók, the serialists and Xenakis). However, perhaps none of them made symmetry as much the crucial point of their music and their thinking about music as Andrzej Panufnik did. Symmetry, and also—later—geometry, is the main element of the construction of his whole output—externally, at least. In Panufnik's music (spanning over 60 years) the symmetrical figures are present at every stage of his compositional career. Even more, symmetry—and geometry—has been always present in composer's thinking about music, in his aesthetic: we can find proof of this by reading what he said or wrote about his music, telling us a lot not only about Panufnik's creative consistency but also how much his musical (and perhaps not only musical) world was ordered.

The symmetrical figures can be found in every musical genre composed by Panufnik, although the examples presented in this paper are taken from the symphonies only—as the symphony is the genre most representative of this composer. I will attempt to explain here how he used symmetry in all three structural aspects of his symphonies—in harmony, musical syntax and form.

Symmetry in the aspect of harmony and tonality

Panufnik's tonal language, as well as other elements of his music, is highly organised. The kinds of chords and sound combinations used by the composer in each piece are determined usually by a basic

---

[*] This article is based on Beata Bolesławska's book *Panufnik* (Kraków: PWM, 2001), pp. 372–400.

three-note cell and the possibilities of development that cell offers—
with its reflections and transpositions. The composer consciously
limited his tonal language—he was reluctant to use any complicated,
complex sound combinations. Panufnik's harmony is neither tonal (in
the major-minor meaning) nor avant-garde. He kept away from using
dodecaphonic or serial techniques (although some elements of his
method are similar to some rules of serialism), and put little
dissonance into his music (he avoided using clusters, and only rarely
used some quarter-tones). Panufnik's tonal language, and the great
role it gives to symmetry, is highly original and—together with other
elements—gives his music its characteristic voice.

Many kinds of symmetrical figuration can be found in Panufnik's
harmonies. He most often used mirror symmetry (axe symmetry) and
transposition symmetry (symmetry of parallel transpositions). Sometimes he combined these two—the most popular—kinds of symmetry.

Mirror symmetry

The most obvious examples of mirror symmetry from a tonal point
of view are the symmetrical chords. The harmonic structure of
Vision I from the *Sinfonia Sacra* (1963) is based on one symmetrical
chord consisting of perfect fourths [Example 1]. It is played by the
trumpets, the only instruments taking part in this movement. This
chord in its full form (as shown at the example) can be heard just
in the last bars of *Vision I* before it turns into a unison "c" at the
very end (see Example 1).

Two symmetrical twelve-note chords are the basis of the harmonic
structure of the *Sinfonia di Sfere*, his 5th Symphony (1974). Panufnik
indicated these two chords at the graphic diagram which is the visual
reflection of the symphony's structure. He emphasized the role of them
in building the harmonic world of *Sinfonia di Sfere* (see Example 2).

Both chords have the axis of symmetry in the same place—between
'b' and 'd'. As shown in the composer's diagram, chord A is responsible
for the harmonic structure of Sphere 1 and 2, chord B for the Spheres
3–6, but in the coda composer uses the intervals from both chords,
mixing them.

Controlling the harmonic aspect with two twelve-note chords does
not mean that they are present in all the musical material all the
time. They are just a kind of key for choosing the intervals which are
used in particular Spheres. Actually in Sphere 1 and 2 Panufnik
operates only with the intervals from chord A, and in Spheres 3–6
there appear only the intervals present in chord B (except the coda
which is—as mentioned above—the mixture of chord A and B). During

b flat
f
c   **axis of symmetry**
g
d

Ex. 1. *Sinfonia Sacra, Vision I*
© Copyright 1967 by Boosey & Hawkes Music Publishers Ltd.
Reproduced by permission of Boosey & Hawkes Music Publishers Ltd.

chord A	chord B
a	e
f	c sharp
d flat	b flat
b flat	g
f sharp	f
d	d
b	b
g	g sharp
eflat	f sharp
c	d sharp
a flat	c
e	a

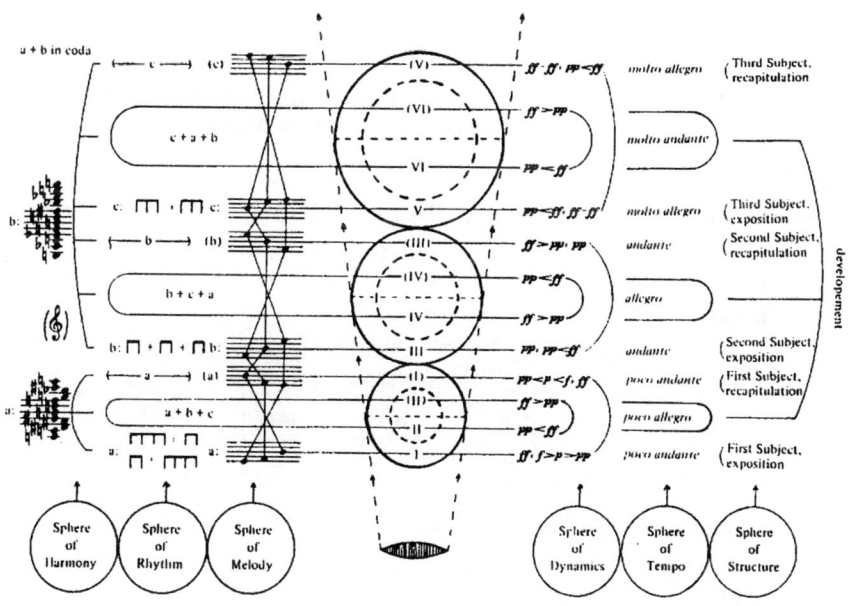

Ex. 2. *Sinfonia di Sfere*, composer's diagram

the musical process in this symphony Panufnik operates three tonal plans—each of them has a melody created by the different transposition of the basic cell—*e-f-b*. These three sound layers produce—by keeping the minor third interval between them—the symmetrical triads:

e.g. **d** (d flat – a)   **b** (c – f sharp)
      b (c – f sharp)   **g sharp** (a – d sharp)   etc.
      g sharp (a – d sharp)   **f** (g sharp – c)

consisting of minor thirds in Spheres 1 and 2 — Ex. 3a

Ex. 3a. *Sinfonia di Sfere*, Sphere 2
© Copyright 1976 by Boosey & Hawkes Music Publishers Ltd.
Reproduced by permission of Boosey & Hawkes Music Publishers Ltd.

consisting of major thirds in Spheres 3–6 — Ex. 3b

e.g. **f sharp** (g – c sharp)   **e flat** (e – b flat)
      d (e flat – a)   **b** (c – f sharp)   etc.
      b flat (b – f)   **g** (a flat – d)

Ex. 3b. *Sinfonia di Sfere*, Sphere 6
© Copyright 1976 by Boosey & Hawkes Music Publishers Ltd.
Reproduced by permission of Boosey & Hawkes Music Publishers Ltd.

It is worth adding that these triads are transposed down a minor third—which means that in this case the composer also uses the interval common to chord A and B. Moreover, moving chords of the same interval is an example of transposition symmetry.

Triads consisting of only minor or major thirds are symmetrical in themselves, but in the same symphony we can also find the example of the symmetrical structures built from the intervals of the melodic cell (*e-f-b*). This kind of structure can be found in the piano part in Sphere 4. This part is developed melodically, but as a harmonic structure it looks as follows:

b	d		
f sharp	a		
c	e flat	etc.	**axis of symmetry**
g	b flat		
c sharp	e		

Ex. 4. *Sinfonia di Sfere*, Sphere 4, piano part
© Copyright 1976 by Boosey & Hawkes Music Publishers Ltd.
Reproduced by permission of Boosey & Hawkes Music Publishers Ltd.

The perfect mirror symmetry is broken here by changing the order of the perfect fourth and diminished fifth in the reflection.

Transposition symmetry

There is no doubt that this is the kind of symmetry most often present in the music. All parallel interval or chord transitions, progressions and transpositions are nothing more than examples of transposition symmetry, or maybe rather transposition-temporal symmetry (as they proceed in time). The most simple examples of this kind of symmetry in Panufnik's symphonies are, for example, the transpositions of perfect fifths in *Vision II* or diminished fifths in *Vision III* in *Sinfonia Sacra*.

More sophisticated examples of transposition symmetry are to be found in *Sinfonia di Sfere*, where—in Sphere 6—there are the following structures (p. 115, vl, vc, db):

```
b              c              c              c sharp
g              g sharp        g sharp        a
e flat         e              e              f
      ────────────►                 ────────────►
          7<↓                            7<↓
```

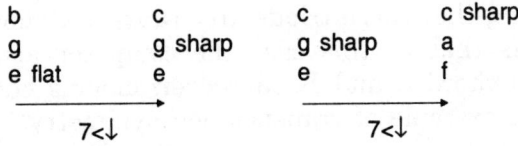

The triad consisting of major thirds (symmetrical themselves) is here transposed a major seventh down. Also, in the same place, in the piano part we can see symmetrical six-note chords (consisted of major thirds). They are also transposed a major seventh down:

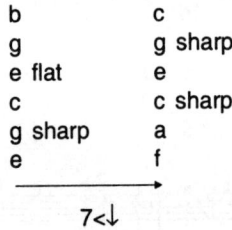

```
b              c
g              g sharp
e flat         e
c              c sharp
g sharp        a
e              f
      ────────────►
          7<↓
```

Ex. 5. *Sinfonia di Sfere*, Sphere 6
© Copyright 1976 by Boosey & Hawkes Music Publishers Ltd.
Reproduced by permission of Boosey & Hawkes Music Publishers Ltd.

This kind of symmetry is also described as a 'reflection with slide' and is very often present in visual arts, especially in ornaments.

Besides of the examples based on mirror or transposition symmetry, Panufnik uses as well the structures being the combination (mixture) of these two kinds of symmetry.

Mirror-transposition symmetry

This kind of symmetry is usually the result of transposing some structures already based on mirror symmetry. An interesting example of this situation can be found in *Sinfonia di Sfere*. In Sphere 4 there is a chordal structure reflected as if in a mirror, but the second part of this figure has been also transposed a minor third up. The whole structure looks as follows:

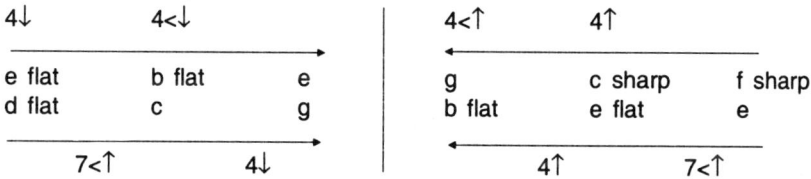

4↓	4<↓		4<↑	4↑
e flat	b flat	e	g	c sharp	f sharp
d flat	c	g	b flat	e flat	e
7<↑	4↓		4↑	7<↑

Ex. 6. *Sinfonia di Sfere*, Sphere 4
© Copyright 1976 by Boosey & Hawkes Music Publishers Ltd.
Reproduced by permission of Boosey & Hawkes Music Publishers Ltd.

Actually, the examples of mirror-transposition symmetry are already the part of musical syntax, so the others will be shown in the part concerning this aspect of Panufnik's symphonies.

Symmetry in the aspect of musical syntax

Mirror symmetry

Mirror symmetry was certainly Panufnik's favourite kind of symmetry. It is the element of composer's technique most often used by him. Examples of mirror reflections can be find in short motifs, as well as in the slightly longer phrases and in the whole thematic structures. Often symmetry in these examples is connected with symmetry in the harmony, and in more long-range context, with musical form.

Mirror symmetry in musical motifs

The reflections in short, usually two-note motifs are actually the constant element in Panufnik's symphonies—present already in his first works (*Sinfonia Rustica*). Over the years they seem to have gained more and more importance, often filling large spaces of each piece (e.g. *Sinfonia della Speranza*). Perhaps the most conspicuous example of this kind of symmetry we can find in Panufnik's last symphony where the lower line of the harp part is consequently developed on the base of reflected octaves.

Ex. 7. Symphony No. 10, harp part
© Copyright 1993 by Boosey & Hawkes Music Publishers Ltd.
Reproduced by permission of Boosey & Hawkes Music Publishers Ltd.

The composer often uses this kind of structure in the moments of emotional tension which, together with full orchestration, lead towards the climax (*Sinfonia della Speranza*). In any case, short, two-note motifs with their reflections do not have an independent role and most often are used in the development sections.

Mirror symmetry in musical phrases

An example of a short phrase of great importance for the construction of the whole movement of a symphony is the trumpet fanfare from *Vision I* of *Sinfonia Sacra*—which was already shown as an example of the symmetrical chord structure. Thus, it is an example of two kinds of symmetry at the same time—in the aspect of harmony and musical syntax (see Ex. 1).

The whole construction of this movement is based on the constant flow of this phrase, together with its reflections and transpositions, as well as mixture of them both. This also causes the appearance of transposition symmetry and—in vertical dimension—the symmetrical chord consisting of perfect fourths. This phrase also has significance in the final part of the symphony—by recalling it in the last bars the composer closes whole work with a symmetrical brace.

The three-note cell (*d-a-c*) plays the main role for building the melodic layer of Panufnik's fourth symphony, written in 1973, *Sinfonia Concertante*. The harmonic layer is determined by another cell—that most often used by Panufnik: *e-f-b*. The composer, carrying the melodic cell on the different pitch levels of flute and harp, creates the musical phrase which together with its mirror reflection built a calm, wavy melody:

Ex. 8. *Sinfonia Concertante*
© Copyright 1977 by Boosey & Hawkes Music Publishers Ltd.
Reproduced by permission of Boosey & Hawkes Music Publishers Ltd.

In this example, as well as in previous one, we can observe the conjunction of two most popular kinds of symmetry—mirror and transposition symmetry. This happens usually when the basic phrase in its reflected part starts not from the same note but it is moved of some interval up or down. We call this kind of symmetry a *topologic symmetry*[1] because the intervals in two parts of mirror structure are not exactly the same—but they keep the same (but inverted) way of development as well as the analogous rhythmic structure.

The rule explained above is the basis for the construction of almost whole part of flute and harp in *Sinfonia Concertante*. And it is worth adding that in the strings accompanying the soloists we can also find the symmetrical figures—usually based on the reflected two-note motifs.

---

[1] See: Ewa Kofin, 'Fenomen symetrii w muzyce' (Symmetry in music), in: *Symetrie w sztuce i naukach humanistycznych* (Symmetry in Art and Humanities) (Wrocław, 1993).

Symmetry in the thematic structures

One of the most interesting examples of the symmetrical structure in the thematic idea (which is also an example of connection between symmetry of musical syntax and symmetry in harmony) is the main thematic idea of *Vision II* from *Sinfonia Sacra*:

Ex. 9. *Sinfonia Sacra, Vision II*
© Copyright 1967 by Boosey & Hawkes Music Publishers Ltd.
Reproduced by permission of Boosey & Hawkes Music Publishers Ltd.

This structure has a clear symmetrical axis in one point for harmony and syntax. Moreover, it is the basis for the construction of whole *Vision II* as it is transposed in later part of this movement. Thanks to this transposition it is also, of course, influenced by transposition symmetry.

Another interesting example of mirror symmetry structure can be found in *Vision III* of the same symphony, in the string parts. This time symmetry is also very easily heard (see Example 10).

Ex. 10. *Sinfonia Sacra, Vision III*

© Copyright 1967 by Boosey & Hawkes Music Publishers Ltd.
Reproduced by permission of Boosey & Hawkes Music Publishers Ltd.

Two parts of this structure have been here very clearly separated by using the general pause and the 'entrance' of brass and percussion. The second, reflected part is not a perfect reflection (except of the first few notes), which means that there is a kind of topologic symmetry. Additionally, in this structure we can also observe transposition symmetry because the first motif is taken by next instrument (it is transposed).

Transposition symmetry

Transposition symmetry as part of musical syntax will appear mostly as transposition and imitation of the short motifs or longer thematic ideas. But it is worth stressing that this kind of symmetry is not so often used by Panufnik as mirror symmetry. This is perhaps because Panufnik seldom used fugal techniques and—clearly—these kinds of techniques determine usually the presence of transposition symmetry. And although composer in his programme notes often wrote that the basic cell is reflected and transposed during the musical process, he usually set together two consecutive forms of the basic cell and they were transposed later. We can find the example of the transposition of the structure consisting of two forms of basic three-note cell in *Sinfonia Mistica*:

Ex. 11. *Sinfonia Mistica*
© Copyright 1978 by Boosey & Hawkes Music Publishers Ltd.
Reproduced by permission of Boosey & Hawkes Music Publishers Ltd.

In the first movement of *Sinfonia Concertante* we find a very interesting example of mirror-transposition symmetry:

3> 4< 2> 3> 2> 4< 3> 4< 2> 3> 2> 4< 3> 4< 2> ‖ 2> 4< 3> 4< 2> 3> 2> 4< 3> 4< 2> 3> 2> 4<

Ex. 12. *Sinfonia Concertante*
© Copyright 1977 by Boosey & Hawkes Music Publishers Ltd.
Reproduced by permission of Boosey & Hawkes Music Publishers Ltd.

This structure seems to be symmetrical just from the first point of view, which is additionally marked by changing the instrument. Indeed, when we analyse it in detail we can see that the flute part is the perfect reflection of the harp part (except of two first notes, creating the interval of minor third).

The second, reflected part of this figure has been transposed a minor third up.

It is also worth adding that the analogous structures caused by the connection of two kinds of symmetry are present inside this long figure, too. Each motif consisting of augmented fourth and minor second is immediately reflected with moving the second part of the minor third up. This is thus an example of a highly organised musical structure—symmetry within symmetry.

Symmetry in the aspect of form

The significant thing for the formal construction of Panufnik's symphonies, as well as that of his other works, is that very often the extra-musical inspiration determined the structure of particular piece. For instance, in his *Sinfonia Rustica* the composer wanted to infuse his music with some elements of the naive art of paper-cuts made by Polish peasants. This inspiration influenced the whole structure, which is full of mirror symmetry, not only in harmony or musical syntax, but also in the whole form, which although in a classical four-movement shape, refers to the idea of mirror symmetry.

In later years, starting from the *Sinfonia di Sfere*, written in 1974, geometric shapes determined the structure of Panufnik's symphonies. He used to indicate the shape of the geometric figure that inspired him, on a diagram, usually added to the score and showing the construction of each work.

But before the geometric shapes began to influence the structure of Panufnik's compositions, the form he most often used was arch form. This kind of form has been known in musical tradition as ABA form, with the central part in the middle and symmetrically designed outside movements.

Arch form

Arch form is in some way similar to mirror symmetry. It refers especially to this kind of symmetry but with a more abstract meaning—as the middle section "B" is the centre of composition and turning point for the musical action. It is also the axis of symmetry for the sections "A", usually very different in character. But in the real musical material the repetition of section "A" is the example of the transposition-temporal symmetry.

Panufnik frequently used arch form in his works, especially in those written up to the middle of 1970s. For instance, his first four symphonies are the examples of arch form, where it is connected with the emotional character of the composition. Creating the arch, composer starts his work from the fast, jolly, dance-like movement, then introduces the slow, melancholic part and returns to the atmosphere evoked at the beginning. He also uses the opposite possibility—starting from a slow, sorrowful and contemplative atmosphere, then going through dramatic and turbulent expression and going back to the contemplation. This first variant is used in the *Sinfonia Rustica* and—only in the outline—in *Sinfonia Sacra*, where composer creates a symmetrical brace by recalling in last bars the trumpet fanfare from the beginning. More often we can find the second variant, e.g. in *Sinfonia Elegiaca*, where the similar character of the outside movement is additionally stressed by keeping the same tempo, dynamics and the similar metrical structure.

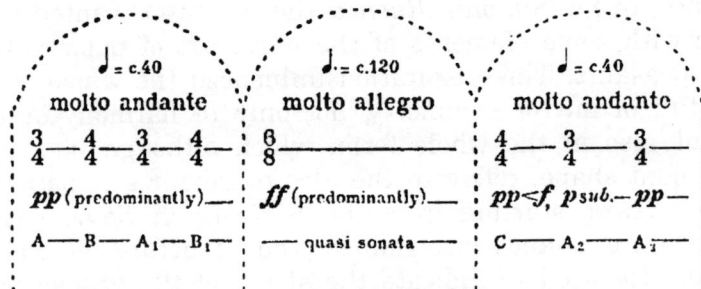

Ex. 13. *Sinfonia Elegiaca*, composer's diagram

The same variant is used in *Sinfonia Concertante*, where after the strongly contrasted movements *Molto cantabile* and *Molto ritmico* the composer introduces short *Postcriptum*, bringing back the atmosphere of the first part—and the whole composition draws an emotional arch.

It is worth saying that the musical action of the emotional arch cannot be connected strictly with dividing the form into separate movements—e.g. his *Sinfonia Rustica* is the four-movement piece and *Sinfonia Sacra* has only two movements. Also, arch form is represented in one-movement *Nocturne* for the orchestra (1947).

Mirror form

Mirror form is actually the development of arch form. The difference is that the material of the repeated movement 'A' is introduced as a mirror reflection. The axis of symmetry is in this case the middle section of the piece, since which the action starts going back to the ideas and expressions evoked at the beginning of composition.

The most precisely organised mirror form can be found in Panufnik's fifth and ninth symphonies. In these two works we have the example of mirror reflection on real sound material.

Sinfonia di Sfere (1974–5) is based on a geometrical diagram; it is also the first of Panufnik's work composed on this basis. Looking at the formal plan of the particular Spheres we can see that the second part of Sphere 1 (as well as 3 and 5) is the mirror reflection of the first part of the same Sphere. For instance, Sphere 1 starts with the melody played by trumpet with the accompaniment of strings, and is gradually joined by other wind instruments and piano. Sphere 1 ends with piano and cello. Then we have Sphere 2 (No. 9 in the score) played only by woodwinds and percussion. After it Sphere 1 (No. 16) returns and—very importantly—is played now from the end—we can hear cello and piano first, and gradually we are going back until the first trumpet melody. Thus, this is the evident example of using mirror symmetry, where the axis of the symmetry is the Sphere put in the middle of each circle. Additionally, each of this middle Spheres (2, 4 and 6) is built on the similar rule. The whole structure of this is consistent with the composer's idea of including the form of symphony in the circles. And, as we know, mirror symmetry is the typical feature of any circle.

It is worth adding that Panufnik, although precise and clear about this mirror structure, himself saw the form of the *Sinfonia di Sfere* as a modified sonata allegro with three subjects—as he indicated in the diagram. But in this conception there is no adequate explanation for the middle Spheres, unless they are recognised as developmental material. However, the reminiscences of the classical sonata allegro form are rather weak, especially in comparison with the role played here by mirror symmetry.

A similar construction, based on mirror symmetry in the whole structure, with a clear axis in the middle of piece, is Panufnik's Symphony No. 9—*Sinfonia della Speranza* (1986). The graphic visualisation of this symphony—as a Symphony of Hope—is a rainbow arch.

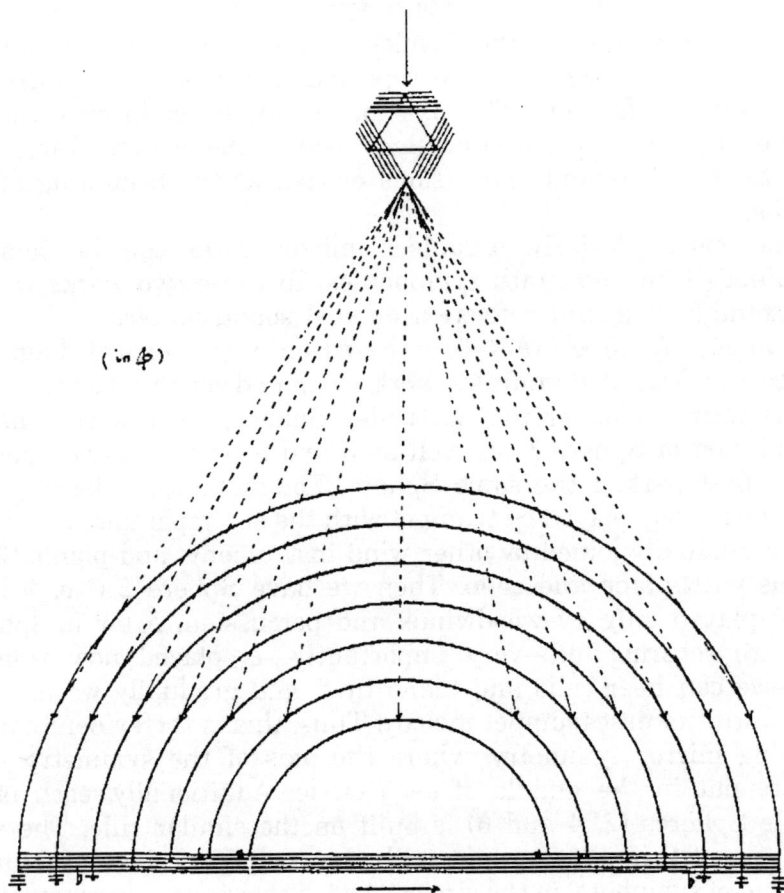

Ex. 14a. Symphony No. 9, composer's diagram

And the element determining the whole structure is the three-note cell *e-f-b*, known also from the other Panufnik's works. This cell is here juxtaposed with the tonal lines (the same technique is also used in the eighth and tenth symphonies). The diagram of *Sinfonia della Speranza* is clearly divided in two mirror parts and going through the music material we can also find the analogous dividing line—the axis of symmetry. Analysing this material we can see that the main plane of symmetry here is the fast, middle part of the piece—*Molto vivo* (figures 30–50). From figure 50 the musical material is being reflected, which means that figure 50 is the reflection of figure 29, etc. This fast middle part is constructed similarly, as figures 42–49 are the reflection of figures 30–37 and the section between figures 38–41 constitute the plane of symmetry. So, we have here again an example of symmetry within symmetry.

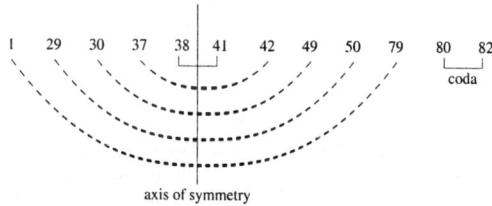

Ex. 14b. *Sinfonia della Speranza*
© Copyright 1987 by Boosey & Hawkes Music Publishers Ltd.
Reproduced by permission of Boosey & Hawkes Music Publishers Ltd.

The whole formal structure of this symphony refers to the circular construction of *Sinfonia di Sfere*. The symmetrical shapes of Panufnik's fifth and ninth symphonies gain more clarity by keeping the analogous instrumentation in reflected parts. It is obvious that the reflected movement is not based exactly on the same musical material—that would be too simple and perhaps not right for creating music which should explore not only technical elements but also the emotional ones (as we know, the perfect balance of these two elements was the main aim of Panufnik's output).

In Panufnik's other symphonies the use of mirror symmetry as part of the formal construction is not so clear or precise. But we can still find some elements of it in the particular elements of form, e.g. in the metrical system of the composition (*Sinfonia Mistica, Metasinfonia*).

Summary

As shown above, Andrzej Panufnik used symmetrical structures not only in the aspect of harmony or musical syntax but also in constructing the form shapes of his symphonies. It is thus no exaggeration to say that the structure of his works is deeply influenced by symmetry of all kinds. There is no doubt that the most important achievement of this composer is the creation of mirror form—and not only in the emotional sense (arch form) but also, and first of all, in the real sound material (mirror form).

The analysis of the three aspects of Panufnik's symphonies shows beyond all doubt the importance of symmetry and geometry in the music of this composer. He used symmetry not only in symphonic pieces but in the all other genres composed by him—in orchestral music, concertos, choral music, chamber music and solo pieces. Even more important, it should be noted that he used it throughout his creative life, starting from the first pieces (*Tragic Overture*) and up to the last ones (Symphony No. 10, Cello Concerto). Considering this, there is no doubt that symmetry (and geometry) set into the music is the main characteristic of Panufnik's compositional style. This feature is very important as it influences very deeply the formal and structural face of his compositions. Symmetry designates the whole Panufnik's output—an output which was evolving slowly, free from the sudden stylistic breakthroughs. Symmetry and geometry ordered Panufnik's musical world, remaining for him not only the element giving unity to the construction of his works but also facilitating the 'unconstrained flow of thoughts, feelings and emotions'. For Andrzej Panufnik both these—perfect construction and the element of emotion ('impulse and design', as he used to say)—were always the main aim in the creation of his music.

Translated by Beata Bolesławska with John Allison

Panufnik's 'musica mensuralis'. The Problem of Isorhythmic and Metrical Organization of Musical Time

Alicja Jarzębska

> The phenomenon of music is given to us with the sole purpose of establishing an order in things, including, and particularly, the co-ordination between man and time.
>
> I. Stravinsky, *Autobiography*

In their analyses of Andrzej Panufnik's compositional work, theorists have tended to concentrate their interest primarily on the question of pitch organization, (which in early music theory is termed as *musica plana*) while paying little attention to issues related to the organization of metre and rhythm[1]. However, in relation to problems concerning the concept of *musica mensuralis,* an analysis of Panufnik's music shows that for almost 20 years (i.e. since the late 60s) he was making use of an original method of time organization. This method relies on a synthesis of early and contemporary compositional principles, in other words, (1) an amalgamation of the medieval concept of music *senza misura* and the modern day idea of music composed within a framework of a constant or changing metre, an

---

[1] See Krzysztof Stasiak, *An Analitycal Study of the Music of Andrzej Panufnik,* doctoral thesis, Faculty of Arts, Queen's University, Belfast 1990, pp. 194–230. The author used the concept of module as a time duration of pitch cell. He wrote that "The module is the most direct rhythmic equivalent of the pitch cell, and its use is allied exclusively the pitch cell arranged as melody. The earliest models are to be found in *Reflections* and *Universal Prayer*. These types contain certain common features which enable them to be classed together as a group. Each contains three durations which are paired exactly with the three-note pitch cells" (p. 197).

(2) the amalgamation of isorhythmic patterns with strongly contrasted tone-colour and the concept of *Grundgestalt* interpreted as a pre-compositional 'cell' (i.e. Panufnik's famous three-note cell or cell of three rhythmic values).

The composer often emphasized his identification with the view expressed by the English poet, Alexander Pope, that "Order is Heaven's first law", which explains why he wanted his scores to be "lucid and clear" and his music to convey to the listener a distinct impression of order and harmony (performed in accordance with his instructions in the score regarding relative duration and tone-colour). The composer stated:

> I never was tempted by the trend to construct music of such density and intellectual complexity that even finest musical ear cannot discern inaccuracies in performance[2].

He might added that anyone reading the score should find himself able to identify the clear principle governing the composer's notation. He challenged the opinions of so-called avant-garde composers who claimed that auditory perception of clearly defined differences in time values is unimportant, since the need for order can supposedly be 'satisfied' through use of the pre-compositional conceptual relationships between serial numbers (e.g. the Fibonacci series). He was not attracted—as for example Messiaen was—by the 'charm impossibility' in mathematical permutations of serial numbers that determine rhythmic values of notes in any specific composition.

Though Panufnik in keeping with Romantic traditions maintained that "Music expresses emotions and feelings", at the same time he stressed that his ideal was a composition with a perfect balance between intellect and emotion, heart and mind. He particularly valued compositional tools associated with principles of stability as in *ars componendi*, i.e. principles which guarantee order and organized musical structure without curtailing the composer's inventiveness, thus allowing him to make full use of his creative imagination. Panufnik was in accord with St. Augustine's view, as expressed in *De ordine* (II 41) "*Unde ista disciplina sensus intellectusque particeps musicae invenit*", in other words he was convinced that music in conjunction with the concept of beauty should satisfy both the senses and the intellect. St. Augustine often repeated that he took pleasure "Only in beauty, in the beauty of proportional shapes and numbers" (*De ordine* II, 15, 42).

---

[2] Andrzej Panufnik, *Composing Myself* (London: Methuen, 1987), p. 348.

In my paper I will discuss the principles related to organization
of metre and rhythmic order; I will identify pre-compositional sets of
rhythmic values as well as patterns of repeated rhythmic structures
and discuss their relevance to instrumentation and the famous
three-note cell (i.e. three pitch cell), drawing attention also to the
issue of polyrhythm.

Organization of metre

Sections and movements of cyclic works composed *senza misura*

Panufnik categorically dismissed the avant-garde concept of chance,
which caused radical departures from musical traditions in terms of
the ordered process of sound. He maintained that "the element of
chance is contrary to my passion for order which in my eyes is the
intrinsic core of a viable work of art"[3]. Nor was he interested in the
effect of contrast between sections defined as "controlled aleatory"
(where patterns of notes are performed simultaneously *ad libitum*)
and sections organized metrically and rhythmically.

One of the fundamental principles in Panufnik's music which he
used to form his clearly-defined, extended structures of 'music-buil-
ding' material is contrast between (1) a sequence of notes with regular
or variable accents and (2) a sequence of notes without metrical
accents but with a freely chosen duration of rests between the notes
(i.e. *senza misura*). This contrast between sequences of notes *senza
misura* and those with metrical accents is usually enhanced by
combining these fragments with two clearly defined types of timbre
(i.e. different orchestration, articulation and level of register). However, the rhythmic correlation between notes (or between groups of
notes) is precisely ordered both in sections marked *senza misura* and
those with metrical accents. In both types of musical process Panufnik
exploits an analogous method of organizing rhythm, which relies on
a hierarchic montage of three rhythmic values treated as a pre-compositional 'cell'.

Universal Prayer (1969) provides an example of structure created
according to this principle of contrast. Its form is generated by a
hierarchic montage of 45 sections, 23 of which have metrical accents
while 22 are marked *senza misura* (see Example 1). The effect of
contrasts resulting from these two types of metrical organization in

---

[3] Andrzej Panufnik, *Composing Myself, op. cit.*, p. 348.

enhanced by the previously mentioned contrasts of timbre: the *senza misura* sections are always performed by the organ (solo or accompanied by the chorus) while the sections with metrical accents are performed by the 3 harps and 4 solo voices. The complete structure illustrates the composer's creation of a mirrored symmetry, the axis of which is to be found in section no. 13. This logically consistent montage of sections of two different types of timbre and two types of organization of metre (i.e. *senza misura* and with metrical accents), also bears the hierarchic characteristics of an architectural design.

The function of pillars which divide this work into larger structural entities has been assigned to two types of sections, (a) numbers 6 and 20 arranged in parallel and (b) numbers 10 and 16 arranged in symmetric patterns (see Example 1).

[0]	1	2	3	4	5	6	7	8	9	10	11	12	13	14	15	16	17	18	19	20	21	22	23	24	25	26
A	B	A	B	A	B	AB AB AB AB	B	A	B	A B A	B	A	B	A	B	A B A	B	A	B	AB AB AB AB	B	A	B	A	B	A

↑
axis

Ex. 1. *Universal Prayer*. Structural scheme
A = *senza misura* sections, **B** = sections with metrical accents

The principle of the symmetric montage of sections composed without metrical accents (A) or within a bar-line with metrical accents (B) also was used in the structural design of the Violin Concerto (1971) where the 1st movement (*Rubato*) is divided into five sections (in the form ABABA) (see Example 2). The *senza misura* sections are played in constant tempo (crotchet =40), whereas the sections with regular metrical accents in the rhythmic values are played in changing tempo.

Senza misura	$\frac{4}{4}$	Senza misura	$\frac{4}{4}$	Senza misura
crotchet = 40	crotchet = 56 *accelerando* crotchet = 96 *rall. poco a poco*	crotchet = 40	crotchet = 60 *accelerando* crotchet = 96 *rall. poco a poco* crotchet = 56	crotchet = 40
A	B	A	B	A

Ex. 2. Violin Concerto, 1st movement *Rubato*. Structural scheme
A = *senza misura* sections played in constant tempo,
B = sections with metrical accents and changing tempo

Panufnik's cyclic works also contain movements composed entirely *senza misura*, for example the 1ˢᵗmovement (*Prelude*) of String Quartet No. 1 (1971), the 6ᵗʰ movement of *Arbor Cosmica* (1983) and the 2ⁿᵈ movement (*Recitativo I*) of the Bassoon Concerto (1991). Movements and sections marked *senza misura* have a dual character, because the quasi-melodic phrases are divided (a) by rests of unspecified rhythmic values (marked as *fermata* or as a 'v' sign symbolizing a 'breath' effect, or (b) by rests of precisely specified rhythmic value. In the *senza misura* sections one can observe a precise and clear relationship between different rhythmic values without metrical accent. To make this clear to the performers the composer invented the idea of "interrupted" bar-lines. He also inserted instructions in his scores; for example in the *senza misura* movement of the *Bassoon Concerto*, where the performers (solo bassoon, flute and 2 clarinets) are requested to take a breath when necessary, but never simultaneously with any other instrumentalist, nor the soloist, nor just before a quasi-bar line. In the *Arbor Cosmica* score (for 12 solo string instruments) the composer wrote:

> Please note it is necessary for the players performing trills and tremolos to avoid a tendency to accentuate the beginning of each quasi-bar.

The fact that composer indicates the duration of each rest appearing between groups of notes is also of importance. For example in *Arbor Cosmica* (6ᵗʰ movement) he wrote:

> The sign 'v' in the parts of any instrument playing a solo indicates a rest, which should each time be a slightly different length to the previous one. But start with very long rests (cb), and very gradually shorten them towards the end of this evocation.

However, in the Bassoon Concerto (2ⁿᵈ movement *Recitativo I*) the sign 'v' indicates a breath, i.e. a rest, the duration of which fluctuates between a quaver and semiquaver. The composer also emphasizes that the melodic line in the bassoon part should to be played 'always very freely', i.e. creating an impression of a relaxed yet rhythmical singing sound. In the 1ˢᵗ movement (*Prelude*) of String Quartet No. 1, he indicates that this section also should be played very freely, *molto rubato*, while the duration of the rests marked with a *fermata* should seem to be chosen spontaneously during the performance, though they must be no shorter than one second nor longer than three seconds.

Sections composed with regular or variable metrical accents

In his music Panufnik also created contrasts between sequences of notes by means of regular or irregular metrical accents (i.e. notated in regular or variable metre). In his works variable metrical accents conform to a series of natural sequence of numbers or to clear proportions. Bars with variable metre are arranged consecutively or divided by fragments composed in a regular metre. The duration of these contrasting musical fragments may be equal or varied, however the variable metre remains in agreement with the principle of clear proportions. An example of this type of structure can be seen in *Metasinfonia* (1978) as well as in *Prologo, Aria* and *Epilogo*, three of the five movements of the Bassoon Concerto (1985). In *Metasinfonia* variable metre in successive 14-bar groupings corresponds to a natural sequence of numbers (from 8/4–7/4–6/4.... to 2/4) and the mirror image of the sequence (2/4–3/4–4/4...to 8/4) (see Example 3).

8/4	7/4	6/4	5/4	4/4	3/4	2/4	2/4	3/4	4/4	5/4	6/4	7/4	8/4	senza misura	8/4
[..2]	[2]	[4]	[6]	[8]	[10]	[12]	[14]	[17]	[19]	[21]	[23]	[25]	[27-29]		

Ex. 3. *Metasinfonia*. Scheme of variable metre (crotchet = 56)

Similar relationships between bars with variable metre appear in the outer movements (movements 1 and 5) and the 4th movement of Bassoon Concerto. In this instance the composer alternates sections composed in regular metre with sections in variable metre, where they conform to a natural sequence of numbers and mirror symmetry (8/4.... 1/4.... 8/4)(see Example 4).

3/4		3/4		3/4		3/4		3/4		3/4		3/4		3/4		3/4
	8/4		7/4		6/4		5/4		4/4		3/4		2/4		1/4	
8 b.		4 b.		4 b.		4 b.		3 b.		3 b.		3 b.		3 b.		16 b.

Prologo   (crotchet = 96)

4/4		4/4		4/4	
8 7 6 5 4 3 2 1 1 2 3 4 5 6 7 8 4 4 4 4 4 4 4 4 4 4 4 4 4 4 4 4		1 2 3 4 5 6 7 8 8 7 6 5 4 3 2 1 4 4 4 4 4 4 4 4 4 4 4 4 4 4 4 4		senna misura	
[5-8]		[12-15]			

Aria   (crotchet = 40)

	3/4
8 7 6 5 4 3 2 1 4 4 4 4 4 4 4 4	
	from no. 2

Epilogo   (crotchet = 96)

Ex. 4. Bassoon Concerto (*Prologo, Aria, Epilogo*)
Scheme of sections composed in regular metre or in variable metre

As previously mentioned, *Universal Prayer* also is a fascinating example of a compositional structure of sections *senza misura* in a montage together with sections composed in regular or variable metre which conform to a natural sequence of numbers (10/8–11/8–12/8; 3/4–4/4–5/4–6/4) or to clear proportions (3/4–6/4–9/4) (see Example 5).

(0) & 26	*senza misura*						
1 & 25	10, 11, 12 / 8 8 8						
2 & 24	*senza misura*						
3 & 23	3 6 3 9 / 4 4 2 4						
4 & 22	*senza misura*						
5 & 21	3 4 5 6 / 4 4 4 4						
6 & 20	*senza misura*	3/4	*senza misura*	3/4	*senza misura*	3/4	*senza misura*	3/4
7 & 19	3 1 3 / 4 4 4						
8 & 18	*senza misura*						
9 & 17	4 5 6 / 4 4 4						
10 & 16	*senza misura*	3/4	*senza misura*				
11 & 15	3/4						
12 & 14	*senza misura*						
13	4 6 / 4 4						

Ex. 5. *Universal Prayer*. Structural scheme
Montage of sections composed in regular or a variable metre
and sequences of notes *senza misura*

Simultaneous polymetre

In Panufnik's music also the effect of simultaneous polymetre is particularly interesting. For example in *Procession for Peace* (1983), the composer creates two simultaneous 'musical events', in other words two sound-layers, the first sound-layer (a) making use of sound-colour of unspecified pitch, played by timpani and drums, producing a constantly repeated rhythmic formula in 2/4 metre; (b) the second sound-layer consisting of quasi-melodic line (therefore of specific pitch) played usually in 3/4 metre and sometimes in 4/4 or

5/4 metre. The repetitions of the melodic phrases (a group of 12 or 24 crochets) are divided by rests of various duration. Panufnik thus combines the simultaneous polymetre with the effect of simultaneous contrast in timbre, i.e. between the sound-layer of unspecified and specific pitch. Successive changes of timbre—as a result of specific instrumentation—creates the effect of the gradation in the dynamics: consecutive sections are performed first by (1) a few brass instruments (*con sordini pp*), then by (2) wood-winds, (3) the strings, (4) the wood-wind and brass, and finally (5) the whole ensemble (wood-wind, brass and strings) (see Example 6).

$\frac{3}{4}$	$\frac{3}{4}$ $\frac{5}{4}$ $\frac{3}{4}$ $\frac{5}{4}$	$\frac{3}{4}$ $\frac{4}{4}$ $\frac{3}{4}$ $\frac{4}{4}$	$\frac{3}{4}$	$\frac{3}{4}$
12 (3) 12 (3) 12 (3) 12 (3)	24 (2) 12 (2) 12 (2) 12 (2) 12 (2)	24 (1) 12 (1) 12 (1) 12 (1) 12 (1)	24' 12' 24'	24' 12' 12' 24
A	B	C	D	E
	(repeated rhythmic pattern in regular metre: 2/4) X			
	[2]	[4]	[6]	[8]

Ex. 6. *Procession for Peace*. Structural scheme
X – timpani and drums (they play repeated rhythmic pattern in regular metre). The melodic phrases (as a group of **12 or 24** crotchets separated by rests which duration takes 3, 2, or 1 crotchet) are played by **A** – brass (*con sordini, pp*), **B** – wood-wind, **C** – strings, **D** – wood-wind and brass, **E** – the whole ensemble (wood-wind, brass, strings)

Organization of rhythm

Pre-compositional rhythmic cells

> For me, economy of means and my responsibility over each and every note I put on paper is crucial

the composer wrote in his autobiography[4]. This economy of resources used in the formation of rhythmic patterns is confirmed by analysis of the composer's scores, in which he makes use of the principle of isorhythm in a specific way. Panufnik's method of formulating repeatable rhythmic pattern usefully illustrated his concept of 'basic

---

[4] Andrzej Panufnik, *Composing myself, op. cit.*, p. 348

cells'. Elements of a given cell can be of single rhythmic value (or a group of notes of equal rhythmic value) connected with each other by the rule of proportion. Various rhythmic cells used in such works as *Universal Prayer*, Bassoon Concerto, String Quartet No. 1, *Arbor Cosmica* and *Sinfonia di Sfere* are illustrated in Example 7.

examples	three elementary components of motion			proportion	tempo	metre
	a	b	c			
Universal Prayer, nos. 2 & 24	𝅝.	𝅝	𝅗𝅥	3:2:1	broadly	*senza misura*
Universal Prayer nos. 6 & 20	♪	♪	♪.	1:2:3	quite fast not so fast rather slowly very slowly	*senza misura*
Universal Prayer nos. 10 & 16	𝅗𝅥	𝅗𝅥.	𝅘𝅥	4:3:2	moderately	*senza misura*
Bassoon Concerto (*Prologo* - segments played by celli & double-basses)	♫	♫ ♫	♫ ♫ ♫	1:2:3	♩ = ca 96	3 4
String Quartet No. 1 (1th movement, part of 1st violin)	♬	♬ ♬	♬ ♬ ♬	1:2:3	♩ = 56-76	*senza misura*
Arbor Cosmica, (6th movement)	♬³	♪ ♬³	♪ ♪ ♬³	1:2:3	lento moderato allegro vivacissimo	*senza misura*
Sinfonia di Sfere nos. 31 - 44	♫	♬ ♫	♫ ♫	1:3:2	change of rhythmic values in propotion 1 : 1/2 : 1/3 : 1/4	1 4

Ex. 7. Rhythmic cells

Rhythmic structure designs

In Panufnik's compositions, recurring rhythmic structures are shaped in accordance with clearly defined designs, which form a montage of greater or lesser complexity of a given rhythmic cell. The general principle of this montage is the rotation of elements in a given set and the mirror-image (symmetrical) projection of the resulting rhythmic pattern. Methods of creating hierarchical rhythmic structures of increasingly complex design are presented in examples 8 & 9. Design I exploits the principle of rotation, Design II – rotation/symmetry, Design III – symmetry/rotation/symmetry and Design IV – the repetition method with some modification. Fragments of *Universal Prayer* illustrate the use of Design III (Examples 10ab, 11ab, 12ab).

	Number of elements	Hierarchical scheme of succession of elementary components of motion	Examples
Design I	16	abcd, bcda, cdab, dabc **a b c d**	Symfony No. 10, nos. 20-23 (example 14)
Design II	18	abc, bca, cab / cba bac acb **Q** **/ Z**	*Arbor Cosmica*, 6th movement (example 13ab)
Design III	36	abc/cba bca/acb cab/bac / cba/abc bac/cab acb/bca **X** **/ Y**	*Universal Prayer,* nos. 10 & 16 or 12 & 14 (examples 10ab, 11ab, 12ab)
Design IV	7+7	a a a b <u>c</u> a <u>b</u> / a a a b <u>a</u> <u>c</u> b **A** **/ A'**	*Sinfonia di Sfere* nos. 31- 44 (example 20)

Ex. 8. Rhythmic structure designs

	α β, α β, α β	*String Quartet No.I,* 1th movement	Example 16ab
Parallel patterns	**QZ, QZ, QZ....**	*Arbor Cosmica*, 6th movement	Example 13
	XY, XY, XY...	*Universal Prayer,* nos. 10 & 16	Example 10
Symmmetrical patterns	α β α β α	*String Quartet No.I,* 1th movement	Example 16
	XYX; XYXYX	*Universal Prayer* nos. 12 & 14 and 6 & 20	Examples 11ab & 12ab

Ex. 9. Montage of a rhythmic structure designs

abc/cba	bca/acb	cab/bac	3/4....	cba/abc	bac/cab	acb/bca
	X *(senza misura)*				**Y** *(senza misura)*	

No. 10

cba/abc	bac/cab	acb/bca	3/4....	abc/cba	bca/acb	cab/bac
	Y *(senza misura)*				**X** *(senza misura*	

No. 16

Ex. 10a. *Universal Prayer* (nos. 10 & 16)
Rhythmic pattern modeled on Design III:
a = half-note, b = dotted crotchet, c = crotchet

x (a   b   c / c   b   a;   b   c   a / a   c   b; c   a   b / b   a   c)

Ex. 10b. *Universal Prayer* (no. 10)
Rhythmic pattern modeled on Design III: X (abc/cba; bca/acb; cab/bac)
a = half-note, b = dotted crotchet, c = crotchet

abc/cbxa	bca/axcb	cab/bxac	cbxa/abc	baxc/cab	axcb/bca
X			Y		

No. 2

cbxa/abc	baxc/cab	axcb/cba	abc/cbxa	bca/axcb	cab/bxac
Y			X		

No. 24

Example 11a. *Universal Prayer* (nos. 12 i 14)
Rhythmic pattern modeled on Design III:
a = half-note, b = dotted crotchet, c = crotchet

Ex. 11b. *Universal Prayer* (no. 12)
Rhythmic pattern modeled on Design III:
X (abc/cba; bca/acb; cab/bac) Y (cba/ abc; bac/cab; acb/bca)
a = half-note, b = dotted crotchet, c = crotchet

abc/cba	bca/acb	cab/bac	cba/abc	bac/cab	acb/bca	abc/cba	bca/acb	cab/bac	cba/abc	bac/cab	acb/bca	abc/cba	bca/acb	cab/bac
X			Y			X			Y			X		

No. 12

cba/abc	bac/cab	acb/bca	abc/cba	bca/acb	cab/bac	cba/abc	bac/cab	acb/bca	abc/cba	bca/acb	cab/bac	cba/abc	bac/cab	acb/bca
Y			X			Y			X			Y		

No. 14

Ex. 12a. *Universal Prayer* (nos. 2 & 24)
Rhythmic pattern modeled on Design III:
a =dotted half-note, b = half-note, c = crotchet, x = semiquavers

Ex. 12b. *Universal Prayer* (no. 2)
Rhythmic pattern modeled on Design III:
X (abc/cbxa; **bca**/axcb; **cab**/bxac) **Y** (cbxa/ abc; **bxac**/cab; **axcb**/bca)
a = half-note, b = dotted crotchet, c = crotchet, x = 2 semiquavers

x (a b c/c b x   a;   b   c a / a   x   c b ; c a   b/ b   x   a   c)

y (c b x   a / a   b   c; b   a   x   c/c   a   b; a   x   c b/ b   c a)

Relationship between repeated rhythmic cells, pitch cells and tone-colour

Panufnik created a variety of combinations of relationships between repeated rhythmic cells and a chosen tone-colour (connected with a specific instrumentation and articulation) which sometimes is gradually changing and sometimes contrasted. One can observe three types of these relationships in his compositions:

(1) a constant use the same tone-colour, as in *Universal Prayer* (see above), where in the sections marked *senza misura*, the repeated rhythmic pattern (based on Design III) always appears in the organ part (see Examples 10ab, 11ab, 12ab);

(2) increasingly varied tone-colour, for example in the 6th movement of *Arbor Cosmica* also *senza misura*, where the six-times repeated rhythmic pattern (modeled on Design II) is performed in succession by double-bass, cello, viola and violin (Example 13ab);

(3) the alternation of two different tone-colour, as in Symphony No. 10 in bars 20–23, where a twice-repeated 4-element rhythmic structure (based on Design I, notated in 9/8 metre), is treated either as continuity of tones of specified pitch (played by almost all the orchestral instruments), or as a sequence of unspecified pitch (played by percussion instruments) (see Example 14).

instrumentation	Repeated rhythmic pattern Design II	
	Q	**Z**
double-bass to [B]	abc, bca, cab abc, bca,	cba, bac, acb
cello [B]- [D]	cab abc, bca, cab	cba, bac, acb cba,
viola [D]-[F]	abc, bca, cab	bac, acb cba, bac, acb
violin [F] to the end	abc, bca, cab abc, bca, cab	cba, bac, acb cba,

Ex. 13a. *Arbor Cosmica*, 6th movement
Scheme of relationship between repeated rhythmic pattern (Design II)
and gradually changing tone-colour (double bass, cello, viola and violin)

Vl b   c   a ; c   a b / c   b   a ; b   a   c   ;

Vn Solo   *until one bar before the end.)*

ff molto agitato
(a b   c   ; b   c   a ; c   a b   /

Vl (————— *ff*)
 a   c   b)

Vc I (4)   (4)
 c   b a ; b   a c   ; a   c   b) (a b   c   ;

Vn *pizz.*   (⌢)
 fff ————————
 b   c   a ; c   a b / c   b   a ;

Ex. 13b. *Arbor Cosmica*, 6th movement
Repeated rhythmic pattern modeled on Design II played by double
bass, cello, viola and violin
© Copyright 1983 by Boosey & Hawkes Music Publishers Ltd.
Reproduced by permission of Boosey & Hawkes Music Publishers Ltd.

Rhythmic pattern (Design I)	abcd	bcda	cdab	dab	c abcd b	c d	a cdab d	a	b c abcd
Tone-colour	T	**P**	T	**P**	T	**P**	T	**P**	T
Number of bars	4 b.	4 b.	4 b.	3 b.	6 b.	2 b.	6 b.	1 b.	6 b.
	[20]			[21]			[22-23]		

Ex. 14. Symphony No. 10, nos. 20–23
Scheme of relationship between repeated rhythmic pattern modeled on
Design I (abcd, bcda, cdab, dabc) and two contrasted tone-colour; T = tones
of specified pitch (sections played by almost all the orchestral instruments),
P = a sequence of unspecified pitch (played by percussion instruments)

A repeated rhythmic cell integrated with consistent tone-colour is sometimes used in variable metre. For example in *Prologo*, the first movement of the Bassoon Concerto, the bars of variable metre (sequentially from 8/4 to 1/4) are played always by celli and double-basses. The rhythmic structure of these bars is a result of a varied montage of three groups of notes of the same rhythmic value (2–4 – 6 semiquavers) (see Examples 15ab).

	[1]	[2]	[3]	[4]	[5]	[6]	[7]	[8-9]
metre	3/4 3/4 8/4	3/4 7/4	3/4 6/4	3/4 5/4	3/4 4/4	3/4 3/4	3/4 2/4	3/4 1/4
	a b c	b c a	c c	b c	a c	b a	c	a
bars	4 bars 4 bars	4 bars	4 bars	4 bars	3 bars	3 bars	3 bars	3 bars

Ex. 15a. Bassoon Concerto (1st movement, *Prologo*)
Scheme of the relation between variable metre and various montage of three groups of notes of the same rhythmic value (played always by celli and double-basses): a – 2 semiquavers, b – 4 semiquavers, c – 6 semiquavers

Ex. 15b. Bassoon Concerto (1st movement, *Prologo*)
Various montage of three groups of notes of the same rhythmic value (played always by celli and double-basses): a – 2 semiquavers, b – 4 semiquavers, c – 6 semiquavers
© Copyright 1986 by Boosey & Hawkes Music Publishers Ltd.
Reproduced by permission of Boosey & Hawkes Music Publishers Ltd.

In Panufnik's music a sequence of rhythm in successive notes sometimes also conforms to a montage technique in which each rhythmic cell is repeated in the relevant tone-colour. A good example of the relationship between a chosen rhythmic cell and tone-colour is the first movement of *String Quartet No. 1*, which constitutes a "conversation" between four instruments. Four rhythmic cells are individually realized by the four instruments (cell 'α' by the 1st violin, cell 'β' – by 2nd violin, cell 'γ' by viola and cell " by cello) (see Examples 16a and 16b).

Imagining musical "conversation" between four people of very different character, the composer combines the effects of these four rhythmic cells and four tone-colours. According to his comment in the score:

> In Prelude, the players individually introduce themselves in a kind of conversation, making their own statements about the subject which will appear later in Transformation. In this introduction, written *senza misura*, each player performs his solo independently, always with his 'own' characteristic expression, dynamics and sound colour. As one would find in different people's speaking voices. They represent totally different personalities: one agitated, very aggressive (Violin I), one ironic, witty (Violin II); one rather pompous (Viola); and the last calmly philosophical (Cello)].

rhythmic cells		elementary components of motion: a,b,c (numbers of notes in one component)		
		a	b	c
α	semiquavers, played (*staccato*) by 1st violin	3	6	9
β	demisemiquavers played by 2nd violin	10 [4 (4) 6] or 6 (4) 4]	16 [10 (4) 6] or [6 (4) 10]	16 [8 (4) 8]
γ	rhythmic pattern played by viola	(3x)	(2x)	(1x)
δ	quavers played by cello	9 [2 (1) 2 (1) 2 (1) 2 (1) 1]	12 [2 (1) 2 (1) 2 (1) 2 (1) 2 (1) 2]	6 [2 (1) 2 (1) 2]

Ex. 16a. String Quartet No. 1, 1st movement, *Prelude*
Four rhythmic cells connected with tone-colour:
α – semiquavers, played by 1st violin *staccato*, β – demisemiquavers played by 2nd violin, δ – quavers played by cello, γ – rhythmic pattern (dotted crochet and 2 semiquavers) played by viola.

α β, α β, α β,	γ δ, γ δ	α β α β α,	δ γ δ γ δ	β α β α β,	γ δ γ δ γ	α β, α β,	γ δ γ	β α β α β,	γ δ
	[1]		[2]		[3]		[4]		

Ex. 16b. String Quartet No. 1, 1st movement, *Prelude*
Scheme of montage of four rhythmic cells

Analysis of this work—considering the relationship between four rhythmic cells (connected with four tone-colours determined by various instruments and articulation) and the recurring pitch cells (the famous three-note cell)—reveals highly refined structural procedures. The composer uses in consecutive order, three groups of pitch cells (A – abc, B-def; C – ghi), modified by a mirror reflection of tones in a given cell and by transposition (by an equivalent interval: major third raised and lowered in the scale) (see Example 17a). Pitch organization in successive segments in the 1st movement of this Quartet corresponds with a variable montage of three-pitch cells in keeping with a symmetrical design of ABCBA. The correlation between recurring rhythmic cells performed by relevant instruments and pitch cells is illustrated by Example 17bc.

Pitch cells	Structure of pitch cells [i.e. number of semitone up (+) or down (-)]	ambitus of pitch cell	succession of pitch in pitch cells		succession of pitch in pitch cells (transposition by major third up in the scale)		succession of pitch in pitch cells (transposition by major third down in the scale)	
A a b c	+6+5 -5 -6	11	**(a)** C-F# -B / B -F# - C	**(a')**	**(b)** E- A# -D# / D# -A# - E	**(b')**	**(c)** G# -D -G / G - D - G#	**(c')**
B d e f [nos. 1 - 2]	-1+7 -7+1	7	**(d)** D# -D-A / A-D -D#	**(d')**	**(e)** G- F#- C# / C#- F#- G	**(e')**	**(f)** B - A# - F / F- A#- B	**(f')**
C g h i [nos. 2 - 3]	+5+1 -1-5	6	**(g)** C -F - F# / F# -F-C	**(g')**	**(h)** E - A - A#/ A# - A - E	**(h')**	**(i)** G# - C# - D / D - C# - D	**(i')**
B₁ d₁ e₁ f₁ [nos. 3 - 4]	+6-7 +7-6	7	**(d₁)** D# -A - D/ D-A-D#	**(d'₁)**	**(e₁)** G - C# - F# / F# - C#-G	**(e'₁)**	**(f₁)** B -F -A# / A# - F - B	**(f'₁)**
A a b c [from no. 4 to the end]	+6+5 -6-5	11	**(a)** C -F# -B / B- F# -C	**(a')**	**(b)** E - A# -D# / D# -A# -E	**(b')**	**(c)** G# - D- G / G- D- G#	**(c')**

Ex. 17a. String Quartet No. 1, 1st movement, *Prelude*
Succession of pitch in pitch cells

from the beginning to no. 1

Vn I	Vn II	Vn I	Vn II	Vn I	Vn II	Vla	Vc

A

a	a'	a	b'	b	a'	a	b'	c	c'	b	a'	a	c'	b	b'	c	a'
↑	↓	↑	↓	↑	↓	↑	↓	↑	↓	↑	↓	↑	↓	↑	↓	↑	↓

nos. 1 & 2

Vla	Vc	Vn I	Vn II	Vn I	Vn II	Vn I

[A]   **B**

a	d	f	f	e'	f	d'	d	e'	E	f	f	e'	e	f	e	e'	d
↑	↑	↓	↑	↓	↑	↓	↑	↓	↑	↓	↑	↓	↑	↓	↑	↓	↑

nos. 2 & 3

Vc	Vla	Vc	Vla	Vc	Vn II	Vn I	Vn II	Vn I

[B]   **C**

d'	g	g	g'	i	i'	h	h'	i	g'	g	h'	i	i'	h	h'	g	g'
↓	↓	↑	↓	↑	↓	↑	↓	↑	↓	↑	↓	↑	↓	↑	↓	↑	↓

nos. 3 & 4

Vn II	Vla	Vc	Vla	Vc	Vla	Vn I	Vn II	Vn I

[C]   **B₁**

g	d_1	d'_1	e_1	e'_1	f_1	e'_1	e_1	e'_1	e_1	d'_1	d_1	f'_1	f_1	e'_1	f	f'	d
↑	↑	↓	↑	↓	↑	↓	↑	↓	↑	↓	↑	↓	↑	↓	↑	↓	↓

from no. 4

Vn II	Vla	Vc	Vla	Vn II	Vn I	Vn II	Vn I	Vn II	Vla	Vc

[B_1]   **A**

d_1'	a'	a	b'	b	c'	b	b'	a	a'	c	c'	b	c'	c	a'	a	b	b'	a'	a	a'
↓	↓	↑	↓	↑	↓	↑	↓	↑	↓	↑	↓	↑	↓	↑	↓	↑	↑	↓	↓	↑	↓

Ex. 17b. String Quartet No. 1, 1ˢᵗ movement, *Prelude*
Scheme of the relation between pitch cells and rhythmic-timbre cells:
↑ – succession of pitch up to the scale, ↓ – succession of pitch down to the scale

Ex. 17c. String Quartet No. 1, 1st movement, *Prelude*
© Copyright 1978 by Boosey & Hawkes Music Publishers Ltd.
Reproduced by permission of Boosey & Hawkes Music Publishers Ltd.

Simultaneous montage of rhythmic structures design

In Panufnik's compositions, a chosen recurring rhythmic structure is not only successively applied, but also simultaneously. Polyrhythmic patterns can be seen among others in *Universal Prayer* where in the solo organ part (no. 6 and 20, *senza misura*) two quasi-melodic sequences (reminiscent of medieval diaphony) of variable pitch and rhythm, are exploited simultaneously. Their rhythmic structure is an outcome of a variable montage of rhythmic cell (i.e. its three rhythmic values: semiquaver, quaver, dotted quaver) applied in accordance with Design III (see Example 18).

sensa misura Quite fast	3 4	sensa misura Not so fast	3 4	sensa misura Rather slowly	3 4	sensa misura Very slowly	3 4
X		**Y**		**X**		**[Y]**	
abc/cba bca/acb		cab/bac cba/abc bac		/cab acb/bca; abc/cba		bca/acb cab/bac; cba/-	
cba/abc bac/cab		acb/bca abc /cba bca		/acb cab/bac; cba/abc		bac/cab acb/bca; abc/-	
Y		**X**		**Y**		**[X]**	

No. 6

sensa misura Very slowly	3 4	sensa misura Not so fast	3 4	sensa misura Not so fast	3 4	sensa misura Not so fast	3 4
Y		**X**		**Y**		**[X]**	
cba/abc bac/cab		acb/bca abc/cba bca/		/acb cab/bac; cba/abc		bac/cab acb/bca; abc/-	
abc/cba bca/acb		cab/bac cba/abc bac/		/cab acb/bca; abc/cba		bca/acb cab/bac; cba/-	
X		**Y**		**X**		**[Y]**	

No. 20

Ex. 18a. *Universal Prayer*, nos. 6 and 20
Polyrhythmic patterns as a results of a simultaneous montage of rhythmic structure Design III:
a = semiquaver, b = quaver, c = dotted quaver

x (a b   c   /   c   b   a;   b   c   a;
y (c   b   a/ a b   c;   b   a   c /   c   (b)   a

Ex. 18b. *Universal Prayer* (no. 6)
Polyrhythmic pattern modeled on Design III used simultaneously
X (abc/cba; bca/acb; ...)
Y (cba/abc; bac/cab; ...)
a = semiquaver, b = quaver, c = dotted quaver

On the other hand, an example of a highly refined rhythmic canon can be seen in a fragment of *Sinfonia di Sfere* (nos. 31–44) where the chosen rhythmic pattern (see Example 19) is repeated dozens of times by various instruments, and is presented simultaneously in variable diminution (this scheme is marked in various rhythmic values: Z- quavers, Y – semiquavers, X – semiquavers triplet, Q – demisemiquavers which highlight the diminution in accordance with the harmonic series 1 : 1/2 : 1/3 : 1/4; the duration of a given rhythmic value remains constant [crotchet=56]). The structure of rhythm as well of tone-colour conforms to mirror image symmetry (see Example 20).

Ex. 19. *Sinfonia di Sfere*
Scheme of the repeated rhythmic "theme" (in the form A A', as a theme of canon):
a – 2 quavers, b – 6 quavers, c – 4 quavers, (1) – quaver rest

	Repeated rhythmic „theme"				Repeated rhythmic „theme"		
Q	vni +vle +vc ----- tr		percussion ------piano		percussion ------piano		vni +vle +vc ----- tr
X		vle+vc; vc+cl+fg ---- cr... -----piano				vle+vc; vc+cl+fg ---- cr... -----piano	
Y	percussion ----- piano		cb pizz. +cfg *stacc.* ----- tn, tb *stacc.*		cb (*pizz*) +cfg *tacc* ----- tn, tb (*stacc*)		percussion ----- piano
Z	percussion	.....(percussion)	percussion		percussion	.....(percussion)	percussion
nos.	31-33	33 -35	35--37	**37-38**	38 - 40	40 - 42	42-44

Ex. 20. *Sinfonia di Sfere*, nos. 31–44
Scheme of mirror symmetry of the repeated rhythmic "theme" and tone-colour.
The rhythmic "theme" is performed by various instruments and in diminution in accordance with the harmonic series: 1; 1/2: 1/3: 1/4 ; it is played as:
Z = quavers (duration of rhythmic theme takes 16 bars), Y = semiquavers (8 bars),
X = semiquavers triplet (6 bars), Q = demisemiquavers (4 bars)

In his works, Panufnik's masterfully composed metro-rhythmic proportions combined with tone-colour variety serve on the one hand in the building of clearly defined and symmetrically proportioned musical structures, and on the other, are a source of differentiated and sublime sound expression associated with such terms as *con grazia, espressione, vigore, tenerezza, cantabile, ritmico, tragico* etc. His astounding creative disciple, seen among others in the precision of his organization of time, was not a manifestation – fashionable among avant-garde composers and American theorists – of a fascination with mathematical group theories or principles of permutations. It is a testimony to a creative furtherance of isorhythm traditions and at the same time a proposal offering new compositional techniques, which accentuate the significance of tone-colour in the organization of time and combine euphonic sounds with the principles of proportion and symmetry that for centuries have been associated with the concept of beauty, yet during the last hundred years have sadly been banished.

The Role of the Major-Minor Chord in Panufnik's Compositional Technique

Charles Bodman Rae

Panufnik's music, like that of many other composers, can be considered from the outside, gradually looking in to the detail, or from the inside, gradually looking out to the whole. In deciding to focus this study on a particular item of detail I was conscious that other contributors would be considering the broader picture, both in terms of approach to aesthetics and concepts of structure. Hopefully, the combination of these two approaches will help us better to appreciate the content of Panufnik's music and the means through which his creative conception was realized.

Here I wish to focus on one particular feature of Panufnik's harmony. It is one of several features which link the music of Panufnik, Lutosławski, and Bartók. The focus is on a particular type of four-note chord which can be described as 'major-minor': the triadic configuration which contains both major and minor thirds in relation to the same root (see Example 1). This type of pitch collection could also be classified in integer terms. Allen Forte identifies it as pitch class set 0347 and gives it the set 'name' of 4–17(12). The Forte method of identification has certain disadvantages, most significantly the way it obscures the distinctive disposition of actual intervals (as opposed to interval classes). It does, however, present one advantage: the six-digit interval 'vector' which explains the total intervallic content of a chord. A four-note major-minor chord has an interval vector of 102210, and this indicates the presence of: one minor second (diminished octave or major seventh), no major seconds, two minor thirds, two major thirds (minor sixths), one perfect fourth, and no tritones.

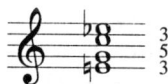

Ex. 1. a 'major-minor' chord

This type of chord has some interesting properties. It is vertically symmetrical; the interval of a perfect fourth provides the central axis, with minor third intervals on either side (these interval classes, 3–5–3, are shown in Example 1). The symmetry is significant. Much of Panufnik's music shows a fascination for symmetry of various different kinds, applied to different levels of a composition (as with Bartók). The symmetry is often formal, or structural, and there are diagrammatic schemes for several of his pieces which clearly demonstrate this approach.[1] But the symmetry also occurs at a local, more detailed level, within the harmonic structures. At this level the 'major-minor' chord appears to be one of the most significant building blocks of his music. Not only is the compact, basic form of the major-minor chord vertically symmetrical, but the notes can be distributed across a wide range, with doublings, and still symmetrically (see Example 8, below).

When the chord is used in its basic layout (Example 1), it has the major third component of the triad at the bottom and the minor third component of the triad at the top. So these notes provide the dissonant interval of a diminished octave, but the aural effect of the dissonance is softened by the symmetrical disposition of minor thirds. The interval vector of 102210 reminds us that there are, in fact, *four* intervals of thirds/sixths embedded in the chord (2 minor thirds, plus 2 minor sixths).

As part of my investigations into Lutosławski's harmony I have identified ten types of four-note chord which he often used in order to construct his twelve-note chords.[2] These twelve-note chords were used from 1957 onwards; but the four note chords, on which many of them are based, appear considerably earlier (for example, in

---

[1] See: Andrzej Panufnik, *Impulse and Design in my music* (London: Boosey & Howkes, 1974).

[2] This first appeared in Chapter 3, 'Vertical Pitch Organisation: Harmony', in *Pitch Organisation in the Music of Lutosławski since 1979* (PhD thesis, University of Leeds, 1992). See also Bodman Rae, *The Music of Lutosławski* (London: Faber and Faber, 1994), p. 54 (Polish edition: *Muzyka Lutosławskiego*, trans. S. Krupowicz, Warszawa: PWN, 1996), pp. 67–68, and 'Organizacja wysokości dźwięków w muzyce Lutosławskiego' (Pitch organisation in the music of Lutosławski) in *Muzyka XL*, 1995 No. 1–2, pp. 46–49.

sketches made as early as 1944). I identified these chords simply
with letters (from A to K). The 'major-minor' chord was identified as
'type H', in the group of chords each containing one perfect fourth
and two minor third intervals. But this was my own labelling, not
Lutosławski's. When I first had an opportunity to look through all
his sketches, at his home in the mid-1980s, I noticed that there were
many pages labelled with the code 'OWD' (Organizacja wysokości
dzwięków). On such pages he would work out, in great detail,
relationships between complementary pitch collections, usually three
groups of four (making up all twelve). Some of these four-note chords
seemed to have a more 'special' status than others, because they were
labelled with particular letter codes (and usually enclosed in double
inverted commas), for example "W", or "D", or "R", sometimes "Ro",
or "P".[3] I asked Lutosławski on several occasions what these codes
represented, but he was initially reluctant to explain. Eventually,
however, he did tell me what they signified. This is not the place to
reveal the meaning of all the letter codes, but it is certainly the place
to reveal one of them: the code "P".

Ex. 2. A page from Lutosławski's sketches for *Les espaces du sommeil*

[3] Some of these codes (W, D, R, Ro) can be seen in a page from the sketches for
the Third Symphony, reproduced in my article for *Muzyka* in 1995, p. 47.

Example 2 shows a page of 'OWD' pitch material from Lutosławski's sketches for his work for baritone and orchestra, *Les espaces du sommeil*. Two sets of letters are used. The ones from A to H relate to the adjoining sketch materials and simply identify the order in which the various pitch collections appear. (These letters have no connection with the ones which I used in my own classification of his four-note chords.) The other letters, which Lutosławski has shown in brackets, enclosed in double inverted commas, identify the particular four-note chords present in the top register of the various pitch collections. Pitch collection A ("P") has a major-minor chord at the top: C natural, D sharp, G sharp, and B natural.

The code "P" represents 'Panufnik'. It is always attached to a major-minor four-note chord. Lutosławski explained to me that, during their student years, and during the café-duo collaboration of the war years, Panufnik would play 'jazz' improvisations in which he would use major-minor melodic inflections and major-minor chords. Thus Lutosławski always associated this type of chord with Panufnik, even when it occurred in a more abstract context and unconnected with a jazz idiom. Incidentally, even though Lutosławski used the term 'jazz', he seemed to be using the term loosely. The major-minor inflection (a minor third inflected in a melodic line above a major triad) has a more specific connection with the Blues tradition.

One can understand Lutosławski's reluctance to disclose the meaning of these chord labels. Although he had some personal associations for the chords and their aural qualities it does not follow that there are any intended allusions to other composers or other works. It could easily give rise to a rather silly kind of analysis which might give undue importance to a comparatively trivial issue. The chord is not used in Lutosławski's music in order to allude to 'jazz', or blues, or even to Panufnik. The chord is used in an abstract way, as one of several kinds of distinctive sonority. It most commonly occurs as the central strand of a twelve-note pitch collection which has minor-seventh chords in the high and low strands. Thus the intervallic symmetry of the central strand is enhanced. The letter code 'P' was merely a memory device for Lutosławski when working out these kinds of complex pitch collection. There are many other such memory devices in his sketches, but this one is a rather touching little gesture towards his old friend and colleague.

There is one other curious link. Lutosławski habitually made his compositional sketches on pieces of manuscript paper cut in half, in order to create small, 'landscape' sheets of approximately A5 size. This can be seen from Example 2 (which has ten staves, but is from a 20-stave sheet which has been cut in half). He once mentioned to me that he copied this idea from Panufnik, during the time of their studies at the Warsaw Conservatory. This point may seem trivial, but it illustrates a degree of closeness between the two student composers. This was the time of Lutosławski's Sonata for Piano (1934), and major-minor chords feature in the middle harmonic strand of some of the big sonorities in the first movement.[4]

Is the major-minor chord really a 'jazz' (or blues) phenomenon? Personally, I think not, in spite of Lutosławski's comment about Panufnik's improvisations. The chord can be identified in some of the most significant works of Bartók and Stravinsky (and others), and these influences on Lutosławski and Panufnik were certainly stronger than any so-called 'jazz' ones. The minor third melodic inflection over a major triad is also highly characteristic of Eastern European folk music, hence it finds its way into the music of Bartók and Stravinsky (and many others). One need only recall the opening of *Le Sacre du Printemps*. The bassoon solo, beginning on C natural, outlines a minor triad rooted on A (with the minor seventh G). The entry of the second part (the second horn) is on middle C sharp. The implied harmony is thus (from the bottom): C sharp, E, (G), A, C natural (see Example 3).

Ex. 3. Stravinsky, *Le sacre du printemps,* opening

As one would expect, especially in view of its properties of mirror symmetry, the chord appears in many contexts in the music of Bartók. Perhaps the most extensive use of the chord (with additions) comes in the second movement of Bartók's Sonata for Two Pianos and

[4] See bars 218–219 reproduced as Example 1 in: Chrles Bodman Rae, *The Music of Lutosławski, op. cit.,* p. 9.

Percussion. According to Adrian Thomas, Panufnik got to know this piece before the war.[5] This must have been very soon after the first performance (in Basel, in January 1938). The most striking passage of major-minor chords in the Bartók work comes in the slow movement. Between bars 48 and 56 of the second movement (Example 4) there is a passage marked *molto espr. la melodia*. From this point the first piano part has a succession of major-minor chords in parallel, in both hands, at the interval of a tritone. Each strand actually contains five-note rather than four-note chords. The major-minor chord provides the outer notes of each harmonic strand, and there is one additional note in each chord, which alters the intervallic structure to three minor-thirds and one major-second. It has to be said that this passage of parallel harmony, rich in tritones and minor thirds, sounds remarkably like Messiaen, even though the method of construction is different. One bar later, the second piano part (left hand) adds a third layer of the same types of chords (initially in canon with the right hand of piano). This is just one example from the Sonata for Two Pianos and Percussion; there are many others. The second idea of the second movement is a six-note rhythmic motif which articulates a minor-third, and in several cases this happens over the major triad.

The Bartók connection may, in fact, lead us back to 'jazz'; not the jazz of the Black-American tradition, of Louisiana, or even the blues tradition, but the Jewish, Eastern-European tradition, as exemplified by New Yorkers such as Gershwin. One suspects that the so-called 'jazz' which Lutosławski recalled from his youth was, in fact, Panufnik re-working the Eastern-European inflections which Gershwin had in common with Bartók (or possibly even assimilated from Bartók). So it is possible that Panufnik may have found the chord, in equal measure, in Polish and other folk music, in the music of Bartók, and in American popular music.

Many of Panufnik's works make extensive use of the four-note major-minor chord. There are instances of pitch collections, or intervallic cells, which are individual to a particular work. But the major-minor chord appears to be one of the most significant pitch collections which can be found across different pieces. It is thus one of the elements of his musical vocabulary and a hallmark of his style.

---

[5] Adrian Thomas, 'Panufnik', in *The New Grove Dictionary of Music and Musicians*, ed. S. Sadie (London: Macmillan, 2001), vol. 19, pp. 45–48.

Ex. 4. Bartók, Sonata for Two Pianos
and Percussion, II, bars 48–55

In the early 1990s I was led more deeply in to some of Panufnik's works through numerous discussions I had with my former student and colleague, Philip Greenwood.[6] The detailed analyses were his, and I was merely looking over his shoulder (sometimes metaphorically, sometimes literally). I recall, in particular, our discussions about the second movement of *Sinfonia Sacra* (*Vision II*, for strings); and the *Katyń Epitaph*. These two pieces are defined by major-minor chords. I also recall his thoughts on some of the expressive properties of this type of harmony. He observed that, when the major-minor idea was used by Panufnik in his earlier works (pre 1954) it tended to be with folk music inflections, whereas from the 1960s onwards it tends to have a different musical purpose. He suggested that the chord's ambivalence between major and minor came to represent psychological oppositions in the music between ideas such as hope and sorrow, or heroism and suffering. The works which make this kind of expressive use of the major-minor sound are, indeed, from the 1960s: Piano Concerto (1961); *Autumn Music* (1962); *Sinfonia Sacra* (1963); and *Katyń Epitaph* (1967). In the Piano Concerto, it is the climactic passage in the final movement which makes emphatic use of the major-minor harmony. In *Sinfonia Sacra* the second section, Vision II (for strings) uses the chords (with some subtle melodic movement) in a much more intimate manner. But in the *Katyń Epitaph*, the major-minor principle dominates.

Example 5 shows the beginning of *Katyń Epitaph*, as the opening solo for violin is taken up and developed contrapuntally by the woodwinds. The composer very helpfully includes natural signs in brackets just to confirm that he really does intend the minor third to be played above a major triad (eg, bars 15, 17, 20, 21, 22). The modal inflections between C sharp and C natural, or F sharp and F natural, can also be seen and heard in the violin solo, which also has cautionary accidentals. Example 6 shows the last page of the score of *Katyń Epitaph*. One can see that the final, emphatic chord is a widely spaced E major triad with octave doubling of G natural in the first violins contradicting the octave doubling of G sharp in the second violins and violas.

---

[6] During the time I was at Leeds College of Music.

Ex. 5. Panufnik, *Katyń Epitaph*, opening, bars 1–24[7]
© Copyright 1972 by Boosey & Hawkes Music Publishers Ltd.
Reproduced by permission of Boosey & Hawkes Music Publishers Ltd.

---

[7] The cor anglais part in the score is transposed, so it should be read down a perfect fifth.

Ex. 6. Panufnik, *Katyń Epitaph*, ending
© Copyright 1972 by Boosey & Hawkes Music Publishers Ltd.
Reproduced by permission of Boosey & Hawkes Music Publishers Ltd.

Sinfonia Sacra is in four movements: *Vision I*, Vision II, Vision III, and *Hymn*. *Vision II* is scored for strings, only, and lasts just over three minutes. Fifteen of its twenty-nine bars (including the first and last bars) contain major-minor chords. Example 7 shows the first five bars of the score, with the strings in six parts. The opening harmony has a widely spaced A major triad with a C natural at the top. Bar 3 has a B major triad with a D natural in the second violins contradicting the D sharp played by the cellos (bar 5 is similar). Again the composer provides natural signs in brackets just in case we are tempted to assume that the false relations are misprints.

Ex. 7. Panufnik, *Sinfonia Sacra*, *Vision II*, bars 1–5
© Copyright 1967 by Boosey & Hawkes Music Publishers Ltd.
Reproduced by permission of Boosey & Hawkes Music Publishers Ltd.

At the end of *Vision II* the six-part texture is thickened to eight parts. The purpose of this further subdivision of parts is to enable Panufnik to present the final chord in a vertically symmetrical layout (see Example 8). The last bar has a widely spaced E major triad with G natural in the upper middle register. Working from the outer intervals to the centre the symmetrically disposed intervals are: perfect fifths, major sixths, minor sixths, with a perfect fifth in the centre.

Ex. 8. Panufnik, *Sinfonia Sacra*, *Vision II*, bars 26–29
© Copyright 1967 by Boosey & Hawkes Music Publishers Ltd.
Reproduced by permission of Boosey & Hawkes Music Publishers Ltd.

The harmony of *Vision II* returns towards the end of the *Hymn* (from Fig. 40 onwards), but this time the strings are not alone. The contrapuntal woodwind lines develop the melody of the *Hymn* against the string harmony and introduce additional major/minor melodic inflections against the chords as well as within and between the lines themselves. This passage builds in intensity to the culminating point where we reach the fortissimo Maestoso section (from Fig. 54) where the fanfares from *Vision I* reappear (this time with horns joining the four trumpets). The harmony at this point (Fig. 54) is a widely spaced A major triad 'contradicted' by a high C natural from the first trumpet. (see Example 9)

The modal contradictions between emphatic major triads and minor third inflections in the fortissimo trumpet motifs persist right to the end of the work. The last three bars present a sustained, fortissimo A major triad, played tutti, with the minor third (C natural) blaring out from repetitions of the fanfare motif (see Example 9). In the final bar, Panufnik raises the first and second trumpets by an octave and gives us the motif, with the C natural, at a dynamic of

Ex. 9. Panufnik, *Sinfonia Sacra*, *Hymn*, ending [p. 72]
© Copyright 1967 by Boosey & Hawkes Music Publishers Ltd.
Reproduced by permission of Boosey & Hawkes Music Publishers Ltd.

ffff followed by a crescendo taking the dynamic level as loud as 'possibile'. This is as emphatic a presentation of the major-minor principle as one could possibly have. The harmonic ambivalence between major and minor thirds is the dominant characteristic of the symphony.

All these are mere details, taken out of context. Naturally, this brief discussion of them does not do justice to the complete works in which they appear. It does, however, provide evidence of Bartókian symmetry at the micro, local level. It raises the issue of Stravinskian contradictions. But above all, it may provoke us to consider the psychological properties of chordal/modal ambivalence. This type of harmony does, indeed, seem to reflect or express internal psychological conflicts. Such conflicts are universal, part of the human condition. Most of us learn ways of living with them. Not all of us find ways of expressing them. But here we have one of Panufnik's ways. Here we have one element of the musical vocabulary which helped to express his inner world and which served his distinctive voice.

Organization of Pitch
in Andrzej Panufnik's
Concertos for Solo Instrument and Orchestra

Alina Królak

Analysis of the linear and vertical structures in Andrzej Panufnik's four solo concerti: for piano (1962)[1], for violin (1972), for bassoon (1985) and for 'cello (1991) shows common characteristics of pitch organization in these works, as well as basic elements of the composer's individual style. A trait particular to Andrzej Panufnik's compositional technique is utilization of tone cells as the basis for the form of a given work. These cells are microstructures comprised of a few tones, representing the basis for formation of higher-level units, e.g. a theme or chord progression.

The tone cell as main constructional idea found application already in one of Panufnik's early works—the *Uwertura tragiczna* [*Tragic Overture*] of 1942. The composer described it in his autobiography[2] and in the book *Impulse and Design in My Music*[3]. He utilized a four-tone cell containing the following intervals: major third, major second and minor second. This microstructure permeates the entire work; it is transposed and augmented, appearing in orchestral *tutti* and in individual instruments.

In the solo concertos, written in a mature and late period of the composer's *oeuvre*, the most important role is played by three-tone cells, though two- and four-tone microstructures are also present, as

---

[1] A second version of the concerto was written in 1972; and a third, with added first movement, in 1982.

[2] Andrzej Panufnik, *Composing Myself* (London: Methuen, 1987).

[3] Andrzej Panufnik, *Impulse and Design in My Music* (London: Boosey & Hawkes, 1974).

well as structures based on pentatonic and hexatonic scales. The cells are subjected to various transformations, utilizing inversions, transpositions, internal permutations, retrogrades, expansions and contractions.

Linear tone structures

Among the three-tone cells, it is possible to distinguish several types, of varying intervalic content: minor second – major second, minor third – major third, second – third, second – fourth, second – tritone and fourth – tritone.

The entire first movement (*Entrata*) of the Piano Concerto is based on a cell built from two seconds: minor and major. Of the eleven segments comprising the *Entrata*, it appears in as many as nine of them (except for segments from nos. 3 and 8). The concerto begins with a fanfare comprised of the tones *A-flat–B-flat–A*. In the subsequent course of the work, this microstructure is transposed, starting from the tones *g-flat* and *d-flat*. In the introductory segment of the *Entrata*, in a quasi-cadenza for the piano, there is a deviation from the given intervalic pattern—namely, substitution of the major second with a minor third. This is a result of permutation of the cell tones from *E-flat–F–G-flat* to *E-flat–G-flat–F*. Another deviation from the basic pattern is external expansion of the cell via addition of another major second: *A-flat–B-flat–A–B*. Three-tone cells sometimes occur simultaneously, in contrary motion, e.g. in the first movement, in segments from nos. 4–7, 9 and 10.

Ex. 1. Piano Concerto, I. Simultaneous occurrence of cells

In the fourth movement (*Aria*) of the Bassoon Concerto, the composer used the three-tone cell *F–A-flat–G*, which he treated as the beginning of the primary theme. He transposed and expanded it, creating phrases greater in length by one to four notes. The theme of the *Aria* appears in segments from nos. 1–4, 8–11 and 16–19.

Ex. 2. Bassoon Concerto, IV, no. 1. Theme of *Aria*

Another type of three-tone cell is comprised of two thirds, equal or different in size. Panufnik used it in his concertos: for piano, for violin and for 'cello. In the Piano Concerto, a linear structure built of two minor thirds appears in several fragments of the third movement of the work (in nos. 0–5, 18–23 and the cadenza). In the 'Cello Concerto, a cell comprised of minor thirds appears in the second movement, in segments from nos. 7–8, as well as in retrograde, in nos. 11–12. Such a cell also appears in the third movement of the Violin Concerto as material for the secondary theme (nos. 5–9, 28–32), also as episodic (nos. 15, 17, 19 and 21) and cadenza material (no. 33).

The Violin Concerto also used a three-tone cell (*G–C-sharp–A*) which takes on various forms resulting from changes in the order of the tones: *G–C-sharp–A* (tritone – minor third), *C-sharp-G-A* (tritone – major second) and *G–A–C-sharp* (major second – major third).

After 1968, the most characteristic and frequently-occurring three-tone cell affecting the horizontal and vertical structure is a tritone-fourth microstructure and two other forms thereof (inversions): fourth-minor second and minor second-tritone. This cell appears many times in the fourth movement of the Bassoon Concerto, in the *Aria* (nos. 5–7, 12–13), as well as in the entire first movement (*Prologo*), in the following forms: fourth-tritone in nos. 1, 5, 9, 11; fourth – minor second in nos. 2, 6, 9, 11; and a fifth – minor second variant thereof in nos. 3, 7, 10, 11. In the 'Cello Concerto, the following intervals: minor second, fourth and tritone have become the fundamental building blocks of the entire cycle, i.e. the first and second movements; they appear in linear, diagonal and vertical structures. In this concerto, a three-tone cell based on the intervals of a minor second and tritone predominates, but also utilized is a tritone-perfect fourth interval structure, which the composer used to compose the six-tone theme in the second movement of the cycle. This theme, like the concerto as a whole, was composed according a palindromic principle. The means by which the theme is constructed is retrogradation of the perfect fourth – augmented fourth interval sequence.

Ex. 3. 'Cello Concerto, II, no. 4. Palindromic theme

Two-tone cells play an important role in the third movement (*Recitativo II*) of the Bassoon Concerto, both in the bassoon part and in the accompanying string ensemble. A basic two-tone cell, comprised of a minor second up or down, appears as an autonomous unit, as well as in three-, four- and six-tone structures. In the fifth movement (*Epilogo*) of this concerto, on the other hand, fundamental significance is attained by a two-tone microstructure based on the interval of a perfect fourth (nos. 3–9).

Ex. 4. Bassoon Concerto, V, no. 3, bassoon solo

Two-tone cells appear most frequently as abbreviated versions of a three-tone cell, or as part of a four-tone cell created on a retrograde principle. We find an example of a two-tone cell which appears first independently, and later as part of larger structures in the second movement (*Molto tranquillo*) of the Piano Concerto. Initially, only a minor second down *E-flat–D* and its retrograde, i.e. a minor second up, appear; later, this microstructure becomes part of the three-tone cell *E-flat–D–C*, comprised of a minor second and major second; and at the end of this movement, it represents a fragment of a longer melodic structure, presented in retrograde.

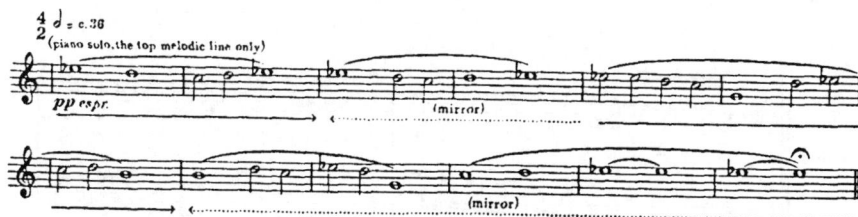

Ex. 5. Piano Concerto. Retrograde tone structure

In the third movement (*Molto agitato*) of the Concerto, the basic intervals are, on the other hand, thirds (major and minor), often linked by a minor second. In this manner, four-tone cells are created.

Ex. 6. Piano Concerto, III. Four-tone cell

Four-tone cells, based on intervals of a minor third and major third, represent the basic material for the second movement (*Adagio*) and the third movement (*Vivace*) of the Violin Concerto. They create thematic and harmonic structures. For example, the violin theme in the second movement is based on a broken form of the major-minor chord typical of Panufnik's music.

Ex. 7. Violin Concerto, II, no. 1. Violin theme

Structures based on pentatonic and hexatonic scales appear in the first movement (*Entrata*) of the Piano Concerto. Pentatonic runs played on the white and black keys occur, for example, in the coda of this movement. Structures based on a hexatonic scale, utilized in this movement of the concerto, contain an intervalic model comprised of major and minor seconds: 21121 and its retrograde 12112.

Ex. 8. Piano Concerto, I, no. 1, hexatonic scales

In the third movement of the Piano Concerto, on the other hand, a scale of intervalic structure 2121212 occurs in four transpositions, starting on the following tones: *E-flat, C-sharp, G-sharp, F-sharp*.

The entire *Recitativo I* of the Bassoon Concerto is based on a symmetrically-formed scale 22122, and on the tones *A-flat*, *G-flat*, *F-flat*, *E-flat*, *D-flat*, *C-flat*. The material of this same tone row was used to create a beautiful, lyric bassoon melody.

Scales of symmetrical structure were also utilized in the third movement of the Bassoon Concerto. These are interval structures as follows: 11211211 as well as 12112112. In the *Epilogo*, another structure also appears: 13131.

In the 'Cello Concerto, based almost entirely on a three-tone cell containing the interval of a minor second and a tritone, we find the following tone progression: *F–G–A–B–C–D–E* (as in an F-major scale) in no. 2 of the *Adagio* movement.

Vertical tone structures

Harmonic analysis of Andrzej Panufnik's four solo concertos has shown that the composer used two types of chords: 1) chords constructed in thirds, including the so-called 'Panufnik chords', as well as 2) chords built of fourth-tritone cells and inversions thereof.

K. Baculewski writes about the significance of triads in Panufnik's harmonic language as follows: 'In the area of harmonic language, the composer oscillates around the issue of third-based chord construction or mixed construction in which the role of the third appears to be, nevertheless, fundamental. This does not mean, however, that this harmonic language is closely related to the major-minor system, though certain sound associations are unavoidable and result from its intentionally third-based character, but the influence of functional tensions is missing here, while the full twelve-tone scale is used freely [...] most characteristic for Panufnik are triads of third-based construction, especially the 'Panufnik chord' occurring from the *Tragic Overture* to the *Sinfonia sacra*, the Piano Concerto and the *Song to the Virgin Mary*, to *Arbor cosmica*, which contains two thirds: minor and major (most often in different octaves).'[4] A chord containing both thirds in its structure is not uncommon in 20th-century music literature. According to Zofia Helman: 'This chord has found broad application in music already since the beginning of the century—and this, in the *oeuvre* of composers completely independent of each other, e.g. Scryabin, Bartók, Stravinsky, Schoenberg, Berg, Webern [...] This

---

[4] Krzysztof Baculewski, *Polska twórczość kompozytorska 1945–1984* (The oeuvre of Polish composers 1945–1984) (Kraków: PWM, 1987), p. 261.

chord can be used in various ways and is notated in different ways, e.g. (Cc). Sometimes the minor third clearly has the character of a leading tone to the major, occurring simultaneously with its resolution; visible in such cases will thus be a traditional, still functional treatment of this chord."[5]

The sound values obtained as a result of using two thirds in one chord, differing in size, represent the criterion for selection of chord elements in Panufnik's compositions. For it is not possible here to discern any application of the old functional system. Chordal progressions do not result from use of the tonal system which reigned for over two centuries; but neither are they random. Rather, they are included in the composer's individual system.

On account of the frequency with which the 'major-minor' chord occurs in Panufnik's music, we follow Baculewski in adopting for it the name 'Panufnik chord'. Often, the major and minor thirds designate a frame for this chord and create the *ambitus* of a major seventh (diminished octave), giving it a harsh sound. We find examples of the Panufnik chord in, for example, the Piano Concerto, in the second movement, nos. 4–5 (*E–G–C–E-flat*); in the Violin Concerto, in the second movement, at the beginning of the violin part with orchestra (*D–F-sharp–D–F–A*); as well as in the Bassoon Concerto, at the end of the third and fifth movements.

In Panufnik's concertos, major, minor and diminished chords also appear. We find an example of simultaneous juxtaposition of chords of third-based sound—thus, bi-chordal structures—in the piano part, in the coda of the first movement of the Piano Concerto. On the other hand, in the 'Cello Concerto, in the second movement *Vivace* (nos. 8 and 11), diminished chords in closed and open position have found application.

Andrzej Panufnik's consistent use, after 1968, of the fourth-tritone cell *F–B–E* (as well as inversions and transpositions thereof in horizontal and vertical structures) lent a new aura of sound to his works. In the Bassoon Concerto and the 'Cello Concerto, all structures were dominated by minor second-fourth, minor second-tritone and fourth-tritone chords. In the entire first movement of the Bassoon Concerto (nos. 0–12), three-tone microstructures occur, taking the forms, for example, *A-flat–D–G* (augmented fourth, fourth), *D–G–A-flat* (fourth, minor second) and *G–A-flat–D* (minor second, augmented

---

[5] Zofia Helman, *Neoklasycyzm w muzyce polskiej XX wieku* (Neo-Classicism in 20th-Century Polish Music) (Kraków: PWM, 1985), p. 103.

fourth). In the *Prologo*, the basic cell was first introduced in the accompaniment plane in vertical structures, and next transferred to the melodic line on a principle of delay relative to the vertical plane.

1	2	3	4	5	6
h f sharp c	d g a flat	b flat e flat e	c f sharp b	d a e flat	f b flat c flat
g	e	g flat	g	b flat	g
d	e flat	c	d	f	f sharp
a flat	b flat	c flat	a flat	b	c sharp

Ex. 9. Bassoon Concerto, I, nos. 1–6.
Relationships among cells in linear and vertical planes

In the 'Cello Concerto, the composer uses cells of which the most frequent is a linearly- and vertically-utilized minor second-tritone formation. Such chords fill the entire space of the work. The two movements of the concerto, I *Adagio* and II *Vivace*, are contrasted with each other in tempo, texture, dynamics and orchestration, on the principle of a photographic negative; but are closely related by occurrence of the same cell, which is developed and exposed in every possible form and inversion, in closed and open positions. The intervalic model of the cell is sometimes interrupted by rests, and fragments of it sometimes belong to two different bars. The vertical and linear structures, as well as the formal architecture, are closely related. The two-tone cell *F–E*—exposed at the beginning of the concerto, in the 'cello solo—with its retrograde *E–F* represents, as it were, an anticipation of the symmetrical form of both movements of the concerto. In the first movement, the axis of symmetry falls in no. 8 of the score; and in the second movement, in no. 10.

The above description of the linear and vertical organization of his works shows that Andrzej Panufnik imposed on himself enormous discipline, creating symmetrical constructions based on selected cells, mainly three-tone. From their constant inversions and transpositions grew not only concertos, but also many other works, e.g. *Universal Prayer* and *Arbor Cosmica*. As the composer informs us in his autobiography, such a manner of composition required creative discipline and economy in disposition of tones, but it led him to aesthetic values satisfactory to him[6]. The interdependence of linear

---

[6] Andrzej Panufnik, *Composing Myself, op. cit.*

and vertical structures is so great that there is no way to unambi-
guously describe the harmonic plane without reference to the melodic
plane, and vice versa. On the example of Panufnik's solo concertos,
we have presented the role of tone cells, which fill out larger structures
and construct entire sound planes, as well as main musical ideas
(phrases, themes). Resulting from the voice leading are chords of
third-based construction, mainly major triads, as well as the major-
minor chord—the so-called 'Panufnik chord'. Characteristic in Panufnik's compositions appears to be the fifth relationship, which affects
the manner of developing themes, as well as chord progressions of
third-based construction (e.g. in the second movement of the Violin
Concerto). This peculiar tonality is clear in Panufnik's works, and
though it is not devoid of elements characteristic of the tonal system,
the presented manner of pitch organization represents an original
and uncommonly coherent concept. Andrzej Panufnik's sound system
perhaps did not influence the developmental direction of contemporary
music, but it represents an important and valuable contribution to
the history of 20th-century music.

Translated by Cara Thornton

The Idea of Note-Cell
in Andrzej Panufnik's String Quartet No. 3

Renata Suchowiejko

Chamber works by Andrzej Panufnik—although somewhat over-shadowed by his orchestral work—hold a very important place in his music, not only because of their intimate character, but also because of the concentration of features typical of his musical language. In these works we can find the most characteristic elements of his style in their most condensed form. Except for the early Piano Trio (1934) and *Hommage à Chopin* (1949) all the chamber music was composed in England. It was created during the period when Panufnik was following a new path of artistic exploration triggered by his discovery of the 3- and 4-note-cell. In *Triangles* (1972), String Sextet (1987), *Song to the Virgin Mary* (string sextet version, 1987) and in all three quartets we observe a constant revelation of new possibilities of its uses, and at the same time his immense curiosity in exploring the potentials of chamber music sound.

Two string quartets were composed by Panufnik in 1976 and 1980; the third, ten years later, in 1990, was one of his last works.[1] All three quartets are dedicated to his family and carry a non-musical message clarified by the composer in his programme notes. He explains that String Quartet No. 1—originally only two movements (*Prelude* and *Transformation*), with the later added *Postludium*—is a kind of musical conversation among four different people, whose individual characteristics are portrayed by each instrument. Panufnik refers here to classical tradition; in the time of Haydn and Mozart the comparison of a quartet with a conversation of four persons of

---

[1] Cf. Anna Seweryniak, *Kwartety smyczkowe Andrzeja Panufnika* (Andrzej Panufnik's String Quartets), MA thesis, Kraków, Uniwersytet Jagielloński 2001.

different degrees of intelligence and eloquence was quite popular.
String Quartet No. 2 entitled "Messages" conjures up reminiscences
from his childhood: the mysterious hum emitted from telegraph posts
which stimulated his youthful imagination. These sounds become
more universal in character as a kind of "message" which may be
individually interpreted by each listener.

String Quartet No. 3 entitled "Paper-cuts" also refers to the past.
The composer explains that this piece

> "emerged from my lifelong attachment to Polish folk art, especially
> paper-cuts—symmetrical patterns, full of magical, abstract beauty and naïve
> charm. Wanting to transform these small geometrical structures into sound,
> I tried to imagine five paper-cuts from different Polish regions, strongly
> contrasted in form and colour, expressing the character and the temperament
> of the person who designed them. On this basis I composed a piece in a
> form of five short studies, each testing different aspects of string quartet
> playing skills".[2]

This title and the commentary together supply information about
both the structure and the meaning of the composition. It may be
seen as a key to understanding the form, although the form itself
does not keep within these limits: after all, the logic of musical syntax
has its own rules and this work comprises a far richer content than
a mere title could suggest. So the folk associations have less
significance in Panufnik's programme note, compared to two more
important aspects of this work—"form and colour"—which the composer treated with exceptional care.

String Quartet No. 3 is another example of the note-cell idea
which preoccupied the composer's mind in the late 1960's. He mentions
this important moment in his autobiography *Composing Myself,*
describing how "ear and intuition" revealed "some evocative and
strangely expandable qualities" of a three-note cell "f–b–e".[3] This cell
became the basis of the material of his works and the primary
principle of construction. Through it the composer built up his original
pitch organization system. He uses this fundamental three-note
structure to create both horizontal lines and vertical harmony. The
four cells can be labelled as $\alpha \beta \gamma \delta$.[4] The cell is created by a combination

---

[2] Andrzej Panufnik, "Composer's Note", String Quartet No. 3, Boosey & Hawkes
1991.

[3] Cf. Andrzej Panufnik, *Composing Myself* (London: Methuen, 1987), Polish edition entitled *Panufnik o sobie*, translated by Marta Glińska (Warszawa: NOWA, 1990).

[4] Cf. Krzysztof Stasiak, *An Analytical Study of the Music of Andrzej Panufnik*,
PhD thesis, Belfast, Queen University 1990.

of a third or a fourth with a second or by only thirds. The modification of these original cells (the change of the size of the intervals, or the change in the order of their appearance: inversion, transposition) stimulated his creative process on both microform and macroform levels.

String Quartet No. 3 consists of five movements, contrasted in "form and colour", but unified by the material. Each movement makes use of different forms of the cells α β and γ (see the attached table). In addition, there are other units with a less clear structure, difficult to interpret univocally. The form of each movement is clearly structured, sustaining the proportional dispositions of elements while the applied symmetry assures its inner stable equilibrium.

Table. String Quartet No. 3: Note-cells

Movements	Form	Note-cells
I	A A1 A'	β ...
II	A B A' bcc'b'	γ ... α (Ir, z', z, II') ...
III	A B C A'B'C'	α (I, I, I, I / II, z, I, I) ... α (I, I, I, I / II, II, II, II) ...
IV	A B A'	γ ... [α] ... α (z', I) ...
V	A A' A"	β ...

In the first movement we can trace four kinds of motivic groupings derived from cell β. The original shape of the cell, its inversions and reverse forms are equally treated. The diversity of variants is the consequence of the manipulation of size, order and the direction of the intervals. These modifications do not weaken the identity of the cell. Its inner integrity is secured by the application of repetitions, transpositions and subsequent inversions. We can observe an effect of "mirror construction" in a single melodic line as well as amongst the separate voices. Symmetrical "mirror structures" are created consecutively by the following instrumental pairs: upper (1st and 2nd violins), middle (2nd violin and viola) and lower (viola and cello) and in the last section by 1st violin and cello. The first movement of the quartet has the form AA_1A', where the equal units are broken by rests: (3+4) + (4+4) + (4+2). The last unit is a symmetrical reflection of the first. The clarity of structure is allied with the clarity of homogenous sound.

The second movement also consists of three heavily contrasted parts (ABA'). The symmetry can be observed on two structural levels. It determines the complete form (A' is a reversed variation of A); also in the central part, the inner units use a "mirror structure". The interval of the third dominates in the motivic layer, both linearly and horizontally. It is not only the basis for the construction of the melodic line, but it also provides the vertical sounds between the accompanying voices. The melodic line is entirely built from three-note cell γ moved through a progression of fifths, first in the upper and then in the lower register. The "accompanying" thirds simultaneously progress together with the seconds. The central section of this movement is based on cell α, the original form of which reappears regularly with its inversion creating the inner order of units.

Cell α becomes particularly important in the third movement where it is used vertically and horizontally. However, each section (ABCA'B'C') exploits it in a different way. At the beginning the cell is used only for the horizontal line. The cello part shows its variants while the 1st violin creates a background based on a repetition of the first inversion of the cell. In the following section cell α provides the vertical harmony. Three voices produce a chord based on the second inversion. One voice, however, always remains independent, exploiting the first inversion in the melodic line. The first inversion of the cell circulates regularly all the time throughout the whole work. Section C preserves the method of overlapping different forms of the cells, creating horizontal and vertical constructions, but the motivic layer becomes more varied. A new grouping appears in the cello and

1st violin parts (at the end of section C and C') as well as the first, basic form of cell α (two intervals: a third and a second) which is presented independently or in interaction with the first inversion.

In the fourth movement, cell γ again plays an important role in the shape of the minor third motif, appearing successively in all voices (except cello) and dominating in the polarised sections. The minor second motif heavily contrasts and outbalances the cell, especially where the motif is used in the melodic line and in the harmony. It could be seen here as a residual element of cell α. In the middle section of the fourth movement the harmonic element is "switched off". Only a single melodic line remains, led by two complementary instruments (1st and 2nd violins). It is motivicly varied, with greater emphasis on the reverse movement. The source of this melody is cell α, especially its first inversion and its modified primary form. The reversed motion of these notes used in consequence result in the absolute symmetry of the melody, which continues through from the end till the beginning.

The last movement of the quartet clearly refers to the beginning of the work, not only with regard to its emotion but also to its motifs. The same note-groupings return, especially cell β. Although the number of its variants is reduced, the frequency of its reappearances increases. The canon is based on this cell while the accompanying voices create the major and the diminished chords. The last movement is closely linked to the first but the accompaniment becomes more varied.

From the analytical point of view String Quartet No. 3 seems to be a coherent construction (the use of the same material) with a perfect balance of elements (repetitive and symmetrical principles). Both the mathematical precision in the use of the melodic cell and the planning of the whole cycle demonstrate Panufnik's control over material on macroformal and microformal levels. The composer's main aim is to balance proportions; he always searches for the "golden rule" in the balance between variety and homogeneity. Could one not say that the construction indeed is a reflection of the "golden rule", and at the same time a way of communicating with the listener? The composer somehow comes nearer the listener by giving him/her the key to understanding the form—the key which is the form itself. We recognize the shape when we perceive the whole arrangement of the elements. This impact survives even though we cannot identify all the note-cells and their variants while listening to the piece. Only an analytical, "intellectual" approach enables us to determine the functions of the cells. The composer appeals, however, to the listener's other senses. The emotional sphere is awakened by the sound.

The "form" cannot exist for Panufnik without the "colour", which combine to provide the overall expressiveness and the stimulation of effective aesthetic reactions. The sonorities open a new plane for communication between the composer and the listener. This must surely be the plane on which the emotions meet?

Because of the pictorial quality of all the movements we can venture to state that each movement is a kind of sound picture. The contour and background play the most important role in the structure and the skilful manipulation of these elements provides the variety of colours. The first picture is monochromatic. The subtle dissonances of the leading voices emerge from the unison of accompanying voices, exposing the tone "g" and lightening the sound with harmonics (flageolets). This long sustained sound recurs at successive moments, lightening other passages. It provides a subtle background to the melodic line, which is heard in mirror reflection by the two main voices. (Example no. 1) The overall effect is homogeneous and static due to the delicate form, subtle dynamics, linear voices and stability of rhythm and meter. It presents a memorable impression of a suspension in time.

Ex. 1. String Quartet No. 3. First movement, beginning
© Copyright 1991 by Boosey & Hawkes Music Publishers Ltd.
Reproduced by permission of Boosey & Hawkes Music Publishers Ltd.

In the second "picture" we can observe more variety of colours. The melodic and rhythmical diversities are created by irregular phrases and pulse as well as by more varied motivic material. The movement is played louder, and there are more dynamic differences. These changes, besides a new combination of instruments, create new layers, and the central climax provides a sudden contrast. (Example no. 2) The second movement sustains the division: the melody plus the accompaniment but in slightly changed proportions. Two voices remain in the same register and lead the melodic line, complementing each other rhythmically, the two remaining voices accompanying in parallel thirds. This change alteration affects the relationship between the contour and the background. Pairing the instruments results in fewer voices, but does not weaken the actual potential of the ensemble because other parameters are strengthened.

Ex. 2. String Quartet No. 3. Second movement, beginning
© Copyright 1991 by Boosey & Hawkes Music Publishers Ltd.
Reproduced by permission of Boosey & Hawkes Music Publishers Ltd.

The third "picture" brings a radical change with enlivening articulation and dynamics. Pizzicato modifies the colour and the duration of the tone, and, combined with the dynamics, it creates a new quality: *sul tasto* in piano-pianissimo, *sul ponticello* in forte and the string strike hard against fingerboard in forte-fortissimo. The presence of many rests prevents melodic continuity. The pulse is based now on dynamic accents. (Example no. 3) The harmony of the voices is also changed in the third movement. In the beginning they are often paired, but later on they gain their independence, which enables the smooth transition of cell α. There is no "horizon" between the melodic line and the background due to this dispersed material. The structure of this "picture" can be described as "pointillistic".

The line and the background or the line and the "splash" gain a new meaning in the fourth movement, through the contrast between tutti and solo. The aggressive tone of tutti is based on the seconds, with loud dynamics and homorhythmical repetitions. The minor third motif is introduced as a contrast. The proportions between these elements gradually evolve. The dark "splash" in tutti shrinks and the melodic motif develops into a longer line. This process is then reversed so as to come back finally to the opening moment. (Example no. 4) The last "picture" is a reflection of the first. We can observe the same linearism, soft melodies, static sound, interrupted sometimes by glissandi in lower voices. Two-note chords in the part of cello and the high register of violin create a rather darker atmosphere. (Example no. 5)

Panufnik's String Quartet No. 3 intrigues and delights not only because of its "geometrical" precision, but also because of the rich variety of its content. The composer's invention was not limited by the instruments or by severe discipline in his treatment of them. On the contrary, overcoming these constraints inspired the composer to look for new solutions and made him reveal the best potential aspects of these reduced resources. Perhaps this is the strength of the cell, its "magical power", in that the cell is born again and again, bringing new results each time.

String Quartet No. 3 is another attempt to find "the equilibrium between feelings and intellect, heart and mind, impulse and design" as the composer once said. The formal discipline supports emotion, the mathematical precision is allied with expression. Can it be said that the form is governed by the intellect, and the emotion by the sound? This is the conclusion of the analysis. The construction of the work—precisely designed, obeying all rules of organizing the material—seems to be the domain of the intellect. The sound—full of

Ex. 3. String Quartet No. 3. Third movement, beginning
© Copyright 1991 by Boosey & Hawkes Music Publishers Ltd.
Reproduced by permission of Boosey & Hawkes Music Publishers Ltd.

Ex. 4. String Quartet No. 3. Fourth movement, beginning
© Copyright 1991 by Boosey & Hawkes Music Publishers Ltd.
Reproduced by permission of Boosey & Hawkes Music Publishers Ltd.

Ex. 5. String Quartet No. 3. Fifth movement, beginning
© Copyright 1991 by Boosey & Hawkes Music Publishers Ltd.
Reproduced by permission of Boosey & Hawkes Music Publishers Ltd.

unexpected changes, astonishing colours—seems to be the domain of emotion and the only place left for imagination. This division, apparently logical, is a convenient simplification. In my opinion both spheres must co-exist; their overlapping suggests even symbiosis. The organization of material influences the sound, which in its turn creates the form as well. The intellect helps to overcome difficulties in forming the material and while at the same time it touches the emotions by evoking aesthetic reactions. These are two aspects of the same process, two features of Panufnik's musical language. This characteristic trait of his music can be called "emotional intellectualism" and is clearly seen in *Quartet no. 3*.

Translated by Anna Piotrowska

Piano Works by Andrzej Panufnik. Structures and Timbres

Jadwiga Paja-Stach

The piano can be heard in several of Panufnik's symphonic works, for example in *Nocturne, Rhapsody, Autumn Music* and his Symphony No. 10. The composer accords this instrument diverse roles in terms of harmony, rhythm and tone-colour. In some works he treats the piano as an orchestral instrument; in others he singles it out, giving it an important function in shaping the musical action, its dynamics and its expressiveness. For example in *Autumn Music* the piano *ostinato* constitutes the principal element of the work's dramatic expression. However, Panufnik always exploits the instrument in keeping with its natural properties and capabilities, and uses traditional rather than avant garde methods of obtaining sound. Only in his Symphony No. 10, exceptionally, he asks for modification of the piano's natural tone-colour, marking the score "if possible, amplified with loudspeaker".

Against the background of the sonoristic mainstream, in 20th-century music, and in the context of the search of new tone-colour values through the use of 'prepared piano' or their treatment as quasi percussion instruments, Andrzej Panufnik's piano music shows its adherence to the traditions of the Classical-Romantic era. The diversity of timbre in Panufnik's works is achieved by exploiting the entire compass of the piano, by changing registers, by using extreme registers, or by using the pedal and by varying the dynamics. Although not an innovator in the sense of searching for new ways of playing the piano, Panufnik nevertheless composed music full of strong contrasts and nuances of tone-colour.

Panufnik's compositional legacy includes only three works for solo piano, written in different creative periods with considerable lapses of time between each: *Krąg kwintowy* (Circle of Fifths)[1] composed in 1947, *Reflections* in 1968 and *Pentasonata* in 1984. However, in considering the tremendous contribution of this great symphonic composer—which Panufnik undoubtedly was—these three pieces are by no means marginal works, each of them representing a turning point in his compositional career. In *Circle of Fifths*, the composer presents musical ideas which herald a new direction in his compositional technique; in *Reflections* he formulates his original concept of pitch organisation, whilst in *Pentasonata* he introduces a synthesis of the innovative Panufnik technique with elements adopted from musical tradition. An analysis of these works on one hand reveals the changes in Panufnik's compositional techniques, while on the other it allows for the identification of characteristics in common that testify to the flowing evolution of the composer's style.

The differences between the earlier composed *Circle of Fifths* and the later two works are clearly defined in their formal design—and, more importantly—in their organisation of pitch. *Circle* is a tonal cyclical work consisting of 12 miniature pieces linked by a shared 'theme', whereas *Reflections* and *Pentasonata* are single movement works, each comprising 5 segments, composed in accordance with Panufnik's original concept of pitch organisation, i.e. founded on three-note cells which constitute the basis for defining linear and vertical structures. In *Pentasonata* the composer broadens his material to include pentatonic sound structures, thus combining a traditional element with his own structural concept.

The formal design of these compositions, presented schematically in the following examples, reveal both the individual and the shared conceptual features of the works.

Example No. 1 shows the main principles that govern the schematic order of the miniatures in *Circle of Fifths:* a) the progression of the cycle in relation to the fifths, b) the alternation of interludes and études preceded by a prelude and ending with a postlude, c) the contrast between the miniatures achieved through tonal, agogic and dynamic differences. The 'theme' of the variations, notated below the diagram, is in fact an arrangement of pitches, only rarely used as a melodic theme; fragments of it are clearly heard in *Interlude in D minor* and *Interlude in B-flat minor*. However it primarily serves as basic material, a source for tonal 'manipulation' and the building of structures, which can only be discovered however through discerning analysis.

---

[1] Published in Britain and USA as *Twelve Miniature Studies*.

Ex. 1. The schematic order of the miniatures
and a basic arrangement of pitches in *Circle of Fifth*

This 'theme' in a minor key, i.e. Aeolian A-minor, does not
determine the tonality of the cycle, but appears in transpositions and
in conjunction with structures of the major scale. For example, in
the *Prelude* the 'theme' is transposed to the scale of C sharp minor
(Aeolian minor) and is hidden within the work (see Example 2).

Ex. 2. *Circle of Fifth*. The beginning of *Prelude*

Its beginning can be detected in the first notes of the ascending musical figures. In these figures a major third appears alongside the minor third, giving the effect of iridescence in the major and minor modes. The minor scale is further extended by the introduction of descending melodic figures based on the scale of C major. In this way both types of figures jointly introduce a scale of twelve tones. In other sections of the cycle minor and major thirds are frequently used together as a structural device, (as can also be found, incidentally, in many neo-classical compositions). Another method of extending the scale is seen in the simultaneous introduction of a layer based on the minor scale and a tonal layer based on the chromatic scale, as e.g. in *Interlude in F-sharp minor*. In spite of these pantonal structures, the tonal center is always clearly defined either through persistent repetition of the *quasi* keynote or by giving the tonal layer greater prominence in a given structure. consequently, despite a fusion of major and minor modes as well as additional tones extending their range to twelve, the section of the cycle have contrasting tonal centers.

The alternation of études and interludes offers another form of contrasts between adjacent sections of the cycle. The études remain homogeneous in terms of motion, figuration and articulation, while the interludes differ in their emotional expressiveness, with melody playing a fundamental role.

Comparison can be drawn between *Circle of Fifths* and other 20th-century cyclic works for piano such as Shostakowich's *24 Preludes and Fugues* composed in 1951 or Hindemith *Ludus tonalis* composed in 1942. However, these are merely superficial analogies, sharing only the principle of alternating two types of miniature pieces within a cyclic structure, with analogous opening and closing sections of the cycle.

Reflections also shares several characteristic qualities with the earlier *Circle*.

Amongst these are the strong contrasts between the sections. Contrasts of tempo, texture and dynamics between the five segments that comprise *Reflections* are shown in Table 1.

Table 1. *Reflections*. Arrangement of segments.
Vertical lines represent chords; horizontal represent melodic lines;
and dots represent single, isolated tones which create the pointillistic texture

Segments	Tempo	Dynamics	Texture
1.	moderately = c. 56	*ppp-p*	| | | | |
2.	slowly = c. 40	*poco f-pp, f-pp etc.*	– – – – –
3.	rather fast = c. 84	*ff* (only introduction *pp*)	| | | | |
4.	moderately = c. 56	*sempre pp*	. . . . . .
5.	freely = c. 40–84	*ff-pp, ff-pp, etc.*	– – – | | – – – | |

The principle of assigning moderate and slow tempi in alternate segments is discarded in the final segment where the composer allows the performer the freedom to shape the change of tempo from slow to fast.

The segments are also contrasted in terms of texture (the types of texture are marked in the example with line and dots). The first segment has a design consisting of an undulating melody against a harmonic background of six-note chords, which, through their constant repetition in *piano pianissimo*, are heard as a homogenous line of delicate tone-colour. Segment 2. has a two-voice structure; Segment 3.—a series of chords; Segment 4.—pointillistic structures, and Segment 5. includes contrasting two-voice and chordal sections that differ both in texture and dynamics.

The pointillistic Segment 4. (see Example 3), though reminiscent of other 20th-century compositions based on pointillism, reveals its own distinctive character. In contrast to works such as Roman Haubenstock-Ramati's *Five Works for Piano (Klavierstücke)* composed in 1963–65, or Serocki's *A piacere*, or indeed pointillist-serial works like Bogusław Schaeffer's *Model I* and *II* in which individual tones, chords and motifs are clearly contrasted and diffused creating a flickering structure of indeterminate shape, whereas, Segment 4. of Panufnik's *Reflections* is characterised by clearly defined design where tones move in a diagonal, criss-cross direction, gradually progressing from the lowest. These tones appearing in various registers of the instrument, change their timbre, yet are performed identically in terms of articulation and dynamics (*sempre piano, poco staccato*). Consequently the listener's attention is directed not so much towards the tone-colour variety—which characterises the majority of pointillistic compositions—but rather to the quality of pitch organisation.

Ex. 3. *Reflections*. Section of Segment 4
© Copyright 1971 by Boosey & Hawkes Music Publishers Ltd.
Reproduced by permission of Boosey & Hawkes Music Publishers Ltd.

The contrasted Segments are firmly held together thanks to this organisation of pitch. Chronologically speaking, *Reflections* is the first work in which Panufnik rigidly applies a three-note cell pattern, including in it fourth and tritones and inversions of this cell as the sole material of this work. It forms the work's only compositional material. This organisation of pitch is illustrated in Example No. 5: the melodic line contains intervals from the basic form of this cell and its inversion and transposition. The harmonic layer is made up of six-note chords generated from the simultaneous use of two triads (the first chord is D–A–E-flat and B–B-flat–F). This creates a sound with the character of a cluster (consisting of minor and major seconds and minor and major thirds), remaining strictly related to the melodic line that forms the second layer of the structure in its entirety. Analogous principles of linear and vertical structures are applied in the remaining segments, thus achieving harmonic unity throughout the work.

Ex. 4. *Reflections*, beginning

© Copyright 1971 by Boosey & Hawkes Music Publishers Ltd.
Reproduced by permission of Boosey & Hawkes Music Publishers Ltd.

The title of *Pentasonata* reveals to a degree the structural concept of the work (introduced in Table 2). Incidentally, the correlation between the work's title and its structure was further clarified (in his forward to the published score) by the composer, who informs us that the prefix 'penta' refers to the number of segments in the work, the use of the pentatonic scale and the metrical patterns of all the sections, with the exception of *Contemplativo* which is not given a time signature. According to the composer the formal structure of *Pentasonata* reflects certain features of sonata form, the first segment being equivalent to the principal theme (or first subject), the second segment to the second theme, the middle segment to the development and the final to the recapitulation, in which the thematic material appears in reverse order.

It is noticeable that the characteristic qualities of Panufnik's compositional technique such as the symmetrical design of the five segments and the presence of three-note cells are more predominant than the influence of classical tradition. As already stated, the composer adds to this work material based on the pentatonic scale. He does this according to principles of 'bitonality' by assigning the pentatonic scale to one layer and the three-note cell to the second, simultaneously occurring layer. This principle of simultaneous occurence of both sound structures is used consistently throughout the work, as is the principle of basing the melodic layer on the pentatonic scale and the harmonic and tone-colour layer on the three-note cell, together with its inversion and transpositions.

The work's symmetry of form occurs as a result of the strong resemblance between Segments I and V, also between II and IV.

Table 2. *Pentasonata*. Design of the form

Segments	Metre, tempo and type of expression	Dynamics	Pentatonic
I (A) First theme	5/8 *Allegretto scherzoso molto ritmico*	ff -fff	C-D-E-G-A
II (B) Second theme	5/4 *Andantino amoroso, molto cantabile*	pp-f-pp	A-H-C#-E-F#
III (C) Development	*Contemplativo, molto rubato senza misura* etc.	*ff-pp-ff-pp*	G♭-A♭-B♭-D♭-E♭
IV (B1) Second theme	5/4 *Andantino amoroso molto cantabile*	*pp-f-pppp*	E♭-F-G-B♭-C
V (A1) First theme	5/8 *Allegretto scherzoso molto ritmico*	*ff-fff*	C-D-E-G-A

In the opening and closing segments (A, A1 and B, B1), besides the analogous metric, tempo, expression and dynamic markings seen in Table 2, similar melodic and rhythmic material has also been exploited. The differences between Segment A and A1 as well as B and B1 largely depend on changes in timbre brought about by transposing sound structures to different registers, i.e. structures in lower registers in Segments A and B to higher registers in Segments A1 and B1, and the reverse. The middle segment is varied and is subdivided into three sections: 1. timbre section, 2. melodic and harmonic, and 3. melodic dialogue. In the first section is the characteristic effect of the 'swelling' (the increasing) of chord and the dying away of chord, initially in the lower register, gradually progressing to the higher register, while the motifs derived from the first theme are diffused by rests generating extra-musical ideas associated with birdsong. The second section exploits the melody in the bass accompanied by triads. The third section is a continuous dialogue of musical phrases that alternate between the left and right hand parts, a dialogue that becomes more forceful as the tempo is accelerated and the volume increased from *ppp* to *fff*.

The diagrams of the forms of all three piano works by Panufnik show structural differences, either related to traditional models, as in *Circle of Fifths* and *Pentasonata*, or allied to contemporary forms of montage, as in *Reflections*. Similarities are perceptible however in the shaping of the dynamic profile of the forms, which rely on the frequent undulation of tensions and on sequences of strongly contrasting movements and segments. The principle of contrast between successive segments, in *Circle* as well as in *Reflections* and *Pentasonata*, is achieved in all three by means of agogic, dynamic and textural change; in *Circle* also tonally.

The principle of distinct contrast is conducive to clarity of form, which makes Panufnik's work immediately comprehensible and easy to remember.

However, the composer's piano music, like his symphonic and chamber works, contains rhythmic and melodic structures characterised by a certain order of structural elements, which is difficult, sometimes even impossible for the listener to perceive.

The rhythmic pattern resulting from notes of long duration, doubtless influences to a degree the general impression of order in the work, though its structural basis may be perceptually inaudible. In *Circle of Fifths*, in the second miniature study—*Interlude in F-sharp minor*—there is a rhythmic pattern based on a progression of minims and semibreves, as illustrated by Example 5. In bars 4 and 5, rhythmic regularity is blurred by an *ostinato* F-sharp in the highest register and by lesser rhythmic values (crotchets and dotted minims) in the lower. In the fourth miniature *Interlude in E minor*, two layers of rhythmic patterns appear simultaneously, and this rhythmic pairing marked as *a, b* and *c* in the Example 6, returns to form a pattern *abcb-abcb*. The work ends with three semibreves unrelated to the pattern.

Ex. 5. *Circle of Fifth. Interlude in F-sharp minor*, beginning

Ex. 6. *Circle of Fifth. Interlude in E minor*, the rhythmic patterns

In *Reflections* and *Pentasonata* the rhythmic patterns are subjected to far more complicated compositional procedures, going through various transformations, such as added rhythmic values as well as permutations of values within the pattern.

In his doctoral thesis, Krzysztof Stasiak devoted a lot of attention to the question of the organisation of time in the work of Panufnik. In this thesis he used a concept of a 'module', which he defines as "a distinct rhythmic grouping of fixed duration or fixed definition, which is subject to a repetitive process"[2]. He distinguishes different types of module, including a three-quaver module and seven-quaver module. A variety of rhythmic values appear within these modules.

---

[2] Krzysztof Stasiak, *An Analytical Study of the Music of Andrzej Panufnik* (Belfast: Queen's University, 1990), p. 197

Accordingly, in his analysis of Segment I of *Reflections*, the author analyses the seven-quaver module, which appears in the form of two rhythmic patterns: 1) 2 crotchets and a dotted crotchet; 2) minim, a quaver and a crotchet. Both of these patterns undergo a mirror-image metamorphosis as well as changes in the order of notes. Segment I begins and ends with a 7-quaver module with an added value (semiquaver), realised at the beginning of the Segment in a pattern of 2 quavers, 2 dotted quavers and 2 twice dotted quavers (see Example 4). At the end of the Segment the order of the values is reversed. In the second Segment of *Reflections*, the author identifies a 3-quaver module comprising three patterns (The author incidentally calls them variants of the module) of: 1) three quavers, 2) dotted quaver and semiquaver, 3) crotchet, dotted semiquaver and demisemiquaver.

Principles govering the organisation of time in a given work also apply to rests, as described by the composer in his book *Impulse and design in my Music*[3]

In his commentary on *Reflections*, he mentions the symmetrical structure of the rests in Segment III (incidentally referring to the segments as *microstructures*). This symmetrical design occurs in the middle part of the Segment, while the outer parts are based on a different design where symmetry is broken by some alterations in the sequence of rests. However, in terms of auditory perception this is insignificant as it is the effect of acceleration in those parts of the pattern where semiquaver rests occur and the effect of deceleration where quaver rests occur, that are of importance.

Though in his above-mentioned commentary the composer reveals the main structural principles of the work (symmetry and the 3-note cell), he concludes by adding his wish that the listener should pay more attention to the poetic meaning of the title—referring to 'reflections' in the sense of contemplation rather than to the structural symmetry reflected in his work.

Many principles governing the organisation of time can also be found in *Pentasonata*. For example in Segment I and V a sequence of two semiquavers and quaver forms the dominant rhythmic pattern, which is heard in every bar of these Segments. Pattern II consisting of four quavers and two semiquavers, which appears in two variations of 3 quavers – 2 semiquavers – quaver and 2 quavers – 2 semiquavers

[3] Andrzej Panufnik, *Impulse and Design in my Music* (London: Boosey & Hawkes, 1979), p. 23.

– 2 quavers, is equally important in the construction of these two outer segments. The simultaneous and alternate occurrence of these patterns and the distribution of accents in various parts of the bar create an impression of recurring disturbance in the rhythmic homogeneity of the segment, which as a result sounds like a musical joke.

Once again we meet the problem of correlation between principles of pitch organisation and the resultant sound effect. The principles of construction, consistently applied throughout the composition do not constitute a mere intellectual game on the part of the composer, though that may well have been his intention; rather they serve to elicit a specific emotional mood in the listener. This is also the case with the (fore-mentioned) frequent additions or subtractions of rhythmic values, whether in symmetrical patterns or containing so called 'additive' rhythms. In the perception of a given rhythmic structure, it is not the construction itself, which is intended to draw the attention of the listener. The construction is meant to produce an effect of *decelerando* or *accelerando* which, together with other elements, will eventually be able to elicit particular emotional states—for example, a state of calmness, reflection or contemplation (in the case of *decellerando*) or, conversely, unease or even agitation (in the case of *acellerando*). The composer's works for solo piano embody structures varied in their musical 'character', able to elicit even extreme emotion during the course of listening. His music contains cheerful scherzos, dynamic movement, lyricism, contemplation, thought-provoking monologues and heated dialogues. The source of this wealth of emotional and aesthetic experience are precisely ordered sound structures characterised by immense discipline of pitch organisation.

Panufnik's piano music shows a continuity of classical ideals in its balance of emotional and intellectual elements, the beauty of its symmetrical construction and its clarity of form. It must have been these qualities of classical music which he held most closely when he remarked, "I consider Mozart to be my greatest master"[4].

Translated by Christine Rickards-Rostworowska

---

[4] Andrzej Panufnik, in: Tadeusz Kaczyński, *Andrzej Panufnik i jego muzyka* (Andrzej Panufnik and his Music) (Warsaw: PWN, 1994), p. 69.

Old Polish Music as Adapted by Andrzej Panufnik

Andrzej Sitarz

Those compositions of Panufnik which are adaptations of old Polish works clearly distinguish themselves as a separate trend in his early artistic work. To date, not much space has been devoted to them in reflections on the composer's art, as they do not represent progressive and innovative elements in his creative work. Beata Bolesławska discusses them briefly in her recent monograph,[1] but the fullest discussion of them still remains a fragment of the chapter 'Transcriptions and Stylizations' in Zofia Helman's book (of 1985) about neo-classicism in Polish music.[2] So far, in the musicological writing, only few of old Polish compositions used by Panufnik have been identified, and there is no analysis of the way the composer adapted them to his music.

Panufnik's adaptations of old Polish music were written between 1947–66 and were published together in 1970 by Boosey & Hawkes in London, under the joint title *Old Polish Music*. These four compositions are:[3]

1. *Concerto in modo antico*, Warszawa 1951, rev. 1955
2. *Jagiellonian Triptych*, Twickenham 1966
3. *Old Polish Suite*, Warszawa 1950, rev. 1955
4. *Divertimento*, arr. Kraków 1947, rev. 1955.

---

[1] Beata Bolesławska, *Panufnik* (Kraków: PWM, 2001).

[2] Zofia Helman, *Neoklasycyzm w muzyce polskiej XX wieku* (Neo-classicism in 20th-Century Polish Music) (Kraków: PWM, 1985).

[3] Panufnik also wrote a Quintet for woodwinds (*Quintetto academico*) for 2 fl., ob., cl. and fg., dating from 1952 (world prémiere: Warsaw 1953) and comprised of the following movements: *Quasi Preludio*, *Old Polish Triptych*, *Postlude*, which was published by the Boosey & Hawkes firm only in 1999, edited by the composer's daughter, Roxanna Panufnik. This work is not included in the present reflections.

What induced Panufnik, considered at the end of the 1940's to be one of the leading and most innovative Polish composers, to create music in a conservative mode, stylistically divergent both from the fundamental trend of his own art and from the main trend in the evolution of music?

At the end of the 1940's and the beginning of the 1950's, when the arrangements under discussion were written, Panufnik's compositions were often performed in Poland and abroad. He himself enjoyed the trust of the authorities, received state prizes, performed as a conductor in various musical centers of Europe, fulfilled important functions in Polish musical organizations. However, this was a period only superficially advantageous to his artistic career. The political situation in the country, especially from 1948 onward, was not conducive to the development of artistic invention. This was a time of pressure exerted by state authorities on artistic circles, which manifested itself in the formulation and execution of the so-called socialist-realist ideology. The fundamental idea was to create art which would be accessible to general audiences and, at the same time, be politically committed. Because of this, contemporary musical works devoid of a socialist-realist program were removed from the concert repertoire. Some of Panufnik's works, too, were banned from performance, even those for which he had previously received awards, e.g. the *Nocturne* and the *Sinfonia Rustica*. At this time, the composer wrote one major (*Symphony of Peace*) and several minor works under the pressure of this ideology; he did not, however, subject himself completely to the socialist-realist ideology.

In his autobiography, the composer mentions his dilemmas of the time as follows:

> After lengthy consideration, I finally worked out a way which allowed me to avoid both confrontation and capitulation. Following the example of our architects, who at the time were zealously restoring entire districts of Warsaw, I decided to take up reconstruction of 16th- and 17th-century Polish music which had suffered not so much during the most recent war, as during successive centuries of foreign invasions. I took up early composers whose unfinished and unknown works had been preserved only in fragments, growing moldy in dust-ridden libraries. Working more as an academic than as a composer, I was able in this way to contribute to the rescue of some miniscule portion of our heritage.[4]

---

[4] Andrzej Panufnik, *Composing Myself* (London: Methuen, 1987). Polish edition entitled *Panufnik o sobie*. Authorized translation by Marta Glińska (Warszawa: NOWA, 1990), p. 119.

In this spirit, he composed the *Old Polish Suite* (1950) and *Concerto in modo antico* (1951), which obtained the authorities' approval in the short term and, together with a previous work of this type (*Divertimento*), numbered among the most frequently-performed of the composer's works at the beginning of the 1950's.

However, the desire to circumvent the injunctions of the socialist-realist ideology was not the only, nor even the most important motive for Panufnik's interest in early music. The first of his arrangements (*Divertimento*) was completed in 1947—thus, prior to the period during which socialist realism was in force in Poland, while the last of the arrangements (the *Jagiellonian Triptych*) was written in 1966 in great Britain, at a period when socialist realism had long since dwindled away, and the composer, having emigrated, was not subject to any external pressure.

Works alluding directly or indirectly to early (or 19th-century) music were a manifestation of the neoclassicist trend, at that time still alive and well, and such works had frequently been written by many composers at least since the beginning of the inter-war period. In Polish music, this trend was represented by, among others, Aleksander Tansman (arrangement of Bach's *Toccata and Fugue in D minor* BWV 565 for orchestra—1937, *Variations on a Theme by Frescobaldi*—1937), Witold Lutosławski (*Variations on a Theme by Paganini*—1941), Tadeusz Baird (*Colas Breugnon* —1952), and Roman Palester (*Concertino* for harpsichord and 10 instruments on early Polish dance themes, written in Paris in 1955).

Attention must also be drawn to yet another motive for taking up this subject matter: authentic love for national elements in music, and desire to restore early Polish works to concert life. Andrzej Panufnik mentioned this motive several times in his statements:

> My compulsion to restore some of the early Polish music was engendered as I witnessed the superb reconstruction of beautiful 16th- and 17th-century houses in the old part of Warsaw, which had been flattened during the Uprising at the end of the Second World War. To see this almost miraculous re-growth of seemingly lost architectural treasures so lovingly brought about by my compatriots, filled me with enormous admiration. I felt a strong desire to undertake a similar task with the fragments of Polish vocal and instrumental music of the same centuries which had suffered near-oblivion because of Poland's long and tragic history of numerous foreign invasions. Little of this music survived in a performable state and I wanted to fill the gap, endeavoring to recreate as nearly as possible the true period style, like those ancient houses in Warsaw, and firmly intending not to superimpose

my own musical fingerprints. My intention was to bring alive the spirit of
Poland at that time, and to make use of these precious fragments which
otherwise would have remained lifeless on the bookshelves of libraries.[5]

It should be added that restoration of various early music
compositions—whether Polish or foreign—to concert life became a
frequent element in Panufnik's work as a conductor. As Musical
Director of the Birmingham symphony orchestra, he introduced works
by early English composers to his concert programs, gaining the
reputation of introducing unknown treasures of English music to the
British audiences.

Adaptations of various musical works were, furthermore,
Panufnik's daily bread during the occupation, when, together with
Witold Lutosławski, he played in a piano duo at the *Sztuka i
Moda* and *U Aktorek* cafés in Warsaw. For their performances,
both composers prepared arrangements of works by Bach, Chopin,
Mendelssohn, Paganini, Ravel and Szymanowski etc. All arrange-
ments created by Panufnik were destroyed during the Warsaw
Uprising in 1944.[6]

Divertimento

The *Divertimento* numbered among the group of Panufnik's first
compositions written after a long break (not counting film music).
This group of works from 1947 comprises: *Twelve Miniature Studies*,
Nocturne (for which the composer received first prize at the K. Szymanowski Competition), and *Lullaby*—one of the first Polish compositions to use quarter-tones. *Divertimento* thus represented a significant stylistic contrast in relation to the remaining works that he
composed that year. It was written before the principles of socialist
realism were introduced to Polish cultural life; thus, it probably was
nothing more than the expression of a desire to return these works
to concert life. Its world premiére took place on 9 December 1947 at
a PWM Edition concert in Kraków, but the work could have been
written for Panufnik's trip to Berlin to conduct the Berlin Philhar-

---

[5] Andrzej Panufnik, *Impulse and Design in my Music* (London: Boosey & Hawkes
1974), p. 24. Statement regarding the *Old Polish Suite*, the *Concerto in modo antico*
and the *Jagiellonian Triptych*.

[6] Similarly to his original compositions, among others the *Piano Trio* from 1934,
Symphony No. 1 from 1939, Symphony No. 2 from 1941, *Five Folk Songs* from 1940,
Tragic Overture from 1942.

monic in January 1948, when he was expected to present Polish works[7].

In *Divertimento*, Panufnik most closely approximated the idea mentioned above of not superimposing his 'musical fingerprints'. In other words, he permitted himself minimal indication of his own compositional individuality in this arrangement. This work is a very faithful transposition of compositions by Janiewicz to a larger instrumentation: from a trio (2 violins and 'cello) to string chamber orchestra (string quintet). Panufnik does not add even one sound of his own here, and the only serious interference with Janiewicz's compositional intentions is the substitution of the second movement of Trio No. 1 with the corresponding movement of Trio No. 2 (see Table 1).

TABLE 1.
Divertimento, Kraków 1947, rev. 1955 (First perfomance: Kraków 9 Dec.1947)
ca. 15 min., string orchestra

Title of the movement	The original composition, which has been adapted by Panufnik	Bars	Key	The source, from Panufnik knew the music
Allegro moderato	F. Janiewicz, Trio No. 1, 1st mov.	138 bars	C Major	
Andante	F. Janiewicz, Trio No. 2, 2nd mov.	44 bars	A Minor	PWM archives
Allegro	F. Janiewicz, Trio No. 1, 3rd mov.	165 bars	C Major	

In Janiewicz's Trios, the leading role is played by the first violin, which plays thematic lines, figuration and progressions of conjunct intervals. Panufnik's arrangement consists mostly of dividing this line between the first and second violins of the string orchestra. He divides up the conjunct intervals in Janiewicz's composition, and the individual fragments of themes and figuration are assigned to 1st and 2nd violins in dialogue (e.g. 1st mvt. bb. 42–76, 104–111; 3rd mvt. bb. 73–78, 95–110). Any alterations made by him to the melodic contour of the themes and figuration are the exceptions; furthermore, these changes are very minor.

---

[7] *Panufnik o sobie, op. cit.*, p. 175. At that time, he presented works by Janiewicz, Karłowicz and Kassern, as well as his own *Tragic Overture* (acc. to Bolesławska, *op. cit.*, p. 127).

Old Polish Suite

The next of Panufnik's works in this genre is the *Old Polish Suite*, composed in 1950 (revised version: 1955). All musical material, which the composer used in this composition has been published in *La musique polonaise* of H. Opieński (Paris 1918). Here, the composer combines works from three different 16th- and 17th-century Tablatures into one whole (see Table 2), creating a work comprised of five small movements—three early Polish dances (*Cenar*, *Wyrwany* and *Hayduk*) linked by two slow movements: *Interlude* and *Chorale*[8]. The work is scored for small string orchestra. In the British publication *Old Polish Music*, the composer writes that '[...] the number of performers can be varied according to the size and acoustic conditions of the concert hall. '

In those fragments where the composer cites the works being arranged, he does this essentially without alteration to the original (introducing only minor melodic and rhythmic divergences, as well as ornaments). He preserves the voicing and voice-leading, entrusting the melody to the 1st violin and sometimes to the 2nd violin in dialogue with it. He only occasionally expands the original dance, repeating selected motifs from its finale (*Cenar*, bb. 20–32 and 56–65; *Wyrwany*, bb. 101, 111). The adaptation for small string orchestra can be found in tempo markings, articulation and ornaments added by the composer[9].

However, the essence of the arrangement here is expansion of the form of the original dances. The composer gives each of them a symmetrical ABA form by introducing an additional middle section. In Dance I, *Cenar*, section A is the *Polish Dance* from a lute Tablature by Mateusz Waisselius, while the B section most probably is of the composer's invention. In Dance II, section A is represented by a *Wyrwany Dance* from a 17th-century lute Tablature and the B section is *Gagliarda* of Jakub Polak. In Dance III, the A section is the *Hayducki* from an organ Tablature by Jan of Lublin; and as its B

---

[8] In the first version of the work, the *Interlude* and *Chorale* bear the name 'Przegrywka' ['Interlude' or 'Fragment'] (Nos. 1 and 2)—acc. to Bolesławska, *op. cit.*, p. 138.

[9] In several statements, the composer compared his arrangements of early Polish music to the reconstruction of buildings in Warsaw devastated during the war (cf. above citation). Panufnik's reconstruction of early music was also similar to the reconstruction of Warsaw in that it was faithful though not pedantic.

TABLE 2.

Old Polish Suite, Warszawa 1950, rev. 1955 (First perfomance: Warszawa 1951)
ca. 12 min. string orchestra

Title od the part	The original composition, which has been adapted by Panufnik	Bars	The edition known by Panufnik
Dance I: Cenar	*Taniec polski* (Polish Dance) from Lute Tabulature of Mateusz Waisselius	1 (5)–32	Henryk Opieński, *Dawne tańce polskie z XVI i XVII wieku* (Old Polish Dances of 16th and 17th Centuries), Annex to *Kwartalnik Muzyczny* 1911 No. 1; Henryk Opieński, *La musique polonaise*, Paris 1918, p. LXII
	the composer's invention (?)	33–40	
	the repetition of *Taniec polski*	41–65	
Interlude	Mikołaj Gomółka, *Psalm XIII*	66–82	Henryk Opieński, *La musique polonaise, op. cit.*, p. XVIII
Dance II: Wyrwany	*Wyrwany* dance from Lute Tabulatur from the 17th century	83–112	Henryk Opieński, *Dawne tańce polskie .... op. cit.*; Henryk Opieński, *La musique polonaise*, Paris 1918, p. XVIII
	Jakub Polak, *Gagliarda*	113–130	Henryk Opieński, *La musique polonaise*, Paris 1918, p. LXXVIII
	the repetition of *Wyrwany* dance	repetition of b. 83–112	see above
Choral	the composer's invention (?)	131–152	
Dance III: Hayduk	*Hayducki* from Organ Tabulature of Jan of Lublin	153–166	Henryk Opieński, *La musique polonaise, op. cit.*, p. LXI; Adolf Chybiński: WDMP No. 20, Kraków 1948
	Wojciech Długoraj, *Villanella*	167–202	Henryk Opieński, *La musique polonaise, op. cit.*, p. LXXIII
	the repetition of *Hayducki*	203–231	see above

section (bars 167–202), the composer uses a *Villanella* by Wojciech Długoraj.

The form of the work, in this way, takes on characteristics of symmetry, as it were, at two levels: arrangement of the individual movements (dances in ABA form) and symmetry of tempo in the work as a whole (fast dance—slow interlude—fast dance—slow interlude—fast dance).

Concerto in modo antico

The next work from this series, *Concerto in modo antico* (1950, revised version: 1955), is scored for solo trumpet, tympani, harp, harpsichord and string orchestra[10]. The work was written initially as musical illustration for the film *Wit Stwosz* [*Veit Stoss*], and Panufnik received the State Prize for it in 1952. Shortly after writing the film music, Panufnik decided to make it into an independent concert piece, which was performed for the first time in 1952 by the Warsaw Philharmonic, conducted by the composer.

In its construction, the work alludes to an early Baroque form based on a dramaturgy of contrast. It consists of one continuous movement, comprising seven sections interlocked according to a principle of contrasts in tempo, motific material, meter, texture, key (from F major through D-flat, G-flat, E-flat, G, B A-flat and finally back to F) and is composed in an expressive climate. The musical material is taken from Polish works from the Middle Ages through the Baroque (see Table 3). Again, all the compositions which Panufnik uses here were published in above mentioned *La musique polonaise* by Henryk Opieński.

In this work, the composer treats the original material much more freely than in the *Divertimento* and the *Old Polish Suite*. Jarzębski's *Tamburetta* is cited exactly only in bars 10–77 (and, correspondingly, in the recapitulation at the end of the work, in bars 345–412) of his composition. Bars 1–10 are the finale of Jarzębski's work, and bars 78–132 (and, correspondingly, 412–445 in the recapitulation) are a

---

[10] As the composer writes in the British publication *Old Polish Music*: 'maximum 16 vn, 12 vle, 8 vc and 6 cb; minimum 6–4–3–2 respectively. [...] A second harp may be used with advantage in sections 1, 3, 5 and 7, playing in unison with the first harp. The Harpsichord (under no circumstances to be replaced by a piano) is similarly not obligatory, and may be used purely for coloristic purposes.' The *ad libitum* harpsichord part was added only in the revised version of 1955.

TABLE 3.

Concerto in modo antico, Warszawa 1951, rev. 1955 (First perfomance: 16 V 1952)
ca. 15 min., tr solo, string orchestra, arpa, timpani, (clavicembalo ad libitum)

Title od the part	The original composition, which has been adapted by Panufnik	Bars	The edition known by Panufnik
(1) Allegro giocoso	Adam Jarzębski, *Tamburetta*	1–134	Henryk Opieński, *La musique polonaise, op. cit.*, p. LXXXII; Adolf Chybiński, *WDMP* No. 11, Kraków 1932
(2) Andante, molto espressivo	*Cracovia civitas*	135–169	fragment in: Henryk Opieński, *Dawne tańce polskie..., op. cit.*; Henryk Opieński, *La musique polonaise, op. cit.*, p. VII
(3) Allegretto pasotrale	*Balet polonais du v.* Gallot D'Angers from Milleran Tabulature	170–191	Henryk Opieński, *Dawne tańce polskie..., op. cit.*; Henryk Opieński, *La musique polonaise, op. cit.*, p. LXII
	Danse polonaise from „Poliński Tabulature"	192–207	Henryk Opieński, *Dawne tańce polskie..., op. cit.*; Henryk Opieński, *La musique polonaise, op. cit.*, p. LXVI
	the repetition of *Balet polonais*	208–229	see above
(4) Andantino	Wacław of Szamotuły, *Song of the Nativity of the Lord* (Dies est laetitiae)	230–257	Józef Surzyński: Annex to *Muzyka Kościelna*, Poznań 1885; Henryk Opieński, *La musique polonaise, op. cit.*, p. X
(5) Allegro pesante	Bálint Bakwark, *Czarna krowa* (Black Cow)	258–330	Henryk Opieński, *La musique polonaise, op. cit.*, p. LXVIII; Otto Gombosi: Annex to *Muzyka* 1929 No. 6
(6) Andante, molto cantabile	the composer's invention (?)	331–344	
(7) Allegro giocoso	Adam Jarzębski, *Tamburetta*	345–447	see above

development of motifs occurring earlier in the work. From the hymn *Cracovia civitas*, he uses only the initial fragment (to the words 'vallo tegunt alti montes' in the original), furthermore changing somewhat the melodic contour and rhythm of the song. He welds D'Angers' *Ballet polonais* into one section with the *Danse polonaise* from the Poliński Tablature, constructing from them an ABA form on the same principle as in the dances of the *Old Polish Suite*. He changes the melodic contour in this first work quite significantly; in both, he adds many melodic ornaments. What is more, in the first of them, he repeats the initial fragment of the work, transposing it up a fifth (in the original version of the work, this repetition is notated using a conventional repeat sign). In the next section, he uses only a fragment of Wacław of Szamotuły's *Song of the Nativity of the Lord* (from the beginning to the words 'w Betleem porodziła' ['she bore in Bethlehem'] in the original), again changing somewhat the melodic contour of the original. In the next section, Panufnik cites bars 1–43 and 70–96 of Bakfark's *Black Cow*[11], omitting the middle fragment of the original composition; and in the remaining fragments, treating its melody rather freely. It should be emphasized, however, that the arranged fragments—where they are cited from the original—retain their harmonies, voicing and general emotional expression.

Despite the fact that the work's structure consists of contrasting combinations of stylistically and expressively different works, a clear leaning by the composer towards unification of the work's structure is manifested here. The uniting element is the solo trumpet part. Throughout the entire work, it is treated in the same way—not as a *concertante* or virtuosic instrument, it is always rather one in dialogue with the orchestra, exchanging thematic lines with other instruments.

Above all, however, the work is given unity of form by beginning and closing the composition with the same musical material. But Jarzębski's *Tamburetta*, used in this manner, becomes something more than a simple arch form. While the final section is an almost precise repetition of the musical material from the beginning of the work, the dialoguing lines are, however, very consistently exchanged. What was assigned to the trumpet at the beginning, the composer entrusts to the violins at the end—and vice versa. Schematically, this can be presented in the following manner:

---

[11] Bar numbers according to the edition published in *Muzyka w dawnym Krakowie* (Music in Old Kraków) (Kraków: PWM, 1964).

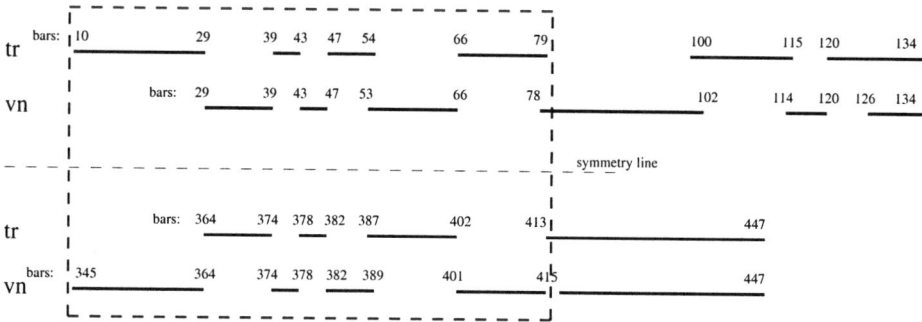

Ex. 1. Dialoguing lines of tr and vn in the beginning (b. 10–79)
and its repetition (b. 345–415) in *Concerto in modo antico*

The ideal symmetry appears here in bar 10–79 and respectively
345–415—e.g. the part of the composition which has been taken
directly from the original piece of Jarzębski. The formal solution
presented here is reminiscent of the mirror symmetry technique
familiar from later works by Panufnik.

Jagiellonian Triptych

The last example of the archaic trend in Panufnik's art is
Jagiellonian Triptych, scored for string orchestra[12]. It was written in
1966 to honor the 1000th anniversary of the Polish state, and was
performed for the first time in London on 24 September 1966 under
the composer's baton, together with his *Old Polish Suite, Divertimento*
and *Landscape*. All compositions, that have been used here by the
composer, appear in the album *Muzyka w dawnym Krakowie* (*Music
in Old Kraków*), which was published in 1964.

In his statements, Panufnik emphasizes many times that the
primary constructive principle of his mature works is symmetry and
use of geometric structure to assist in shaping the form of a work.
Elements of such thinking can already be discerned in his first
arrangements of Polish early music—such as the construction of the
form in the three dances of the *Old Polish Suite,* or the bestowal of
an arch form with an element of mirror symmetry upon the *Concerto
in modo antico.*

---

[12] As the composer writes in the British publication *Old Polish Music*: this work
'[...] may be performed by large or small orchestra: minimum 6 vni I, 6 vni II, 4 vle, 3
vc and 2 cb.'

TABLE 4.

Jagiellonian Triptich, Twickenham 1966 (First perfomance: London 24 IX 1966)
ca. 7 min., string orchestra

Title od the part	The original composition, which has been adapted by Panufnik	Bars	Key	The edition known by Panufnik
(1) Preambulum (vivace)	Mikołaj of Kraków, *Alia 'Poznanie'* from Organ Tabulature of Jan of Lublin	1–63	F D B A-flat F	Adolf Chybiński, *WDMP* No. 20, Kraków 1948; *Muzyka w dawnym Krakowie* (Music in Old Cracow), Kraków 1964
(2) Cantio	Krzysztof Klabon, *Pieśni Kaliopy Słowieńskiej*: Song No. 6 [Hetmanowi koronnemu] (Jeśli greccy Hektorowie)	64–71	C	*Muzyka w dawnym Krakowie, op. cit.*
	Krzysztof Klabon, *Pieśni Kaliopy Słowieńskiej*: Song No. 1 (Słuchajcie mię wszystkie kraje)	72–79	G (A)	Zdzisław Jachimecki: *Wpływy włoskie w muzyce polskiej* (Italian Influences in Polish Music), vol. 1: *1540–1640*, Kraków 1911; *Muzyka w dawnym Krakowie, op. cit.*
	Krzysztof Klabon: Song No. 6 as above	80–87	C	see above
(3) Chorea polonica	Wojciech Długoraj: *Chorea polonica*	88–191	G B E-flat G etc..	Henryk Opieński: Dawne tańce polskie..., *op. cit.*; Zofia Stęszewska: Tańce polskie z tabulatur lutniowych (Polish Dances from Lute Tabulatures), vol. 1, *ZHMP* II, Kraków 1962; *Muzyka w dawnym Krakowie, op. cit.*

Much more clearly, however, this principle explains the form of the individual fragments in the *Jagiellonian Triptych*. In its first movement, the *Preambulum*, the composer used Mikołaj of Kraków's work *Alia 'Poznanie'*. The original work is constructed of two sections: A and B. Panufnik broke up section A into two, A_1 and A_2, and cited it in entirety in his work, in the following order:

$$A_1—A_1—B—B—A_1—A_2$$

Thus, the composer creates here a symmetrical arch form, but the essence of the arrangement consists of transposing its successive sections a minor third down—retaining the harmonic structure of the original in each segment—which in effect creates a closed tonal circle:

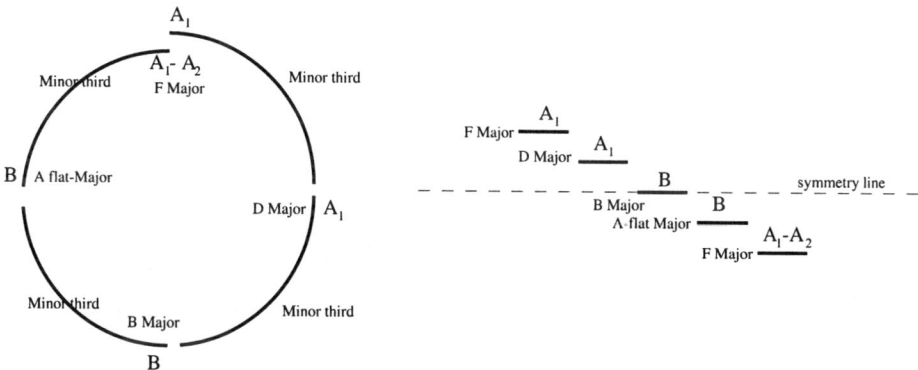

Ex. 2. *Jagiellonian Tripich*, 1st movement: *Preambulum*, the tonal plan

The tonal plan of this section is thus based on a diminished triad, which is by its nature symmetrical.

The A sections are presented each time in the same instrumentation (the theme runs through the 2nd violin, viola, 2nd violin and 1st violin), and the B (middle) sections are contrasted in sound (the theme appears first in the lower instruments of the orchestra, and is repeated in the upper instruments).

The 2nd movement, *Cantio*, is an arrangement of two songs by Krzysztof Klabon, which the composer used to build an ABA form similar to that of the dances in the *Old Polish Suite*. He retained here the precise sound material of the original—with its harmony and relationships among voices. In his arrangement, he constructed the instrumentation of this movement on a mirror symmetry principle: section A is presented initially only by the 1st and 2nd violins (*divisi*—retaining the four-voice scoring of the original); while in the recapitulation, it is played by the 'cellos and basses (*divisi*). Section B was split up into two-bar components identically contrasting in sound. The strict symmetry of this formation is clearly visible in the written score:

Ex. 3. *Jagiellonian Triptich*, 2nd movement: *Cantio*
© Copyright 1968 by Boosey & Hawkes Music Publishers Ltd.
Reproduced by permission of Boosey & Hawkes Music Publishers Ltd.

The last movement of the work, *Chorea polonica*, is an arrange-ment of a composition by Wojciech Długoraj. In the original, this composition has an ABA'B' structure, where the A and B sections are in 4/4 meter; and A' and B', in 3/4. Panufnik maintained the exact melodic contour, harmony, meter and voicing in the individual sections, changing their articulation and differentiating their individual appe-arances by color, combining *pizzicato* and *arco*. The individual sections—very short, barely four- and six-bars—appear in the work many times, but the order of their occurrence is different here than in Długoraj's original. They are presented in the fundamental tonality and transposed to the tonalities a major third up and a major third down—preserving their harmonic structure. Długoraj's composition, in itself, is based on an interesting harmonic progression, which, in combination with the sudden and frequent transpositions made by Panufnik, yields a very interesting sound effect. The formal and harmonic structure of this movement presents itself as follows:

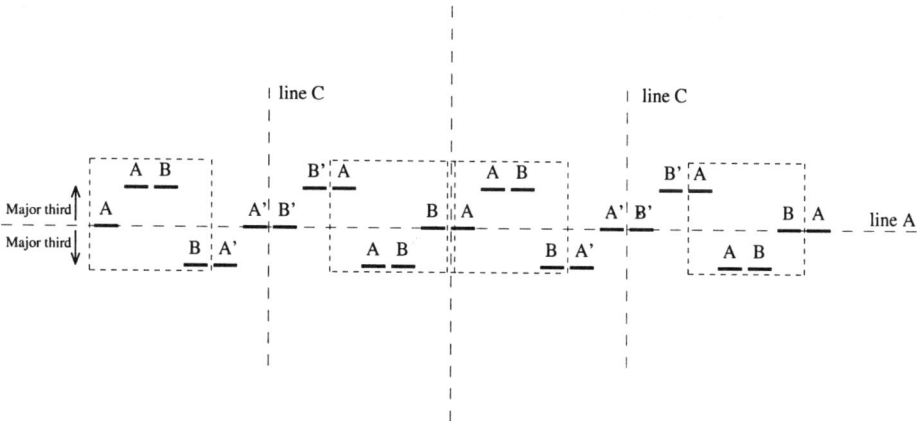

Ex. 4. *Jagiellonian Triptich*, 3rd movement:
Chorea polonica. Scheme of the form and its tonal plan

The tonal plan of this section is based on an augmented triad, again symmetrical by its nature. Here the fundamental tonality is a sort of axis of symmetry around which the 'harmonic plot' of the work developes (line A on the scheme). The symmetry occurs furthermore at several levels. The arrangement of section groups is symmetrical: AABB A'A'B'B' AABB (lines C on Example 4). Their repetition in the same structural and harmonic arrangement creates another axis of symmetry in the middle of the work (line B on the scheme). The structural and tonal arrangement of the first group (AABB) is a mirror image of the third group (where the first A of the first group correspond to the last B of the other group—on the opposite side of the tonal symmetry line, etc.). In the same way, in terms of tonality, the second group (A'A'B'B') is also constructed on a mirror-image principle. It is important to note here, that the composer was able to establish here such a precise symmetrical structure, while still using means restricted to the traditional tonality.

Conclusion

While the works discussed above do not add to already existing resources in 20th-century musical language, they are nonetheless interesting in their own right, not only as testimony to a neoclassical trend in Polish music. At least fragments of them, as well as the entire *Jagiellonian Triptych*, are a manifestation of a an individual instinct for structural discipline properly related to the mature compositional language of Panufnik: as such, they deserve the attention of researchers into his art, as well as their restoration to the concert repertoire.

Translated by Cara Thornton

Part III
Reception of the Composer's Work

The Reception in Poland
of Andrzej Panufnik's Early Works

Piotr Papla

The compositions and conducting of Andrzej Panufnik (1914–1991) had already aroused the interest of Polish critics before the Second World War, during and immediately after the composer's studies at the Warsaw Conservatory. Around 40 items of information about him of different kinds appeared at this time: in serious cultural journals (*Muzyka, Muzyka Polska, Muzyka Współczesna, Kultura*), in daily newspapers (including *Ilustrowany Kurier Codzienny, Kurier Poranny* and *Warszawski Dziennik Narodowy*) and in concert programme notes,[1] quoted by Beata Bolesławska in her monograph. I use the term "items of information" intentionally here because they are mostly short notices on the performance of a specific work,[2] press reviews,[3] and articles presenting a profile of the composer[4] or attempting to place him within modern musical trends.[5] Apart from a couple in 1934, the first[6] of which is an advertisement for at that time very popular recording by Adolf Dymsza of *Ach pardon*, with words by

---

[1] Beata Bolesławska, *Panufnik* (Kraków: PWM 2001), p. 53.

[2] An example of this can be found in the notice in *Muzyka Polska* 1937, p. 259, with information about the performance of Andrzej Panufnik's *Piano Trio* and *Overture* by the Warsaw Philharmonic under the direction of M. Mierzejewski.

[3] Felicjan Szopski, 'Popis Konserwatorium' (Conservatory concert) in *Kurier Warszawski* (June 18, 1936), p. 8.

[4] Jan Maklakiewicz, 'Kompozytorskie orlęta Warszawy' (Young Warsaw composers) in *Kurier Poranny* (April 11, 1936), p. 8.

[5] Michał Kondracki, 'O kierunkach współczesnej muzyki polskiej' (Trends in Polish contemporary music) in *Muzyka Polska* (1937), pp. 270–271.

[6] *Muzyka* (1934), p. 131.

Marian Hemar and music by Andrzej Panufnik, and the second[7] a review of compositional exercises, which undoubtedly is his *Classical Suite*, they all appeared either in 1936 or 1937. These items of information are of considerable significance for those doing research into Panufnik's works because, with the exception of the Piano Trio, which was reconstructed after the war, all his pre-war works perished.

From the review of *Classical Suite*[8] in *Gazeta Warszawska* in 1934, the only known press item about *Suite*, we learn that the suite was written as a string quartet and was divided into three movements: prelude, gavotte and allegro. On the basis of the opinion of the author of the article, who says: "In keeping with the title, Panufnik's suite is of a classical character", we may suppose that the composer kept faithfully to the classical rules both of type and form. Articles on his Symphonic Variations also supply us with a considerable amount of information on the construction and character of this work. From them we know that *Variations* contained a fugue and a finale,[9] and that "one of the variations was a passacaglia, hence variations upon a variation".[10] When it comes to the general character of the work, the author of one of the articles, signing himself Zast, writes that: "[Panufnik's] score of Symphonic Variations, although contains certain harmonic and polyphonic complications, is generally clear, which indicates the true instinct of the young musician", adding that "the work ...has the marks of orchestral virtuosity..."[11]

Thanks to Bolesławska's[12] quotations from concert programmes, we are also able to form some sort of opinion about the formal construction of *The Little Overture*, which probably alludes, with certain modifications, to the pattern two thematic sonata allegro.

After reading a range of press notes and articles, we must fully concur with Bolesławska's opinion that "Andrzej Panufnik, right from

---

[7] Zast (I), 'Produkcja uczniów konserwatorjum' (Compositions of the Conservatory students) in *Gazeta Warszawska* (November 10, 1934), p. 4

[8] Zast (I), *op. cit.*

[9] Zast (II), 'Młodzi muzycy wchodzą w świat' (Young composers start their adult life) in *Warszawski Dziennik Narodowy* (April 18, 1936) and Piotr Rytel, 'Życie muzyczne stolicy. Popisy absolwentów Konserwatorjum Muzycznego' (The capitol's musical life. Concert of the absolvents of the Conservatory) in *Kultura* (July 5, 1936 No. 14), p. 7.

[10] Konstanty Regamey, 'Recenzje muzyczne. Dwa popisy' (Musical reviews. Two concerts) in *Prostu z mostu* (1936 no. 26), p. 7.

[11] Zast (II), *op. cit.*

[12] Beata Bolesławska, *op. cit.*, p. 53.

the beginning of his career, showed himself to be highly talented."[13] Music critics commented on this fact, usually writing about his compositions in complimentary terms, and referring to him as: "unusually good", "important", "an almost fully mature talent", "an undoubtedly talented composer" or "a very mature and aware musician." The young composer's conducting activities also met with similar approval. The above mentioned Zast wrote: "Panufnik also conducted his own work, and he did it skillful",[14] and Piotr Rytel called him a "professional conductor".[15] We also learn, through a notice appearing in a 1937 edition of *Muzyka Polska*,[16] that the work of Panufnik had already before the war awakened the interest of theoreticians of music as the name of the young composer figured in a lecture "On Polish Contemporary Music" by the Warsaw musicologist Dr Julian Pulikowski.

Certain of the critics, as indicated above, attempted to place the composer on the map of artistic currents or to trace the roots of his work. Michal Kondracki included Panufnik (as well as Bacewicz, Ekier, Kisielewski, Lutosławski, Maciejewski and Szałowski) in a group of "young composers under 30". In his opinion Panufnik belonged to a second group of contemporary composers which came into its own during the concert season of 1936/37. Panufnik and Kisielewski appeared to him "to be admirers of neo-classical trends".[17]

Jan Maklakiewicz, in his perhaps excessively florid and extravagant review in the 7th Programme of the Polish Contemporary Music Society, wrote: "The accents of youthful rebellion, struggles and quests, the strong, decisive accents, the forthright romantic bursts of thematic invention on an incredibly rich and varied emotional scale which we hear in Panufnik's music lead us to certain analogies with the impulsive character of Brahms' music. However, the search for connections with Brahms is not consequent because in the same review he traces the sources of Panufnik's inspiration to an "intrinsically Polish atmosphere of sentiment and emotion".[18] Following Maklakiewicz's line of thought, Felicjan Szopski considers that the

---

[13] Beata Bolesławska, *op. cit.*, p. 54.

[14] Zast (II), *op. cit.*

[15] Piotr Rytel, *op. cit.*

[16] *Muzyka Polska* (1937), p. 481.

[17] Michał Kondracki, *op. cit.*, pp. 267, 270–271.

[18] Jan Maklakiewicz, 'Nowe znakomite kompozycje' (New perfect compositions) in *Kurier Poranny* (December 17, 1936), p. 8.

theme of Symphonic Variations "has some relation to the sounds of our folklore". However, he perceived the modernity of Panufnik's music, since he considered that "its basis [the school of Professor Kazimierz Sikorski of whom Panufnik was a representative] is the modernism of today."[19]

A different view is taken by the reviewer of *Warszawski Dziennik Narodowy*, his identity concealed under the name of Zast. He believed that above Panufnik's *Symphonic Variations* "there hovers the recently fashionable spirit of the east, from the land of Mussorgsky".[20]

As seen in these quotations, which in general are quite reservedly worded, the statements of the music critics did not yet show a fully-formed opinion on the young composer's style of composition or on the artistic direction he was taking.

The aspect of Panufnik's musical works which excited a great deal of interest, and often critical approval, is undoubtedly his instrumentation and orchestration. A review of *Gazeta Warszawska* in 1934, also signed Zast, while discussing the characteristics of *Classical Suite*, informs us that it "distinguishes itself by the limpidity and clarity of the movements, which demonstrates his ability to use a string quartet.[21] The same tone is used in *Kultura* by Piotr Rytel, known for his conservative views, who wrote that Panufnik "knows the orchestra very well and knows how to handle its individual instrumentalists",[22] and by Z. D., reviewing Trio in *Ilustrowany Kurier Codzienny*, who added, "Panufnik reveals splendid instrumental texture in his Trio".[23]

The majority of critics write about the instrumentation and orchestration of Panufnik's works in approving way, but in one of his compositions he used an untypical orchestration which attracted particularly strong attention, namely the exclusion of violins in *The Little Overture*. This drew praised for example in a statement by M. Kondracki that "the search for new paths and new sounds has led him to eliminate the violin section from the orchestra in his *Overture*. Because of this, the character of Panufnik's work benefits from its distinctiveness".[24] However, *Little Overture* also received

---

[19] Felicjan Szopski, *op. cit.*

[20] Zast (II), *op. cit.*

[21] Zast (I), *op. cit.*

[22] Piotr Rytel, *op. cit.*

[23] Z. D., 'Nowe polskie utwory kameralne' (New Polish chamber works) in *Ilustrowany Kurier Codzienny* (December 19, 1936).

unfavourable comments, for instance the opinion of Skołuba in *Kurier Polski,* who wrote: "The concept that a work should be written for orchestra with no violins at all is very unusual. Here there is a big "but". Since there are no violins, the part of the leader must undoubtedly be played by a woodwind instruments. Thus reasons the average listener. But the composer understood things differently introducing his main themes principally through the violas and cellos, in parts even pizzicato, which at a fast tempo are unable to produce the right effect. This constitutes a weak spot in what is otherwise a totally successful composition".[25]

Skołuba's statement shows that reviewers, while praising the young composer, also found weak points in his compositions. In general, the most frequently criticized aspect was the form of Panufnik's works and also sometimes—as above—his instrumentation, which after all was praised by many of them. For example Z. D. wrote rather enigmatically about Trio that "the thematic material is not yet particularly independent, and one may have some slight reservations as regards the form".[26] Skołuba wrote: "It is not satisfactorily balanced in its basic structure and the treatment of instruments".[27] Konstanty Regamey in his appraisal of *Symphonic Variations* also draws attention to "a lack of formal compactness" in the final fugue, but tempers his opinion by stating that "this could have been caused by the rather slow tempo in which the composer, who was making his first appearance with the Philharmonic Orchestra, conducted his own work.[28] Still on the subject of Variations, it should be noted that two critics found this work too long. Szopski declared: "Perhaps [the composition] would benefit from some slight cuts",[29] and Zast, in agreement, wrote in *Warszawski Dziennik Narodowy* that because of Panufnik's already mentioned orchestral virtuosity "the composition as a whole loses somewhat in meaning, becoming too drawn out and at times somewhat verbose".[30]

This review of notes and articles connected with Andrzej Panufnik's pre-war work is not fully comprehensive. I consider however that it

---

[24] Michał Kondracki, *op. cit.*

[25] Quoting from Bolesławska, *op. cit.*, p. 53.

[26] Z. D., *op. cit.*

[27] Quoting from Bolesławska, *op. cit.*, p. 48.

[28] Konstanty Regamey, *op. cit.*

[29] Felicjan Szopski, *op. cit.*

[30] Zast (II), *op. cit.*

gives a certain idea of his reception in the Polish press and provides information on the style and construction of his works, most of which were lost. As we can see from statements made by Polish music critics, they were mostly positive towards the young composer, recognizing his talent and prophesying an undoubted future career as an artist. The critics commented on Panufnik's extraordinary abilities in the fields of instrumentation and orchestration and to his thorough schooling as a conductor. However, they were not yet able to grasp fully the compositional style and artistic direction which the composer was taking.

Translated by Christine Rickards-Rostworowska

In the Public Eye:
Panufnik and his Music, 1948-54

Adrian Thomas

Panufnik must have rued the day that he started to draw the attention of the public to his activities outside what he regarded as his natural musical environment. Within Polish culture during the period of socialist realism, arguably only the writer Jarosław Iwaszkiewicz exceeded Panufnik's eminence as an international figure in the public eye because of his 'non-curricular' functions. Each of them, like others of lesser prominence, played the government-led situation his own way. This paper takes as its starting point what Panufnik said and what he wrote, both during and about the post-war decade.[1] It advises caution in dealing with aspects of his autobiography, such as the history of *Sinfonia Rustica* (1948), it investigates his involvement with the peace issue as both a cultural representative and as a composer, and outlines the problem of musical criticism in the early 1950s, taking *Symfonia pokoju* (Symphony of Peace, 1951) as its main example.

In recent years, there has been a marked growth in interest in the post-war decade of Polish culture. We cannot avoid confrontation with the burning issue of those years: the relationship between the arts and their socio-political context. (The manipulation and conditioning of creative artists is not confined to past political systems, of course, as the power of today's state and commercial patronage testifies.)

---

[1] For reasons of time and space, I have not considered in this paper the published and archival materials which relate immediately to Panufnik's escape to the UK in July 1954.

The years 1948–54 are especially significant even if the artefacts are more interesting for their contextual aspects rather than their artistic qualities. Sometimes the results of recent research have been startling. We now know, for example, that in November 1948 Panufnik composed not just one mass song to mark the formation of the PZPR (Polska Zjednoczona Partia Robotnicza—Polish United Workers' Party)—*Pieśń Zjednoczonej Partii* (Song of the United Party, to a text by Leopold Lewin)—but three.[2] We also know that in April 1950 he planned to write a *Symfonia rewolucyjna* (Revolution Symphony), a work, and a concept, that never materialised. To balance this picture, we must also acknowledge the newly-discovered fact that, in 1949, Witold Lutosławski wrote a mass-song triptych (to texts by Konstanty Ildefons Gałczyński) to celebrate the fifth anniversary of the July Manifesto, the declaration in 1944 of the PKWN (Polski Komitet Wyzwolenia Narodowego—Polish Committee of National Liberation).[3]

Generally speaking, source materials for the period are haphazard, but fairly numerous. They are scattered in various governmental and institutional archives, from the Ministry of Culture and Art and other bodies to the ZKP (Polish Composers' Union), ZAIKS (Performing Rights Society), performing organisations such as orchestras, and Polish Radio. Autobiographical data and composer reminiscences, on the other hand, are much rarer and usually very guarded. When asked about the period and his role in it, Lutosławski was either politely dismissive or aggressively defensive.[4] Zygmunt Mycielski, an inveterate diarist as well as a principal player in the musical politics of the period, made no diary entries at all between late October 1951 and late March 1955, thus depriving us of his characteristically trenchant observations.

---

[2] The other two songs were *Pieśń jedności* (Song of Unity, text by Stanisław Wygodzki) and *Naprzód ludu roboczy* (Onward Working People, text by Leon Pasternak). My thanks to David Tompkins for alerting me to the source of this information: Archiwum Akt Nowych (New Records Archive), KC PZPR 237/XVIII, 85.

[3] See my article: 'File 750: Composers, Politics and the Festival of Polish Music (1951)' in *Polish Music Journal* Vol. 5, No. 1, Summer 2002, (Polish Music Centre, Los Angeles), http://www.usc.edu/dept/polish_music/PMJ/issues.html, in which I discuss these and other newly-discovered documentary sources.

[4] For an example of the latter, see Irina Nikolska: *Conversations with Witold Lutosławski* (Stockholm, 1994), p. 39.

Panufnik's autobiography, *Composing Myself*, therefore provides a unique source of information and opinion.[5] Of course, the historian must treat such reminiscences with due caution. Panufnik's autobiography is no exception: it is compelling reading but cannot be said to be either faultless or comprehensive, especially in the section devoted to the post-war decade. In fact, its errors and selective memory are what make it revealing.[6] Apart from a sometimes imprecise chronology, Panufnik's account of the post-war decade is notable for its tendency not to explain fully, and therefore with greater balance, the circumstances which characterised his own position in Polish culture. This is understandable—the book is *his* memoir—but two instances will illustrate what is more than a slight problem when trying to establish an accurate account of the socialist-realist period.

The first is a simple example, which characterises the anomalies resulting from selective memory. A cursory glance at Polish dictionaries and surveys of these years, written in the late 1950s and through the 60s, reveals that it is not true, as Panufnik had been informed by colleagues, that his music and name were totally erased from Polish musical history after his escape to the West.[7] In the twenty years after his departure (prior to his music's gradual reinstatement from 1977 onwards), the ban on performing Panufnik's music was almost, but not quite, 100% successful.[8] His scores were not all destroyed; many remained, even if they were normally hidden from general view. His name did appear in print, albeit infrequently. He was omitted from the first and second editions of *Almanach Polskich*

---

[5] Andrzej Panufnik, *Composing Myself* (London: Methuen, 1987); Polish translation by Marta Glińska: *Panufnik o sobie* (Warszawa: NOWA [Niezależna Oficyna Wydawnicza], 1990).

[6] For an example of Polish critiques of the autobiography, see Michał Głowiński, 'Pochwała bohaterskiego oportunizmu. Epizod socrealistyczny w biografii Andrzeja Panufnika' (In Praise of Heroic Time-Serving. The Socialist-Realist Episode in Andrzej Panufnik's Biography), in *Rytuał i demagogia: Trzynaście szkiców o sztuce zdegradowanej* (Ritual and Demagogy: Thirteen Sketches on Degraded Art) (Warszawa: OPEN, 1992), pp. 95–103; for my part, I have not attempted in this short paper, except in the most straight-forward terms, to address the claims and counterclaims about Panufnik's privileged position in these years.

[7] Andrzej Panufnik, *op. cit.*, p. 243.

[8] For example, see the review of the performance in Warsaw on 21 and 23 November 1958 of *Uwertura tragiczna* (Tragic Overture), conducted by Henryk Czyż, in *Ruch Muzyczny* (iii) 1959 No. 1, p. 27.

Kompozytorów Współczesnych (Almanach of Contemporary Polish Composers, 1956/1966), but two other dictionaries (1960, 1967) gave Panufnik's life and output to 1954 in as much detail as any comparable Polish composer; indeed, in Śledziński's mass-circulation *Mała Encyklopedia Muzyczna* (Little Musical Encyclopaedia, 1960) Panufnik was given a longer entry than Lutosławski.[9] In broader musicological surveys of post-war Polish music (1957, 1967, 1968), there was a measure of objective comment and reference to several specific pieces; the two later volumes even expanded their coverage to include a few musical examples (from *5 pieśni ludowych* (Five Polish Folk Songs), 1940).[10] Clearly, Panufnik was not entirely written out of recent Polish musical history. He was, however, presented as if in a disembodied state, as if he and his pre-1954 compositions had been pickled in a jar of formaldehyde to be left on a laboratory shelf, with most of his post-1954 output ignored as irrelevant to the ongoing Polish experience. Perhaps the most telling assessment comes in *Muzyka Polski Ludowej* (Music of People's Poland, 1968), where Chomiński's tone, though critical, is more in sorrow than in anger:

> It turns out that, even at a difficult time of administrative pressure, he could realise his compositional ideas, with his music performed, published and recorded. After his departure from the country, this interesting output became somewhat paralysed. And that's a pity, because he was a real, authentic composer.[11]

The implication is, of course, that Panufnik would still have been a real composer had he stayed in Poland along with his colleagues and been part of the post-1956 explosion of avant-garde music.

The second anomaly concerns the efficacy of government control over repertoire in the early 1950s. Panufnik recounts how the

---

[9] Stefan Śledziński, ed.: *Mała Encyklopedia Muzyczna* (Warszawa: PWN, 1960; 30,200 copies), pp. 569–70; Józef Chomiński, ed.: *Słownik Muzyków Polskich* (Dictionary of Polish Musicians) (Kraków: ISPAN-PWM, 1967; 5255 copies), vol. 2 M-Z, pp. 108–9.

[10] Józef Chomiński and Zofia Lissa, eds.: *Kultura Muzyczna Polski Ludowej 1944–1955* (Musical Culture of People's Poland 1944–1955) (Kraków: ISPAN-PWM, 1957; 2156 copies), e.g. pp. 124, 127 and 146; Józef Chomiński, *Muzyka Polski Ludowej* (Music of Peoples' Poland) (Warszawa: PWN, 1968; 2000 copies), pp. 63–7; Elżbieta Dziębowska, ed.: *Polska Współczesna Kultura Muzyczna* (Polish Contemporary Musical Culture) (Kraków: ISPAN-PWM, 1968; 3250 copies), p. 34.

[11] Józef M. Chomiński, *op. cit.*, p. 81.

Vice-Minister of Culture condemned *Sinfonia Rustica* in June 1950 at the ZKP's General Meeting:

> Minister Sokorski, having listened attentively to the political condemnation of this patently innocent piece, announced his verdict in sonorous tones: 'Sinfonia rustica has ceased to exist!'[12]

In fact, if the published account in *Muzyka* is to be regarded as a more or less faithful record of the tone and direction of the debate, *Suita polska* (*Hommage à Chopin*, 1949) was more severely criticised than *Sinfonia Rustica*.[13] Thereafter in his autobiography, Panufnik totally ignores the Symphony, reinforcing the impression that Sokorski's word was law, and that *Sinfonia Rustica* had consequently disappeared altogether from Polish musical life and memory. Other sources, however, reveal that the Symphony was performed on several occasions during the next few years: in Wrocław (Autumn 1950)[14], Warsaw (October 1951, with Panufnik as conductor)[15], in Kraków (February 1952)[16] and in Szczecin (November 1953)[17], each time on two or three evenings. Furthermore, Panufnik conducted *Sinfonia Rustica* at Budapest Radio (February 1951)[18] and it was scheduled by Polish Radio for broadcast on 1 April 1953, in a performance by the Łódź Philharmonic Orchestra, conducted by Bohdan Wodicz-

---

[12] Andrzej Panufnik, *op. cit.*, p. 194.

[13] 'Sprawozdanie z obrad V Walnego Zgromadzenia ZKP' (Report of the Proceedings of the Fifth General Meeting of the Polish Composers' Union), *Muzyka* 1950 (i) No. 5, p. 46–59.

[14] One can imagine Panufnik's frustration when Mycielski at one moment prized him, like Chopin, Beethoven and Debussy, for his 'inventiveness' and yet, according to the report, at another targetted him (and others) for a lack of real engagement with Polish folk music, commenting that *Sinfonia Rustica* was 'an idyll without any conflict' and that the use of vocalise in *Suita polska* was 'a characteristic escape from expressiveness' (p. 52). Witold Rudziński's dismissed Panufnik's treatment of the folk element in *Suita polska* was 'soulless', further declaring that *Nokturn* (1947) was memorable for its 'endless pessimism' (p. 55). Sokorski's comment went unrecorded. *Muzyka*, (ii) 1951 No. 1, p. 59.

[15] On 26/28 October, 1950; *Kurier Codzienny* (285) (31 October 1950), p. 4; *Express Wieczorny* (288) 3–4 November 1950; *Nowa Kultura* (45) 11 November 1950, p. 11; FMP *'Informacja nr 4'*, AAN 750/150–160, sheet 152.

[16] *Muzyka* (iii) 1952 No. 5–6, p. 104.

[17] *Muzyka* (v) 1954 No. 5–6, p. 100.

[18] *Muzyka* (ii) 1951 No. 2, p. 59; interview with Panufnik on his return from Budapest, *Radio i Świat* (Radio and the World) (vii/8) (February 1951), p. 8; Andrzej Panufnik, *op. cit.*, p. 192, remembered his trip as taking place in February 1950, i.e., before Sokorski's condemnation.

ko.[19] On 5 July 1950, just two weeks after Sokorski's unreported condemnation, *Sinfonia Rustica* was nominated by the Polish Committee for the Defenders of Peace for the International Peace Prize in Prague.[20] Three months later it was published by PWM (Polskie Wydawnictwo Muzyczne—Polish Music Publishers), and in December 1950 it was cited by Tadeusz Marek in *Muzyka* as one of the major symphonic achievements of People's Poland.[21] The inconsistency of the history of *Sinfonia Rustica* is not unusual: there were many holes in the system which allowed criticised works to resurface in print and as well as in performance.[22]

Panufnik was unusually prominent in Polish musical life, not least because he combined a career as composer and conductor. Prior to 1949, like some other musicians, he had opportunities to travel abroad. Between 1949 and 1954, he travelled more usually within the communist bloc, but his few trips to Western Europe were a prized rarity: he conducted in Helsinki (1952) and, of course, in Zürich in July 1954. There was also a non-conducting trip to the ISCM festival in Palermo (1949) and two visits to Belgium (1953) to attend music competitions. Other composers had virtually no such openings to the West.

It is beyond the bounds of this paper to explore the vexed question of how or why Panufnik became embroiled in the politics of the day. Undoubtedly such foreign visits were regarded as a bonus, but a bonus which had its darker side—an obligation, at the very least, to play along with the PZPR.[23] One condition of such trips appears to

---

[19] Polish Radio II, 23.10, *Radio i Świat* (ix) 1953 No. 13, p. 2; there were other foreign performances, including two in East Germany (April 1952, which Panufnik attended, and March 1954, when Bohdan Wodiczko conducted *Sinfonia rustica* at the Berlin State Opera) (sources: *Życie Warszawy* (105) 2 May 1952; *Trybuna Ludu* (82) 23 March 1954.

[20] *Nowa Kultura* (i/16) 16 July 1950, p. 1; *Muzyka* (i) 1950 No. 5, p. 70.

[21] *Muzyka* (i) 1950 No. 9, pp. 9–14.

[22] For a discussion, in this context, of Lutosławski's mass song, *Nowa Huta*, see Adrian Thomas: 'Your Song is Mine', *The Musical Times* (cxxxvi/1830) August, 1995, pp. 403–9.

[23] In addition to composing three mass songs to celebrate the formation of PZPR in 1948, Panufnik also wrote *Nowy czas* (A New Time) in 1951 (it was published by PWM as one of twelve songs in *Naszej Partii Pieśń* (Our Party Song) in 1954), as well as the song *Ślubowanie młodych* (Pledge of Youth) for the propaganda film 'Ślubujemy' (We Pledge, 1952); Panufnik's signature also appeared underneath a short eulogy on State support for music in the run-up to the elections in 1952, published in *Kurier Codzienny* 24 October 1952.

have been that Panufnik was obliged to write journalistic reports which toed the party line. The most extreme of the several he wrote from his Western travels was his report in *Przegląd kulturalny* about the 1953 International String Quartet Competition in Liège.[24] He uses strong language to condemn Western avant-garde music, especially the new serialist tendencies and the winning First String Quartet by Elliott Carter. The article's fiery tone is surprising, given Panufnik's gentle nature, but perhaps he genuinely did not like the Carter Quartet and felt free to speak his mind, especially if it fitted in with his brief. The language becomes particularly graphic when he links dodecaphony with the dollar (the $ sign was, of course, a ubiquitous symbol of American imperialism in Polish cartoons) and when he alleges an American fix in awarding the top prize to Carter. Certainly, he accurately perceived the fact that the USA was using its contemporary art as cultural and political propaganda, but then so too was Poland, as on this occasion. Panufnik also took the opportunity to contrast anecdotally, and to the Polish advantage, the context for creative work in Belgium and Poland. All in all, Sokorski must have been delighted with such a sharply drawn account of the perils of non-socialist music.

Panufnik is probably unique in that he does not hide in his autobiography that he was prepared to co-operate with the Party. On several occasions he explicitly cites or implies the material advantages to be gained from awards such as the Standard of Labour First Class or from close proximity to influential Party members.[25] And he lays great stress on how his own efforts, as a senior member of the ZKP board for most of 1948–54, helped his fellow composers, even though this work was, by his own account, unremunerated.

If acting as an intermediary between music and politics was a price worth paying, then Panufnik was not alone, even if at times he seemed to be both one of the principal beneficiaries and victims. If signing open letters in support of peace was tolerable, again he was not alone.[26] But Panufnik's propaganda value for the burgeoning peace movement which followed the Stockholm Appeal in April 1950 proved second to none, and this was arguably the most burdensome part of his unwritten deal with the party. It is not clear why he

---

[24] Andrzej Panufnik: 'Wrażenie belgijskie' (Belgian Impressions), *Przegląd Kulturalny* (ii/43) 28 October–3 November, 1953, pp. 1, 7.

[25] Andrzej Panufnik, *Composing Myself*, *op. cit.*: e.g. pp. 175 & 195.

[26] *Kurier Codzienny* (252) 12 September 1950, p. 1.

became one of the State's cultural representatives in this field, but his involvement may have stemmed at least in part from what turned out to be a genuine lifelong commitment to peace. His involvement went back at least as far as August 1948, when he was present at the World Congress of Intellectuals in Wrocław.[27] The following April, he was listed as a delegate for the Paris Peace Congress[28], but instead went to Palermo with Iwaszkiewicz to attend a performance of Szymanowski's *King Roger* at the ISCM Festival, where the peace issue unexpectedly surfaced. There then followed several occasions when he did contribute internationally to the Polish peace effort, including the Second World Congress of the Defenders of Peace in Warsaw (November 1950) and the Congress of Peoples in Vienna (December 1952), where his role as a Polish cultural emissary was paralleled by that of Shostakovich for the Soviet Union.[29]

The year 1950 marked a crucial moment for Panufnik's public persona as an individual and collective proponent of peace, and it was at this stage that the public eye began to focus on Panufnik for his propaganda activities. Alongside Grażyna Bacewicz, Alfred Gradstein, Zofia Lissa and Mycielski, he signed the Stockholm Appeal on 21 April on behalf of the ZKP.[30] There was the now notorious and apparently doctored interview published in the Russian weekly, *Ogoniok*, on 26 June and its ramifications in the Polish press.[31] There was also the less well-known occasion of a speech at the First All-Polish Peace Congress, held in Warsaw 1–2 September 1950, in which Panufnik reiterated sentiments from the interview in *Ogoniok*. His role as a mouthpiece was never clearer:

---

[27] Panufnik appears again, just after the Congress, conducting *5 pieśni ludowych* (Five Polish Folk Songs) at a reception given for Picasso and other visitors at the National Museum in Warsaw; source: *Kurier Codzienny* (iv/238) 30 August 1948, p. 2.

[28] *Rzeczpospolita* (vi/102) 13 April 1949, p. 1.

[29] Andrzej Panufnik: 'Pokój można obronić' (Peace can be Defended), with accompanying photo of Panufnik talking with Shostakovich at the Vienna Congress, *Przegląd Kulturalny* (ii/1) 8–14 January 1953, p. 1.

[30] 'Profesorowie Politechniki i kompozytorzy polscy kładą podpisy pod apelem pokoju' (Polytechnic Professors and Polish Composers Put their Signatures to the Appeal for Peace), *Trybuna Ludu* (iii/110) 22 April 1950, p. 4.

[31] Panufnik: 'Symfonia Mira. Biesieda s polskim kompozitorom Andreijem Panufnikom', *Ogoniok* 26 (26 June 1950); 'Moje wrażenia muzyczne z ZSRR' (My Musical Impressions of the USSR), *Nowa Kultura*, i/15 (9 July 1950), pp. 5–6; 'Najbardziej zaimponował człowiek. Wrażenia z wycieczki do ZSRR' (Most Impressive were the People. Impressions from a trip to the USSR), *Życie Warszawy* (vi/313) 13 November 1950, p. 2.

I am an artist and I speak on their behalf and I say: which artist does not feel called today to the frontline in defence of peace? I believe that there are no such people among us. Which of us does not realise how important are the tasks that artists have to fulfil on this front? It is enough to look at our Soviet colleagues, who efficiently and with dedication serve the cause of peace in many ways, both directly as advocates for the idea of peace and indirectly as opponents of Western art subjected to the yoke of imperialism. Let us remind ourselves of the role attributed to the arts in capitalist countries, to the musical arts, closest to me, about which I wish to speak.

Music there is characterised by the deliberate avoidance of any programme which could, even in a distant way, touch upon matters close to every man. Western music often gives the impression that it had originated out of hate and contempt for man. Formally complicated, soaked with pessimism, expressing lack of confidence in the sense of peaceful coexistence between nations, it removes the thoughts even of the few, to whom it speaks, from any social problems, from the simplest duty of fighting for a better tomorrow.[32]

To what degree his speech was actively or passively conditioned by the Party (i.e. which parts were written or suggested by others) we are unlikely ever to know.[33] Whatever his private views on the more political sections of the speech, it was certainly brought to a rousing conclusion:

Please forgive me for this handful of not-so-fresh thoughts and personal memories. I am a composer and I am not good at speaking. But we are all striving for the same thing and so we do not have to convince each other. Our deepest desire, constant will, strength and inspiration—yours as well as mine—is the final victory of peace. This is the bright goal for which it is worth fighting and for which we are able to make any sacrifice, as we

---

[32] Andrzej Panufnik: speech at I All-Polish Peace Congress, Warsaw, 1 September, 1950. Archiwum Dokumentacji Mechanicznej, Radio File, P. 1492/50–51. My thanks to Małgorzata Szyszkowska for discovering this recording, which is held alongside many other speeches, including those by Jarosław Iwaszkiewicz and Jerzy Andrzejewski. Panufnik was photographed alongside these two writers at the Congress (*Rzeczpospolita* (vii/241) 2 September, 1950, p. 4. To the best of my knowledge, Panufnik's speech was never published, although a brief summary of early passages did appear in *Rzeczpospolita* (vii/242) 1950, p. 4. Iwaszkiewicz's speech at the same Congress appeared in *Nowa Kultura* (i/24) 10 September 1950, p. 2.

[33] Lady Camilla Panufnik said after this paper was delivered that the recording was not of Panufnik's voice. She suggested that this was probably a typical manipulation from that epoch attempting to connect him with the regime's ideology. Adrian Thomas agreed that there was no absolute proof that it was a recording of Panufnik's voice, although there was photographic evidence and newspaper reportage that indicated that Panufnik had been on the speakers' platform and had given a speech. He suggested that further analysis of the recording and the others in the archive might usefully be a subject for specialist study (Ed.)

know and believe that peace is the most precious gift that we can offer for
the future of our fatherland.

Panufnik delivered his speech after he had spent six weeks at
Obory wrestling with the problems of putting such sentiments into
practice, as a composer. And it was as the composer of *Symfonia
pokoju* (1951) that Panufnik became most publicly the subject of
debate. There was every hope that this work, like other pieces from
1950–51—Lutosławski's orchestral *Mała suita* (Little Suite), Szeligo-
wski's opera *Bunt żaków* (The Scholars' Revolt), Olearczyk's mass
song *Miliony rąk* (Millions of Hands)—would come to symbolise and
promulgate the new socialist-realistic aesthetic in Polish music.

It is strange that in his autobiography Panufnik should recoil so
violently at the memory of his hasty promise in Moscow in May-June
1950 to write a *Symphony of Peace*.[34] It was not, after all, his first
concept for the new symphony. Only a few weeks earlier, on 21 April
1950 (the very same day that he signed the Stockholm Appeal), he
had written a grant application letter to the ZKP declaring that he
wanted to write a *Symfonia rewolucyjna*.[35] How could the idea of a
'peace' symphony have been so unacceptable to Panufnik when he
had just volunteered a much more hard-line propaganda proposal of
a 'revolutionary' symphony? Indeed, given his innate commitment to
peace, it made great sense to switch topics to one which would be
much more amenable to his natural talents and interests. And while
this change of mind may have been a spur-of-the-moment decision
in Moscow, it is not beyond the bounds of possibility that his arm
was twisted 'peacefully' (perhaps by Sokorski) to contribute profes-
sionally to the main political cause of the day.[36]

The publicity machine moved fast. It appears, for example, that,
by the end of July 1950, the new *Symfonia pokoju* was intended for
premiere at the forthcoming Second World Congress of the Defenders
of Peace in Warsaw (then planned for 21–26 October 1950).[37]
Furthermore, the Symphony's texts were reported to be by Władysław

[34] Andrzej Panufnik, *Composing Myself, op. cit.*, p. 200.

[35] See Panufnik's letter indicating his intended contribution to the Festival of
Polish Music, then projected to begin in mid-November 1950, in AAN, Ministerstwo
Kultury i Sztuki, 1950 (Dep. Twórczości Artystycznej, Wydz. Twórczości Muzycznej),
750/67.

[36] Sokorski was to engineer a similar persuasive moment with Lutosławski at the
ZKP meeting in June 1950, as the composer recalled in Nikolska, *op. cit.*, pp. 40–1.

[37] *Kurier Codzienny* (vi/185) 6 July 1950, p. 1

Broniewski and Pablo Neruda and not, as it eventually emerged, by his friend Iwaszkiewicz.[38] It seems evident that such information must have come from government sources, presumably with Panufnik's knowledge, because at that stage he was in isolation at Obory supposedly hard at work on the Symphony. It soon became apparent, however, that it was not going to be finished in time for performance at all that year. In fact, its premiere on 25 May 1951 was no doubt deliberately scheduled to coincide with the culmination of the Polish Peace Plebiscite the following day. As part of the build-up to the concert, Iwaszkiewicz's poem for the final movement, 'Pokój', was published in the press, but without any reference to the premiere.[39]

The reception of *Symfonia pokoju* raises another matter: the function and impact of music criticism in this period. This was a difficult issue for all involved in Polish musical life, from composers and performers to newspaper critics and other participants in peer-review listening sessions (*przesłuchania*). There are many instances of criticisms by party members being given prominence, be they Lissa or a delegate of the ZMP (Związek Młodzieży Polskiej— Polish Youth Union). Panufnik certainly took exception to any negative criticisms, summarising the Symphony's reception in emotive terms:

> ... the authorities damned the symphony on the grounds that my style was 'weak in ideological eloquence', accusing me of an even worse crime, that I was 'praying' for peace instead of 'fighting' for it.[40]

The first accusation refers to an unsigned editorial in *Muzyka* profiling the winners of the 1951 State Prizes.[41] The profile of Panufnik is, in fact, extremely positive, praising the Symphony's

> intense, emotional expression. The Symphony is a great step forward in the composer's output ... an achievement of great stature.

Its criticism of *Symfonia pokoju* is quite specifically localised and stems from an observation that Panufnik's music was unnecessarily archaic for such a contemporary theme:

---

[38] *Kurier Codzienny* (vi/209) 30 July 1950, p. 6. The convoluted history of the venue for the II World Congress for Peace is a topic in itself. Polish papers noted between June and mid-November that it was scheduled to take place first in Genoa, then successively in Warsaw, London and Sheffield, only to be relocated at five days' notice to Warsaw (16–22 November 1950).

[39] *Nowa Wieś* (20) 20 May 1951, p. 3.

[40] Andrzej Panufnik, *Composing Myself, op. cit.*, p. 205.

[41] *Muzyka* (ii) 1951 No. 8, p. 4.

If in *Bunt żaków* [Szeligowski's opera about a student revolt in Renaissance Kraków] the use of 16th-century musical language seems justified and in every way interesting, much of the same language used in some parts of Panufnik's work weakens its ideological eloquence.[42]

In other words, *Symfonia pokoju* was fundamentally regarded as ideologically eloquent, if somewhat flawed in its execution. Aleksander Jackowski's review in the preceding issue of *Muzyka* is more fulsome in its praise:

> Let me stress here only its fundamental asset: the sincerity of expression. It took Panufnik a year to compose the piece, writing it with a creative passion that is rarely to be found.[43]

But his review is also more telling in its criticisms, some of which are sustainable, especially with regard to the three-movement Symphony's overall structural and expressive weighting. Panufnik's second objection arises, I suspect, from Jackowski's opinion on precisely the same archaisms picked up by the anonymous editorial cited above:

> Perhaps the atmosphere of the first movement weighs too heavily on the Symphony as a whole. The fact that this part is based on church modes gives it a specific character, by this token narrowing the image and turning it almost into a Church Requiem.
>
> This kind of impression dominates the piece, all the more so because the third movement does not constitute a sufficiently strong counterbalance. The culmination of the finale with the numerous repetitions of the word 'Peace' lacks active force—the will for peace—while the 'gothic' atmosphere again evokes an image of waiting, of asking for peace.[44]

Such criticisms of *Symphonia pokoju*—primarily of its final section—extended as far forward as Lissa's book *O specyfice muzyki* (1953)[45], Michał Bristiger's often insightful article on Panufnik, 'Reflections without Hagiography', in *Przegląd Kulturalny* in March 1954[46] and Jerzy Broszkiewicz's follow-up article on *Symfonia pokoju* two weeks later:

---

[42] *Ibid.*

[43] Aleksander Jackowski, 'Po pierwszym etapie Festiwalu Muzyki Polskiej' (After the First Stage of the Festival of Polish Music), *Muzyka* (ii) 1951 No. 7, p. 5.

[44] *Ibid.*

[45] Zofia Lissa, *O specyfice muzyki* (On the Specifics of Music) (Kraków, 1953), pp. 117–8.

[46] Michał Bristiger, 'Rozważania bez hagiografii' (Reflections without Hagiography), *Przeglad Kulturalny* (iii) 11–17 March 1954, p. 6.

> The dove of the third movement has emerged from within an archaic frame, almost from among the psalms. It lacks contemporary courage and the impulse of a Picassoesque optimist, both alert and strong ...[47]

Despite the praise it received, the lack of the 'mobilising' factor in the third movement clearly irked many critics.[48] Not for the first or last time, his music was seen by some as artful, refined and noble, but equally distant and hermetic, eschewing conflict or struggle, characteristics which turned out to be immanent in Panufnik's (musical) psychology. Panufnik was not able, even if he was willing, to provide the sort of culmination to *Symfonia pokoju* which would engage in what, for want of a better phrase, we might call a traditional symphonic *durchführung*. In Bristiger's view, there was a basic and unresolvable dichotomy:

> The ideological-artistic problem of this symphony is hard to define, but it is hidden in some sort of discrepancy between its concept and life itself, even though the music responds splendidly to the poems which inspire it.[49]

The problem with the finale is almost entirely musical and distinct from any textual or ideological considerations. It is almost as unconvincing as other contemporary Polish attempts at archaic climaxes, as in the gawky conclusions to Krenz's cantata *Rozmowa dwóch miast* (Conversation of Two Cities, 1950) and Skrowaczewski's *Kantata pokoju* (Cantata of Peace, 1951). Panufnik's setting of Iwaszkiewicz's rather fine text is a stiff and earthbound 'chorale', but at least he did not attempt a quasi-Baroque fugue like Krenz and Skrowaczewski.[50] He does try to raise the spirits by jacking up the

---

[47] Jerzy Broszkiewicz: 'Po koncercie: O Panufniku bez partytury' (After the Concert: On Panufnik without a Score), *Przegląd Kulturalny* (iii/12) 25–31 March 1954, p. 6.

[48] Even so, at least in the initial months after the premiere, the Ministry of Culture and Art was determined to promote the Symphony as one of Poland's musical flagships. In addition to Polish performances, the Symphony was heard in the USSR and East Germany (twice) in 1951–52. Interestingly, three days after the premiere on 25 May 1951, the Ministry decided to make it a priority to obtain not only a commercial release of *Symfonia pokoju* on the French label 'Le Chant du Monde' but also a French performance conducted by the composer; source: AAN/Ministerstwo Kultury i Sztuki/32/Dep.Polityki Kulturalny (Wydział Twórczości Kulturalnej i Kontroli Repertuarowej)/1951/: *protokół 6*, p. 29. At the end of May 1954, it was performed and broadcast nationally and across Europe from Kraków in a performance conducted by the composer.

[49] Michał Bristiger, *op. cit.*

[50] Cf. Bolesław Woytowicz's individual setting of the same text.

tonality from the initial E flat Aeolian through F Aeolian, and thence
by step from C major to D Aeolian, from D major to E Aeolian, and
on to E major for the 19 final utterances of 'Pokój' ('Peace').
Nevertheless, the lasting impression—on a purely musical level—is
one of empty rhetoric, non-organic and lacking in expressive connection with the two preceding movements. His intention to climax the
Symphony with what he called an 'extended and symphonic mass
song' had evidently failed.[51]

It is perhaps not without significance that, even though Panufnik
used *Symfonia pokoju* as his calling card in the USA in 1955[52], he
soon recast it as *Sinfonia Elegiaca* (1957), rededicating it 'To the
Victims of the Second World War'. The first movement's textures were
amplified, and ornamentation and octave transposition applied to
individual melodic lines, but most significantly the end of the
movement was cut by 58 bars, reducing its overall length by over a
third (cf. Jackowski's criticism above). There are local extensions and
re-orchestrations in the central movement, with the short climactic
codetta being more substantially remodelled and strengthened. The
finale's opening section is much as in *Symfonia pokoju*, but at the
very point where the choir originally entered with Iwaszkiewicz's text,
in *Sinfonia Elegiaca* Panufnik introduces a symbolic 'pausa', before
recollecting the main theme from the first movement. He thereby
reinforces the elegiac aspect and, at the same time, gives greater
prominence to the central 'Molto Allegro' (originally marked 'Drammatico') by enveloping it with like material, rather than attempting
a developmental follow-on. There is still an element of patchworking
in the way the finale is put together, but there is no sign whatsoever
of the music which so disappointed Polish commentators. It would
appear, therefore, that in some measure Panufnik did eventually
acknowledge some shortcomings in his original score, even if his
reasons may not have been the same as, or in response to, those of
the critics.

It is clearly difficult, half a century later, to recreate the subtle
and minute subtexts of Polish musical and cultural life in the first
half of the 1950s. This is particularly true of cultural criticism. I

[51] (ibis) (interview with Panufnik): 'Treść narzuciła formę' (The Contents Imposed
the Form), *Życie Warszawy* (143) 25 May 1951.

[52] In 1999, Joseph Herter rediscovered the original Voice of America tape recording
of Stokowski's performance of *Symfonia pokoju*, made in Detroit on 17 February 1955
and broadcast to Poland on 9 April 1955.

believe there is much work yet to be done in teasing out the politically-inspired polemic from the musically-inspired critique, the low-grade review from the perceptive assessment, the vagaries of long-distance memory from archival documentation. Each has its place. The socialist-realist perspective in Poland had both ideals and misconceptions; although it is customarily denigrated for its many negative features it should be respected for its loftier intentions and for the fact that it was not by any means monolithic; where it was operational, it was necessarily responsive to changing circumstances. It could not exist (nor could its antithesis) without its creative realisation by composers and their listeners. The relationship was symbiotic.

In terms of the reception of Panufnik and his music, his own memoirs need to be treated with caution in factual terms but they do represent a valid personal recollection from a distance of over thirty years. His contemporaneous utterances have yet to be assessed fully, not least within the broader cultural and political contexts of the time. As is well known, the ideological reception of his music from within the profession ranged from watchful equivocation and malice at the ZKP meeting in June 1950 to Lissa's very different commentaries in the mid-1950s. Although negative musical views were certainly expressed on aspects of Panufnik's output (cf. the discussion of *Nokturn* at Łagów in August 1949)[53], the balance of *published* comments on *Symfonia pokoju* was overwhelmingly supportive. The discrepancies between Panufnik's account and the published reviews and presluchanie reports concerning the two versions of *Uwertura bohaterska* (Heroic Overture, 1950/52) are also interesting examples of reception and compositional response.[54]

Are we to assume, as Panufnik appears to do with regard to *Nokturn, Sinfonia Rustica, Symfonia pokoju* and *Uwertura bohaterska*, that any negative criticism was automatically and solely the result of the Ministry of Culture and Art's drive for socialist realism? Surely not always, because by the same token all positive responses would be similarly blighted. No creative artefact nor response to it is ever immune from contextual issues, but credence should be given where a musically justifiable critical stance is taken. By and large, Bristiger's article is one such instance, not only for its thoughtful if rather polite

---

[53] *Ruch Muzyczny* (v) 1949 No. 14, pp. 1–10, 12–31.

[54] Andrzej Panufnik, *Composing Myself, op. cit.*, p. 209; *Muzyka* (iv) 1953 No. 3–4, pp. 77–8.

questioning of *Symfonia pokoju* but also for its 'courageous' advocacy of *Kołysanka* (Lullaby, 1947)[55], which was a true and innocent victim of the brave new (and ultimately transitory) world of Polish socialist realism.

As a footnote, but a highly significant one, there is the extraordinary case of the interview with Panufnik by Lucjan Kydryński, published in *Dziennik Polski*.[56] Carried out during Panufnik's visit to Kraków to conduct *Symfonia pokoju* in May 1954, the interview was published in mid-June, barely a month before he flew to Zürich. There is something in the bullish tone of the interview which, in hindsight, suggests that Panufnik may have sensed that an opportunity to escape might soon become a reality and that he felt emboldened to speak out. In any event, Panufnik's replies to Kydryński's questions (which were edited out before publication) are frank and outspoken, especially on two issues. The first of these concerns a speech made by Mieczysław Drobner at the recent ZKP General Meeting, which Panufnik uncompromisingly rebuts.[57] The second concerns the work most criticised at the Łagów conference in 1949, Zbigniew Turski's Second Symphony:

> For me, for example, the fact of the complete withdrawal from the concert platform of Turski's 'Olympic' Symphony, which won the Gold Medal at the 1948 Olympics in London, is mystifying. I can see no formalism there.

Such opinions were almost never allowed to appear in print: their appearance in mid-1954 implies that perhaps the cultural clamps might be changing, but for Panufnik his die was cast and he was committed to leaving, whenever the opportunity might arise. Panufnik's comments here do, however, put his other published utterances into a different perspective. They do not negate them, but they do indicate that his role as a figure in the public eye is a fascinating example of the complexities of the artist's responses to the pressures of socialist realism.

---

[55] We must not, however, forget Stefan Kisielewski's often robust defence of Panufnik's music, which included an article in *Tygodnik Powszechny* (41) (1951) on *Kołysanka* and an earlier one in the same newspaper which strongly resented the labelling of *Uwertura bohaterska* as formalistic.

[56] Lucjan Kydryński, '8 odpowiedzi Andrzeja Panufnika' (Andrzej Panufnik's Eight Replies), *Dziennik Polski* (140) 13–14 June 1954.

[57] Cf. Andrzej Panufnik, *Composing Myself, op. cit.,* p. 225.

Reception of Andrzej Panufnik's Work in the Great Britain

Violetta Kostka

Andrzej Panufnik spent 37 years—almost half of his life—in the Great Britain. During that time (but also earlier and later) his music was performed, published, recorded there, and was the subject of aesthetic and theoretical discussions. How was Panufnik's music received by the British? The first attempt to answer this question was made by Tadeusz Kaczyński in his book *Andrzej Panufnik i jego muzyka*[1]. The author remarks that Panufnik's music is enjoyed by the British musical public, his works are often performed in London and other British cities, and "the Panufnik Memorial Concert" organized in Queen Elizabeth Hall on the first anniversary of the composer's death was received with applause by the large audience. The author suggests that it may be prestigious English publishing house Boosey and Hawkes that is responsible for popularising Panufnik's work. He claims further that the lack of interest in Panufnik's music shown by musicologists and critics is because his music is considered not avant-garde enough for contemporary music specialists, yet too modern for those dealing with "classical" music. Of course, Tadeusz Kaczyński merely "touches" upon this considerable problem which needs further research. Theorists of music reception claim that this kind of research requires the consideration of various types of documents, be they scientific or popular texts, letters, diaries, memoirs, letters to editors, school books, teaching materials, music sheets, school anthologies,

---

[1] See Tadeusz Kaczyński, *Andrzej Panufnik i jego muzyka* (Andrzej Panufnik and his Music) (Warszawa: PWN, 1994), pp. 39–45.

etc.[2] In order to grasp at least something of the above essential
information, I decided to analyse some documents, choosing
comments published in British magazines by British critics and
musicologists. Taking into account the typology of reception
presented by G. Wunberg (and recently brought to mind by
Małgorzata Woźna-Stankiewicz) analytical and analytical-creative
receptions were selected for the purpose of that article[3]. Using
a popular American Bibliography *The Music Index. A Subject-Author
Guide to Music Periodical Literature* I established a list of thirty
five articles about Panufnik's music. These articles appeared in
following magazines (in alphabetical order): *Composer. The
Composer's Guild of Great Britain, The Gramophone, London
Musical Events, Monthly Musical Record, Music and Letters,
Music and Musicians, The Music Review, Musical Opinion, The
Musical Times, Recorded Sound, The Journal of the British
Institute of Recorded Sound, The Strad* and *Tempo. A Quarterly
Review of Modern Music*. Two books on Panufnik's music by
English writers were an additional source.

Andrzej Panufnik decided to emigrate to the Great Britain in July
1954. This event was noticed by the English daily press, and written
about a few times. Five articles dedicated to the composer were
published in the years 1954–57, but afterward there was silence for
a few years[4]. Among publications we encounter essays as well as
reviews, but the bulk consists of fairly short texts. An essay in *London
Events* gives information about Panufnik's nomination as the director
and conductor of the Birmingham Symphony Orchestra. The authors
recall that Londoners had the occasion to listen to *Five Polish Peasant
Songs* for voices and chamber orchestra in 1946, and in 1952 they
had a chance to hear *Nocturne*. A lot of space is devoted to the
composer's life. The authors acknowledge Panufnik's high position in

---

[2] See Małgorzata Woźna-Stankiewicz, *Muzyka francuska w Polsce w II połowie
XIX wieku. Analiza dokumentów jako podstawa źródłowa do badań nad recepcją*
(French Music in Poland in the 2nd half of the 19th Century. Document Analysis as a
Source Base for Research on Reception) (Kraków, 1999), pp. 14–15.

[3] *Ibidem*, pp. 11–14.

[4] See [no author], 'Colin Horsley and Andrzej Panufnik', *London Musical Events*
(October 1954), p. 35; [no author], 'Politics and Panufnik', *Musical Opinion* (November
1954), p. 89; Donald Mitchell, [review of Piano Trio], *The Musical Times* (January
1955,) p. 38; [no author], [review of *Concerto in modo antico, Lullaby*], *Music and
Letters* (October 1956), pp. 410–411; [no author], 'Andrzej Panufnik', *London Musical
Events* (October 1957), p. 30.

Poland as a composer and a conductor. They write that Panufnik is one of the most highly regarded Polish composers. The matter of his immigration is just announced, never commented upon. Only the author of an essay, 'Politics and Panufnik', tries to investigate the subject. He claims that in order to understand this problem Panufnik's music should be viewed in the light of state political intervention in matters of culture. Since the author is unknowledgeable about contemporary Polish music he refers to a concert of modern Romanian music held in London, where he heard *Cantata of Liberation, My Beautiful Homeland, Peace and Friendship among People* (the author does not give names of the composers). Comparing the recently-heard Panufnik's *Nocturne* with the above mentioned Romanian music he concludes that "Mr. Panufnik's sort of music stands in the extremest possible opposition to the new music of Romania. (...) Mr. Panufnik's music was obviously too 'good'—too consciously cultured, too esoteric—for consumption in present day Poland"[5]. Interestingly however, when he proceeds to the more detailed analysis of *Nocturne*, it turns out that this piece although too good for the Polish is not good enough for the British. A lack of interesting form and interesting musical substance is the main argument. The author acknowledges that the sonorities are interesting, but at the same time he claims that the instrumentation is only a technical tool and not an aim of the composition. Other authors of articles about Panufnik are equally severe when assessing his works, which they know either from the concert hall or just from reading the scores. Piano Trio was considered to be too much influenced by French music, whereas *Lullaby* and *Concerto in modo antico* seemed banal in the choice of melodies and simple in the way they were developed. All the publications tend to doubt the credibility of Panufnik's reputation from before his immigration. A short entry in the book *European Music in the Twentieth Century* from 1957[6] written by an English composer Bernard Stevens[7] however, is completely different in tone. According to Stevens Panufnik is "(...) one of the most remarkable composers of his generation. He has unlimited audacity and conviction in his exploitation of novel sonorities"[8].

---

[5] [no author], 'Politics...', *op. cit.*

[6] See Bernard Stevens, 'Czechoslovakia and Poland'. (in:) *European Music in the Twentieth Century*. Ed. Howard Hartog 1957, pp. 316–317.

[7] Bernard Stevens—an English composer born in 1916, the professor of composition, see *The Oxford Dictionary of Music*. Ed. Michael Kennedy. Oxford 1985, p. 692.

[8] Bernard Stevens, 'Czechoslovakia...', *op. cit.*, pp. 316–317.

From 1960 until the end of the 60s only four analytical publications appeared. Three of them were quite substantial, published in the renowned magazine *Tempo*[9], and the fourth one—in *Musical Opinion*—was the abridged version of the last article printed in *Tempo*[10]. Harold Truscott is the author of the first article. The six pages are devoted to the basic information about Panufnik's life, and the analysis of one of (in his view) the best of Panufnik's works, *Tragic Overture*. Truscott gives musical examples and discusses three traits of the composer's style i.e. the atmosphere of the choral, romantic expression and the classical sense of the sonorities. Barrie Hall—the author of the next article—writes about *Sinfonia Sacra* which won first prize at the competition in Monaco in 1963. He analyses the work in detail including comments he had obtained from the composer himself. The concentrated organization of sounds, the perfect use of string instruments and the "remote" atmosphere are viewed as the main original features of *Sinfonia Sacra*. Eventually the author tries to grasp, like Truscott, those traits that might determine Panufnik's individual style but ends up with a completely different set. In his opinion other composers had had little impact on Panufnik's music, which is essentially Polish although not descending from the Chopin-Szymanowski line; Panufnik's approach to folklore is original, different from Bartók's or Stravinsky's. Hall writes about the non-musical elements as an important factor in the process of conceiving the form. The sonorities are hailed as the most important aspect of Panufnik's music.

The third article written in 1968 by Peter French gave British readers the best picture of the Polish composer. The author notices that Panufnik uses a set hierarchy of musical elements. Starting with the most important these are: poetic and spiritual components, musical structure, themes, harmony, sonority. He also writes that, in his search for new techniques, Panufnik does not forget the economy and simplicity of musical means, exploiting free tonality rather than atonality. Specific features of this language include: major and minor chords played simultaneously and the use of chords and phrases based on the twelve-note scale. The author mentions the most obvious

---

[9] See Harold Truscott, 'Andrzej Panufnik', *Tempo* (autumn/winter 1960), pp. 13–18; Barrie Hall, 'Andrzej Panufnik and his 'Sinfonia Sacra'.' *Tempo* (winter 1964/65), pp. 14–22; Peter French, 'The Music of Andrzej Panufnik', *Tempo* (spring 1968), pp. 6–14.

[10] See Peter French, 'Andrzej Panufnik', *Musical Opinion* (April 1968), pp. 375–377.

trait, which is the tendency to build up the work out of three or four-note cells. Eventually the author states that this music is really Polish. French concludes that Panufnik's career so far is interesting enough to merit observation of his progress in future and his works (though not numerous) also deserve attention.

There is a remarkable change towards Panufnik reflected in the musical periodicals of the 70s. As many as nine articles appeared, among them seven reviews of specific compositions, concerts or recordings, as well as two strictly scientific articles paying tribute to his overall achievement. The appearance of seven reviews written by various authors is a proof of the increasing interest in Panufnik's music. All authors regret that this music is rarely performed in concert halls and seldom broadcast on the radio, and it deserves to be recorded on disc. Roger Wimbush states "Like Handel, Panufnik is a British subject, but unlike Handel his music is more often performed abroad than in this country"[11]. All the reviews are about Panufnik's recent works. Stephen Walsh writes about *Universal Prayer* as a cold but interesting composition where the use of modern techniques is similar to the ones exploited by Penderecki and Messiaen, however with original sonorities[12]. Calum MacDonald views Violin Concerto as one of the most successful and ravishing pieces recently composed by Panufnik. This composition is based on the symmetry and the strict confinement of basic music material, which nevertheless does not result in any lack of fantasy or of structural variety or expression[13]. Unlike *Sinfonia Concertante* however, it presents—in the critic's opinion—some weaknesses. The most noticeable is the choice of the note cell that fails to awake the listeners' interest[14]. According to Oliver Knussen *Sinfonia di Sfere* (1975) is a very successful composition[15], while Paul Griffiths thinks otherwise. The latter writes that what strikes is "an impotent note, though more through technical than expressive schematism. (...) the composition seems like an illustration of the diagram rather than the other

---

[11] Roger Wimbush, 'Here and There', *The Gramophone* (January 1972), p. 1193.

[12] See Stephen Walsh, 'Festival in Richmond', *The Musical Times* (August 1971), p. 785.

[13] See Calum MacDonald, [review of Violin Concerto, *Sinfonia Concertante*], *Tempo* (June 1976), pp. 48–49.

[14] *Ibidem.*

[15] See Oliver Knussen, 'Panufnik's 'Sinfonia di Sfere'.' *Tempo* (June 1976), pp. 29–30.

way about. Its palindromic regularity becomes tiresome"[16]. Nicholas Kenyon writes similarly about *Sinfonia Mistica*. In his opinion geometrically determined structures are inflexible and the composition is devoid of organic development. The reason for this is Panufnik's attempt to balance the architecture of the work and the non-musical element. The author concludes: "Mystery (...) cannot be guaranteed by geometry"[17]. The last reviewed composition is String Quartet No. 1. Peter Wright scrutinises the structure of the work and assigns to it such appellations as "solemn and awe-inspiring"[18]. It is worth noting that two scientific articles were published to celebrate the 60th birthday of the composer. Stephen Walsh's text provides considerably more new observations than Meirion Bowen's one[19]. Walsh states that Panufnik is underestimated, not even regarded as a national compo- ser; there are many reasons cited in the article why this should be changed. The author writes about inflated titles of works but considers Panufnik as too conscious to be unreasonably influenced by the public as to the choice of titles. The composer controls the emotional and sensorial impulses by the use of various composing techniques. Walsh ventures to say that Panufnik is more original than Lutosławski, but also concedes that Panufnik's works are uneven, which may be the reason why he is less popular. *Tragic Overture, Lullaby, Sinfonia Rustica* are considered by Walsh as his best works especially in the early phase of Panufnik's life, and he also notices some links with Shostakovitch's music. The author ends his eight page article with his statement underlining the value of Panufnik's music: "He [Panufnik—VK] continues to share with his contemporaries still in Poland a talent for the arresting sonority and texture, along with an unwavering preoccupation with good composition in the old sense of good musical design. Beyond this, it seems quite doubtful whether there is any more original or self-determining composer of his nationality working at this moment"[20].

---

[16] See Paul Griffiths, [review of *Sinfonia di Sfere*], *The Musical Times* (June 1976), pp. 508–509.

[17] Nicholas Kenyon, 'Panufnik's 'Sinfonia Mistica',' *Tempo* (March 1978), p. 26.

[18] Peter Wright, [review of *Universal Prayer*, String Quartet No. 1], *Music and Musicians* (April 1978), p. 40.

[19] See Stephen Walsh, 'The Music of Andrzej Panufnik', *Tempo* (December 1974), pp. 7–14; Meirion Bowen, 'Panufnik at 60', *Music and Musicians* (September 1974), pp. 20–24.

[20] Stephen Walsh, 'The Music...', *op. cit.*, p. 14.

The period of success was from 1981 till the composer's death, as is evident in the musical periodicals. Nine reviews, two articles, interviews with Panufnik's music interpretators as well as interviews with the composer himself all appeared at that time. No more negative opinions are published. Astonishingly the idée fixe in these publications is the geometrical element in Panufnik's music[21]. It is probably so because the critics turned to the composer's diagrams published in concert programmes. Malcolm Miller, writing about String Quartet No. 3, focuses on explaining the phenomenon of symmetry (how and where it is used)[22]. The reviews from that period resemble mainly analysis, aesthetic opinions are rare. Martin Anderson hailed *Sinfonia Sacra* as a masterpiece of the 20th-century orchestral music[23]. Calum MacDonald writing about *Sinfonia della Speranza* stressed its expression, rarely obtained by other composers nowadays[24]. The Bassoon concerto's expression also made an impact on critics. They write about the kind of expression never before associated with the bassoon and describe the piece as "elegiac concerto", "tender elegy", "a sombre work", "a soberly moving act of homage". According to Anderson this is the best bassoon concerto. He writes: "Indeed, there has not been a bassoon concerto to match this one since Mozart's and, to be honest, I have to say that I prefer Panufnik's. It is an unalloyed masterpiece"[25]. This prevailing mode of writing about Panufnik's music was criticized by Stephen Johnson[26]. In order to present different approaches to

---

[21] See Mary Crighton, [review of *Arbor Cosmica*], *The Strad* (February 1985), pp. 728–729; Martin J. Anderson, [review of *Metasinfonia, Universal Prayer*], *Tempo* (September 1986), p. 38; Calum MacDonald, 'Panufnik 9 and Bassoon Concerto', *Tempo* (June/September 1987), pp. 107–108; Rona Hemingway, [review of *Katyń epitaph*], *Musical Opinion* (September 1988), pp. 317–318; Rona Hemingway, [review of Violin Concerto, Bassoon Concerto], *Musical Opinion* (November 1989), p. 383; M.E.O., [review of Bassoon Concerto, Violin Concerto, *Hommage à Chopin*], *The Gramophone* (July 1990), p. 218; J. B., [review of Bassoon concerto, Violin concerto, *Hommage à Chopin*], *The Gramophone* (July 1990), p. 300; Martin Anderson, [review of *Sinfonia Sacra, Arbor Cosmica*, Violin Concerto, *Hommage a Chopin*, Bassoon Concerto], *Tempo* (December 1990), pp. 50–51; Malcolm Miller, 'Panufnik's String Quartet No. 3', *Tempo* (June 1991), p. 53.

[22] See Malcolm Miller, 'Panufnik's String Quartet...', *op. cit.*, p. 53.

[23] See Martin Anderson, [review of *Sinfonia sacra*...], *op. cit.*, p. 51.

[24] See Calum MacDonald, 'Panufnik 9...', *op. cit.*, pp. 107–108.

[25] Martin Anderson, [review of *Sinfonia sacra*...], *op. cit.*, p. 51.

[26] See Stephen Johnson, 'Lines, Colours and Textures', *The Gramophone* (July 1990), p. 177.

this music he quotes Panufnik's musical interpreters. Observations made by Mark Stephenson, the conductor of the group "London Musici", are quite interesting. He basically recognises colours, melodies and the powerful atmosphere in Panufnik's music. The structure of works is simple but effective. But "a strong feeling of suffering in his music"[27] is even more important than a structure alone. This kind of expression is, according to the conductor, difficult to apprehend, which is the reason why works like Violin Concerto are not as popular as they should.

As mentioned before, two large analytical articles appeared in the 80s beside reviews and interviews. Harold Truscott, known from his earlier publications on Panufnik's music, is the author of both[28]. Like Johnson, Truscott believes that non-musical ideas are helpful in the creative process, but are not necessary in the process of perception, hence he neglects the link between Panufnik's diagrams and his music. Basing his views on aesthetic experiences and analyses, the author proclaims Panufnik as an internationally renowned composer[29]. His musical language is individual, modern and traditional at the same time. The expression of his works is personal to him. This music is solemn, even sad. The author assigns this fact to Panufnik's way of thinking, to his ability to sympathize. Panufnik is regarded by Truscott as a symphonic composer. Andrzej Panufnik and Robert Simpson are declared to be the best such composers in the 20th century. Truscott proves wrong all earlier opinions reproaching Panufnik's symphonies for the lack of organic development[30]. He concludes: "This output is a remarkable achievement by any standards, a superb exhibition of symphonic thought (...)"[31].

After Panufnik's death, critics and musicologists again started to write about him. In 1991 two essays appeared[32], and one year

---

[27] *Ibidem.*

[28] See Harold Truscott, 'The Achievements of Andrzej Panufnik', *Tempo* (December 1987), pp. 7–12; Harold Truscott, 'The Symphonies of Andrzej Panufnik', *The Musical Times* (July 1989), pp. 390–393.

[29] See Harold Truscott, 'The Achievements...', *op. cit.*, p. 7.

[30] When Calcum MacDonald writes about *Sinfonia della Speranza* he formulates that Panufnik is putting aside all kinds of organic development normally associated with the symphony, in favour of introducing new ones. According to the author these are: tendency to compose discreet blocks of sound and structure.

[31] Harold Truscott, 'The Symphonies...', *op. cit.*, p. 393.

[32] See John Warnaby, 'Andrzej Panufnik', *Musical Opinion* (December 1991), p. 433; [no author]: 'Obituaries', *The Gramophone* (January 1992), p. 26.

later—two reviews: from "the Panufnik Memorial Concert"[33] and from a new record from "Conifer"[34]. Among reviewed works the critics liked Concerto for Piano and Orchestra the least, Symphony No. 9 and Cello Concerto were described as superb and Symphony No. 10 made the greatest impact. For Calum MacDonald this work even marks the climax of Panufnik's symphonic works. In his opinion Symphony No. 10 is the culmination of Panufnik's harmonic thinking and an example of the perfect structure developing organically. It ends with the fragment which is "some of the most personal and profoundly moving music Panufnik ever wrote"[35]. Panufnik's death made musicologists re-consider his music and his position in the 20th-century music. They all agree that Panufnik did not receive as much attention as he deserved. But when it comes to assessing his work, music critics are less unanimous. Some believe Panufnik is one of the most interesting individuals in the 20th century. Only one critic—John Warnaby—forms his opinion reservedly, acknowledging that Panufnik is a good composer but possibly from the second league due to the lack of certain abilities which for example Witold Lutosławski had[36]. In the following years, there were no publications on Panufnik's music. Only Bernard Jacobson wrote about Panufnik in his book from 1996: *A Polish Renaissance*[37]. This title is dedicated to the most prominent 20th century Polish composers: Lutosławski, Panufnik, Penderecki, Górecki, and two chapters are allotted to Panufnik. One chapter includes the biography of the composer while the other deals with the comparison between Panufnik and Lutosławski. The last chapter is full of interesting remarks. The author starts by stating that both composers are modernists, and then he tries to trace similarities and differences between them. He takes into consideration their attitude towards tonality, notation, musical tradition and the relation between a composer and the public. Each of these points is fully discussed: for example the passage about the technique concludes: "a Panufnik work is impressively 'all of a piece', whereas a Lutosławski work is no less impressively a fusion of contrasting, even conflicting, ele-

---

[33] See Calum MacDonald, [review of Cello Concerto, Symphony No. 10], *Tempo* (September 1992), pp. 27–28.

[34] See David Wordsworth, [review of Symphony No. 9, Piano Concerto], *Tempo* (September 1992), p. 58.

[35] See Calum MacDonald, [review of Cello Concerto...], *op. cit.*, p. 28.

[36] See John Warnaby, 'Andrzej Panufnik...', *op. cit.*

[37] See Bernard Jacobson, *A Polish Renaissance* (London: Phaidon Press, 1996).

ments"[38]. The last pages of this chapter are dedicated to Panufnik's lesser known music. Finally Jacobson says: "Panufnik's music never sounds remotely like that of any of those forerunners or colleagues, for each of these resources and methods is used in an entirely individual way, and in the furtherance of an entirely personal artistic vision"[39]. As a side-note it can also be said that Paul Griffiths (who previously wrote critically about Panufnik's work) did not bother to mention the name of the Polish composer in his book *Modern Music. A Concise History*[40].

The above presented documents concerning the reception of Panufnik's music in the Great Britain enable us to draw some conclusions concerning its history. Firstly it can be concluded that acceptance of Panufnik's music has gradually increased. In the 50s, only the personality of the composer awoke interest, in the 60s actual analysis appeared in just one periodical only. In the 70s although the interest was extended, the critics did not concur in evaluating new compositions. The 80s (until one year after the composer's death) shows itself to be the period of the most intense interest in Panufnik. There are, in my opinion, two groups of writers as far as the aesthetics of the reception is concerned. Some never saw any value in his music, e.g. Paul Griffiths, but others fought from the beginning for the appreciation of his work, e.g. Stephen Walsh, Calum MacDonald, Harold Truscott. In time there were more and more supporters, but they also differed in some aspects. Their sets of priorities as regards Panufnik's characteristic features are ordered differently, and they disagree about the ultimate significance of Panufnik's music. Moreover, some are "frightened" by the complicated texture and cannot think of anything else except the link between music and Panufnik's diagrams, while the others ignore the source of the inspiration and concentrate on what they can hear and experience. Despite these differences both critics and musicologists view Panufnik's work similarly. They underline its original expression, talk about it in the categories of solemnity, sympathy, even suffering. Other important issues are: moderate modernism in this music, its connection with Polish music, comparison with Lutosławski's work and acknowledgement of Panufnik's role in 20th-century music.

Translated by Anna G. Piotrowska

---

[38] *Ibidem*, p. 107.

[39] *Ibidem*, p. 122.

[40] See Paul Griffiths, *Modern Music. A Concise History*. Second edition (London, 1994).

Andrzej Panufnik's Reception
in the United States

Ray Robinson

... my nerves would crack totally if I stayed on; I was on the point of
mental breakdown; I had to burst out of [this] prison, whatever dangers lay
outside. I not only needed peace and freedom for myself in order to compose,
but it was vital that someone should alert the Western world to the sufferings
of the Poles. I could achieve nothing more in Warsaw, in my own work or
for my fellow composers; but perhaps by escaping and making a noise in
the outside world I might be of service to my colleagues, describing our
plight to the free press, possibly bringing outside pressure to help those still
in the trap.[1]

Prologue

My initial contact with the music of Andrzej Panufnik took place in
February 1970 when I met with the legendary conductor Leopold
Stokowski (1882–1977) to ask him to conduct a concert at the
festivities surrounding my inauguration as the fourth president of
Westminster Choir College. At this meeting he indicated that he
would accept my invitation on one condition. When I asked him what
that condition might be, he replied:

That we include a world premiere on the program![2]

He then went on to identify the composer and work to be
performed.

There is a wonderful Polish composer now living in England who has
written a piece entitled *Universal Prayer*. He is a conductor as well as a

---

[1] Andrzej Panufnik, *Composing Myself* (London: Methuen, 1987), p. 230.

[2] Interview given by Leopold Stokowski to Ray Robinson, New York, February 20,
1970.

composer. It is a work for all religions. I would like to conduct this work at your inauguration concert![3]

... This was my special introduction to the music of Andrzej Panufnik and, I might add, the start of a joyful and rewarding thirty-year journey leading to this study of the reception of his music in the United States.

Commissions and premieres in the United States (1949–72)

The Stokowski factor

Without question Leopold Stokowski was the single most important musical influence in Panufnik's early American reception. As illustrated by the story just related he was always "marketing" the music of contemporary composers, and sometimes this penchant for the New Music got him in trouble with conservative American audiences and critics.

Born in London of Polish and Irish parentage, Stokowski first came to the United States in 1905 to accept a position as organist and choirmaster at St. Bartholomew's Church, New York, which he held for three years before returning to Europe to make his conducting debut in Paris (1908). He returned to the States one year later and was appointed conductor of the Cincinnati Symphony Orchestra (1909–12) at the age of twenty-seven. In the 24-year period 1912–36 he built the Philadelphia Orchestra into one of the finest symphonic ensembles in the world. Following a season as conductor of the NBC Radio Symphony (1941–42), he was joined by Arturo Toscanini as co-conductor for the next two years (1942–44). He was appointed principal guest conductor of the New York Philharmonic (1947–49) and co-conductor with Bruno Walter, Dimitri Mitropoulos and Charles Munch during the 1949–50 season. Five seasons of guest conducting followed before he assumed the position of music director of the Houston Symphony (1955–60). He went on to conduct *Turandot* at the Metropolitan Opera (1960) and to create the American Symphony Orchestra (1962) with which he gave the first complete performance of Charles Ives' Fourth Symphony (1965). With his movie star appeal—he founded the Hollywood Bowl Symphony Orchestra (1945) and appeared in the original version of Walt Disney's film *Fantasia*— he was the ideal person to create an American audience for Panufnik's

---

[3] Stokowski interview, 1970.

music.[4] In the period 1949–1972 Stokowski conducted six of the composer's works with six different orchestral ensembles. Three were world premiere performances of works he had commissioned.

Works introduced by Stokowski in the United States

TRAGIC OVERTURE (composed, 1942; reconstructed, 1945; revised, 1955; first performed in America, 1949)

It was under Stokowski that the first performance of a Panufnik work took place in the United States. The site was New York's Carnegie Hall; the year was 1949; and the work was *Tragic Overture*. This American premiere occurred five years before the composer's defection to England and six years before the work's first London performance. At the time Stokowski was serving a two-year appointment (1947–49) as principal guest conductor of the New York Philharmonic. He programmed the *Overture* for concerts on March 24 and 25, 1949, six years after the work's 1943 world premiere at the Warsaw Conservatory.[5] With the Second World War still a vivid memory, the poignant circumstances that led to the composition and dedication of the work resonated with war-weary Americans.

While *Tragic Overture* did not prove to be Panufnik's most popular work in America (*Sinfonia Sacra* would hold that distinction), the very fact that it was the first of the composer's works to receive a performance in the New World was significant in itself. It proved to be a very important beginning to Panufnik's reception. Panufnik's own written description of the genesis of the Overture was circulated by Boosey & Hawkes, the composer's publisher, and initiated the process of creating an identity for the composer in America. It also revealed how deeply the composer felt about his native Poland.

> In April [1943], the Germans started their destruction of the [Jewish] ghetto. Day after day, week after week, we heard the hammer of machine guns. From my window, in anguish, I saw smoke from the burning houses, and sometimes low-flying German aircraft spewing out their bombs in broad

---

[4] 'Stokowski, Leopold', *The New Grove Dictionary of Music and Musicians,* ed. Stanley Sadie., Vol. 24 (London: Macmillan, 2001), pp. 425–426.

[5] Andrzej Panufnik, *Composing Myself, op. cit.,* p. 351; Program of The Philharmonic-Symphony Society of New York, concerts on March 24 and 25, 1949. The program included, in addition to Panufnik's *Tragic Overture,* Virgil Thomson's *Wheat Field at Noon,* Jean Sibelius' Concerto for Violin and Orchestra in D minor (performed by John Corigliano), Aram Khachaturian's *Music from the Ballet 'Gayaneh',* and Johannes Brahms' Symphony in F Major, No. 3, Op. 90.

daylight. I would sit in my little room, turning away in horror from its rooftop view of yet another pillar of black smoke from the ghetto, yet another salvo of gunfire. I hadn't composed any new music in a year, and my helplessness and inactivity were more painful than action. In order to hold in check the emotions which I felt were threatening my sanity, I decided to write a *Tragic Overture*, and began with the firm intention that it would be totally abstract, with no literary implications.

I returned to my search of a year before [1942] for a new musical language, rooted in the ideal of a stringent economy of means of expression, and chose a sequence of just four notes which would run from the beginning of the Overture right through to the end. It was my intention to explore this four-note cell to the very limit. It might be transposed, augmented, sometimes inverted, but I must strictly guard throughout the entire work the same intervals between notes (minor third, major second and minor second), always within a framework of repeated rhythmic patterns.

Once the work was finished, however, I realized that my intellectual disciplines had failed to control my unconscious, that the *Overture* was interspersed with startlingly onomatopoeic passages—for example, the sound of a falling bomb (percussion); the soft engine noise of an aeroplane disappearing in the distance (trombones' glissando); a volley of machine guns (the burst of percussion in the final bars; the final chord shrieked out by the full orchestra, an agonized wail of despair.

There is no question that his gripping eye-witness account of the destruction of the Warsaw "ghetto" and this first public description of one of the most distinctive elements of his original music language would prove influential in creating an initial image of the composer and his music.[6] When he did defect on July 14, 1954, the event attracted significant publicity in the Western press as is evidenced by two front page news articles that appeared in *The New York Times* on August 23 and 24, 1954.[7]

> **SYMPHONY OF PEACE** *(composed 1951; withdrawn and incorporated into Sinfonia elegiaca, 1963; first performance in America, 1955)*

It was five years before another of Panufnik's compositions would be heard in the United States. *Old Polish Suite* (composed 1950, revised

---

[6] Andrzej Panufnik, *Composing Myself, op. cit.*, pp. 118–20 [paraphrased from the original text].

[7] Four articles about the composer and his defection from Poland appeared in *The New York Times* in July and August 1954. The news stories—'Polish Composer Flees to Britian' (July 16, 1954) and 'Composer Who Fled Says Poles Despair' (July 25, 1954)—were published first in July. Then the two articles authored by the composer appeared on consecutive days on August 23 and 24, 1954.

1955), a work for string orchestra, received its first America reading on January 23, 1954 in Philadelphia with the University of Pennsylvania String Orchestra under the direction of Arthur Cohn. However the very next year (1955) the later to be withdrawn *Symphony of Peace* (1951) was programmed by Stokowski, along with *Tragic Overture*, on a regular subscription series concert of the Detroit Symphony. This concert, which took place on February 20, 1955, also marked Panufnik's initial meeting with Stokowski, as well as the first of thirteen trips the composer would make to America over the 35-year period, 1955–90. (See Table 1, "Andrzej Panufnik's visits to the United States") Occurring just eight months after his defection from Poland, this maiden voyage to the New World made a profound impression on the composer.

> My eyes were wide on my first drive through an American city, trying to take in all the new sights and impressions. The snow-covered streets were full of cars, but the pavements were empty: it seemed that everyone was moving on wheels. I regretted that I was too tired to explore further that night, but planned to walk miles the following day.[8]

Stokowski, who at that point in his career was between permanent appointments, was serving as guest conductor of the Detroit Symphony. Whatever preconceptions Panufnik had about the venerable maestro were allayed in their first meeting in a Detroit hotel.

> I had seen many photographs of him, and the famous Disney film of *Fantasia*, from which I had gained the impression of a tall man, with a proud head carriage and the face of a dreamer, romantic and at the same time rather arrogant. The man who walked into my hotel room was of less than medium height with a slightly stooping posture, his head bowed forward, a mild expression on his face. He was dressed in tweed like an English country gentleman. His voice was not fierce or loud as I had imagined, but soft, gentle, and almost exaggeratedly polite.[9]

The choice of Detroit for this introduction of Panufnik and his music to a mid-American concert audience was obviously a shrewd decision on the part of Stokowski. After the war, more Poles lived in Detroit than in the whole of Warsaw! There were, in the words of the composer,

> Polish churches, shops selling Polish food, Polish newspapers [Perfect Polish continued to be spoken by whole generations born in America, and, in order to earn a living, even a few black Americans have found it essential to learn Polish too!][10]

---

[8] Andrzej Panufnik, *Composing Myself, op. cit.*, p. 251.

[9] *Ibid.*, p. 251.

Panufnik's recent defection from Poland for political reasons and the ethnic make-up of the audience virtually guaranteed a sympathetic reception of the *Symphony of Peace.*

The text by Jarosław Iwaszkiewicz,[11] incorporated by the composer into the musical fabric of the first and third movements of the *Symphony of Peace*, was also a powerful reminder to Americans of the need for peace and tranquility in the world. While the poem was originally selected by the composer for its "Social Realist" text, this fact went over the heads of both the audience and the critics who covered the concerts.

---

[10] *Ibid.*, p. 250.

[11] The text of the poem by Jarosław Iwaszkiewicz is in three parts:

Lamentoso

On an autumn evening among these ruins, flames were
rekindled. Flames burning on the graves. Above the ruins,
above the graves, resounds the mournful lament of mothers
and children. A wordless cry: pain has no words. That cry
is that of the battlefield.

Drammatico

But revolt bursts forth against passive suffering. The right
to live and fight for life is stronger than lamentation. Sometimes
to fight—is to live. Laments and the resistance of the weak—is
too little this with which to oppose the horrors of war. To fight
for peace, to defend peace, the will of peace must be born!

Solenne

Not like the dove-wing calmly descending
Not like the seasons in sure succession
Not like the lightning night's curtain rending
                    Comes peace unending.
Not like the summer flower-scent expending
Nor on the storm-cloud and thunder riding
Nor form the sky a b right rainbow bending
                    Comes peace unending.
But from our will alone it's conceiving
And with the blood of our hearts be nourished
Grow like the corn in sweat of the striving
                    Peace for the living.
Bright shall it spring a flame never dying
From hands and minds to one purpose plying
And from the hearts of all people crying:
                    Peace! Give the World Peace!

The "Peace Symphony" is a tremendous creation written by a man who knows his idiom and writes with profound conviction. When the chorus and orchestra ended in a glorious paean of sound ("Give peace, Give Peace")—there was a spontaneous ovation from the audience.[12]

On his way home to England Panufnik stopped in New York where he was interviewed by *The New York Times* reporter Howard Taubman.[13] In the ensuing published article the circumstances surrounding the Polish reception of the *Symphony of Peace*, and the issues that were decisive in his decision to defect from his native Poland, were revealed.[14]

SINFONIA ELEGIACA [Symphony No. 2] (Composed 1957; revised 1966; first performed in America, 1957)

Houston was the next stop in Stokowski's conducting career and the music of Andrzej Panufnik traveled with him. Among the many contemporary works he led in his five-year tenure with that orchestra (1955–60), *Sinfonia Elegiaca* (Symphony No. 2) was commissioned and premiered by the orchestra on November 11, 1957. It was clear from the articles that appeared in the press prior to the concert, and the reviews that followed, that the reception of the Symphony in Houston would be overshadowed by the controversy that was brewing over Stokowski's "excessive" programming of contemporary music.

The Houston Symphony Orchestra was way out there in the lonelier void during much of its concert Monday evening. As you know, the announced intention of Leopold Stokowski to pursue 'the music of the future' with the resources of Houston this winter, to which end he has made up a season program for the orchestra representing contemporary composers in a ratio of about 50 per cent. This affair at the Music Hall showed something of what that could mean. The contemporaries had 100 per cent of the program.[15]

Oblivious to the criticism of the press, Stokowski's response to Panufnik's second symphony was one of unbridled enthusiasm. In a telegram to the composer following the American premiere, he offered his own encouraging review of the concert.

TONITE WE PERFORMED YOUR POWERFUL AND PROFOUNDLY MOVING *SINFONIA ELEGIACA*. AUDIENCE'S AND ORCHESTRA'S RE-

---

[12] August Maekelberghe, 'Detroit', *Musical Courier* (March 1955).

[13] Andrzej Panufnik, *Composing Myself, op. cit.*, p. 252.

[14] Howard Taubman, 'Troubles of a Pole', *The New York Times* (March 13, 1955).

[15] Hubert Roussel, "Symphony Fired Into Space; Heard Barking In Contemporary List," *Houston Post* (November 12, 1957).

ACTION DEEPLY EMOTIONAL. SHALL REPEAT TOMORROW. THANK
YOU FOR UNFORGETTABLE MUSICAL EXPERIENCE – LEOPOLD
STOKOWSKI.[16]

According to Panufnik, the Houston performance came as a
complete surprise to him. It seemed that, without notifying the
composer in advance, his publisher (Boosey & Hawkes) had sent a
copy of the score to Stokowski, who was looking for new works for
the Houston Symphony to perform. Stokowski reacted promptly and
enthusiastically by slipping it into a regular subscription program
without even informing the composer.[17]

What the Houston audience heard on November 11, 1957 was a
recycled version of the *Symphony of Peace* but without the work's
"Socialist-Realist texts" and the "politically-charged context" in which
it had been originally composed.[18] The revised work extracted material
from only the first and second movements of the *Symphony of Peace*;
sections from the third movement (*Solenne*) were later incorporated
into a separate work for children's voices: *Invocation for Peace* (1972).

Because of the heavily-biased attitude toward Stokowski's programming, the press totally ignored the musical craftsmanship and
the poignancy of the Symphony's message. The subsequent *Houston
Post* review was superficial at best.

> Panufnik, though described as one of Poland's 'most advanced' composers,
> turned out to be rather conventional and quite pretty in his short *Sinfonia
> Elegiaca*.[19]

ELEGY, and other works for dance

Although first introduced to American audiences as a concert work,
Sinfonia Elegiaca became the musical score for a popular ballet in
1967, thanks to the brilliant choreography of Gerald Arpino (b. 1928).
Entitled "Elegy," the dance work incorporated music from the first
and third movements of the Symphony. It was the first concert work
of Panufnik's to be selected as the score for a ballet.[20]

The setting for the ballet, an American Civil War battlefield, was
poignant indeed. As the muffled drums of a death tattoo beat out, a

---

[16] Andrzej Panufnik, *Composing Myself, op. cit.*, pp. 257–58.

[17] *Ibid.*, p. 258.

[18] Andrzej Panufnik, *Impulse and Design in my music* (London: Boosey & Hawkes,
1974), p. 4.

[19] 'Symphony Fired Into Space'.

[20] Andrzej Panufnik, *Composing Myself, op. cit.*, p. 322.

Confederate soldier, under escort, made his way to the barren place of execution. The Union guns are raised for the last shot. The prisoner stands blindfolded facing his death, and remembers his wife and two children. But as the dream fades, the shots of the Union soldiers ring-out through the morning, and the man slumps to his death.

"Elegy" was premiered on April 12, 1967 in New York by the Joffrey Ballet and elicited the following review by Clive Barnes of *The New York Times*:

> This somber score, with its grave and simple measures and broad emotional span, could have been written for the theater, and makes an excellent partner to Mr. Arpino's ballet.

In another New York performance, on September 13, 1967, the same critic wrote:

> Mr. Panufnik may be a composer whom the ballet should use more often. He has a very individual voice and a lyric gift that choreographers in search of fairly conventional yet original music might easily welcome.[21]

And many took this advice. In the ensuing years seven dance companies would offer American productions based on Panufnik's concert works: Dancers Maxiliano Zomosa (1967) with *Sinfonia Elegiaca*, Ballet West (Salt Lake City) (1975) with *Autumn Music*, the Houston Ballet (1978) with *Rhapsody*, the Martha Graham Company in New York (1982) with *Nocturne*, the Batsheva Dance Company (Israel) in New York (1983) with *Sinfonia Sacra*, the New York City Ballet (1987) with *Sinfonia Mistica* (Symphony No. 6), and the Washington Ballet (1993) with the Violin Concerto in a dance work entitled "Stop It!"

SINFONIA SACRA [Symphony No. 3] (Composed 1963; first performed in America, 1965)

Interestingly, *Sinfonia Sacra* (Symphony No. 3) was not commissioned by an American orchestra nor premiered in the United States, in spite of its tremendous success in this country. Nevertheless it did owe its existence and musical success to two American sources: The Kościuszko Foundation of New York City and conductor Leopold Stokowski. The work was conceived in the fall of 1960, while the composer was on an extended visit to the United States. As a result of a meeting with Stephen Mizwa, the President, and the subsequent

---

[21] Clive Barnes, 'Dance: Arpino's 'Elegy',' *The New York Times* (April 13, 1967); Clive Barnes, 'Dance: New Joffrey Asset', *The New York Times* (September 15, 1967).

action by the Foundation Board, Panufnik was granted a ten-month stipend that allowed him to concentrate on the composition of the Symphony in a period when he was without a permanent appointment. The work was completed in 1963.

Shortly thereafter, Panufnik submitted the new Symphony to the Prince Ranier III of Monaco International Competition for Composers, where it won First Prize out of 133 entries (from 38 countries) in the orchestral division. As a condition of the award, it was performed first in Monte Carlo. Then it was heard in Paris at a special United Nations Day concert, and later in Lisbon, Buenos Aires, Rochester (NY) and Birmingham (England) prior to its Carnegie Hall performance on December 10, 1966.[22]

Winning the Prince Ranier Competition marked an important turning point in Panufnik's career as a composer. While he would receive the award again in 1983, for his entire compositional output,[23] this signal achievement gave the composer instant credibility and subsequently led to other performances and commissions.

Sinfonia Sacra (1963) had its American premiere under Stokowski in Rochester (New York) on February 11, 1965, but it received performances in New York City three other times: First by the American Symphony under Stokowski (December 10, 1966), then the Philadelphia Orchestra with William Smith (February 29, 1974) and finally at Hunter College (May 14, 1994). The American Symphony performance under Stokowski drew the wrath of *The New York Times* critic, Howard Klein, not because it was a bad work, nor because it was a sloppy performance, but for the description of the terms of the commission, written by the Foundation's president Stephen Mizwa, and prominently displayed in the program notes of the concert. Mizwa's narrative seemed innocent enough.

> We made only two suggestions to the composer: First, that it [the Sinfonia] not be a concoction of capophonous dissonance in which so many of our contemporary composers indulge; second, that in some way it be tied up with Polish historic tradition.

But Klein took great exception to the Foundation's guidelines:

> A shocking statement, in face of the traditional love of freedom of the Poles... As it turned out, there was dissonance and percussive noise and,

---

[22] Stephen P. Mizwa, *The Kościuszko Foundation. Monthly News Letter* 21:2 (October 1966), p. 1.

[23] *Andrzej Panufnik, Biography and List of Works* (London: Boosey & Hawkes, 1994), p. 3.

since Mr. Panufnik based his four-movement Sinfonia on the old hymn, *Bogurodzica*, there was a tie with tradition.[24]

In spite of the review, Stokowski expressed great enthusiasm for the work during a New York radio interview at the time the Symphony was broadcast.

> I regard this [*Sinfonia sacra*] as one of the greatest compositions of Polish art, with Szymanowski, Chopin, and all other great Polish composers... I greatly admire Panufnik, both the composer and the conductor. His gifts as conductor and as composer make him a really unique person in Polish music. I have conducted the *Sinfonia Sacra* in other places and always the reception has been tremendously enthusiastic.[25]

Following a New York performance by the Philadelphia Orchestra six years later (December 2, 1974), the noted *New York Times* critic Harold C. Schonberg echoed Stokowski's enthusiasm.

> We don't hear much of the music of Andrzej Panufnik in this country... It is not modern music, as modernism goes these days... There is a great deal to admire about the work. Panufnik has handled the various elements with a great deal of skill, and that includes brilliant-sounding orchestration. It is an effective score throughout, one that deserves repeated hearings.[26]

Although *Sinfonia Sacra* received its first east coast performance two years after it was completed, it is curious that it was not performed in Minneapolis (where there was a prominent Polish conductor, Stanisław Skrowaczewski) until 1973 or in Chicago (where there was a large Polish population and a prominent Eastern European conductor and naturalized British citizen, Sir Georg Solti) until 1982, nearly twenty years after its completion. It was even more embarrassing that the music critic who covered the Chicago premiere on November 11, 1982 was forced to write: "None of Panufnik's music has ever been played by the Chicago Symphony." He then went on to give the work and its performance a glowing review.

> One could not fail to draw a parallel between the feelings so intensely expressed by this music and the political struggle and uncertainty that have become emblematic of Panufnik's homeland throughout the century. Yet the symphony makes a strong and deeply moving effect through its musical

---

[24] Quoted in: Howard Klein, 'Music: A Polish Program', *The New York Times* (December 12, 1966).

[25] Leopold Stokowski, manuscript of radio broadcast text, New York (broadcast date, December 10, 1966) [*Sinfonia Sacra*].

[26] Harold C. Schonberg, 'First Philadelphia Orchestra performance in New York', *The New York Times* (December 4, 1974).

means alone... This is music that knows well the cruelty of the powerful,
but it also knows the power of faith to ease the suffering of the oppressed...
The composer received an ovation of such magnitude he seemed overwhelmed,
though happily so.[27]

The New York and Chicago reviews were prophetic of its success:
The reception of *Sinfonia Sacra* would be remarkable. It has turned
out to be Panufnik's most popular work with America orchestras. To
date, it has had 46 performances in the United States. (See Table 2,
"Panufnik Works Most Often Performed In the United States")

KATYŃ EPITAPH *(composed 1967; revised 1969; first performed in America, 1967)*

Following the success of *Sinfonia Sacra*, Stokowski commissioned
another Panufnik work for the American Symphony Orchestra, and
it received its premiere on November 17, 1968, at New York's
Carnegie Hall. *Katyń Epitaph*, which followed in the tradition of
Sinfonia Elegiaca and *Sinfonia Sacra*, reminded the audience of yet
another Polish tragedy of the mid-twentieth century: The Katyń Forest
Massacre of 1940. The score contained the following poignant note
by the composer.

> This piece is dedicated to the memory of 15,000 defenseless Polish
> prisoners-of-war bestially murdered in Katyń Forest in Russia during the
> second world war, by undiscovered and unpunished hands.[28]

Following the premiere, Winthrop Sargeant, writing in *The New
Yorker*, found the work to be

> one of the most original works that has recently come to my attention...
> I hope to hear more of Panufnik's music. It is expressive and at the same
> time highly individualistic.[29]

In spite of its tragic subject matter, its references to "Old Polish
music", and its expressive musical language, *Katyń Epitaph* failed to
catch on with American audiences and conductors. To this point it
has received only one other performance in the United States: The
Northwestern University Philharmonia programmed it along with
Heroic Overture as part of a "Polish Music Festival" held at the
university on November 22, 1998.

---

[27] John von Rhein, 'CSO's introduction of Panufnik shows solidarity with the
Poles', *Chicago Tribune* (November 12, 1982).

[28] Andrzej Panufnik, quoted in the American Symphony Orchestra program, New
York, Carnegie Hall (November 17, 1968).

[29] Winthrop Sargeant, '*Katyń Epitaph*', *The New Yorker* (November 1968).

UNIVERSAL PRAYER (Composed 1968–69; first performed in America, 1970)

The last Panufnik work that Stokowski would conduct in America was *Universal Prayer*, a moving setting of a poem by Alexander Pope (1688–1744). One of Panufnik's more enigmatic works, it reflects two of his personal interests: Religion ("Although I practice no religion I was and am interested in all religions") and the local life and history of the area in which he lived in England, Twickenham on the banks of the Thames in south-west London. It seems that Panufnik's affinity for Alexander Pope stemmed partly from the fact that the poet once lived near the composer's English home. The *New York Times* review, though brief and to the point, was encouraging to Panufnik and confirmed the work's positive reception.

> The composer's sense of word-sound and meaning was impeccable. Beyond that he translated Pope's fervent text into the grandest, most awesome kind of music.[30]

Stokowski conducted the world premiere on May 24, 1970 in the vast Cathedral of St. John the Divine, which was well filled [an audience of approximately 5,000 people attended] for the first performance. Two additional readings were led by Stokowski in the same year: The afore-mentioned Princeton performance (October 19) [which did not turn out to be the world premiere as Stokowski had indicated to me the previous February, but was nevertheless heard as promised by the conductor], and at New York's St. Patrick's Cathedral (November 29). Both drew capacity audiences.

By 1972, the year Stokowski returned to his native England, ten of Panufnik's works had been performed in America and he had conducted six of them. While his contacts with and support of the composer would continue in London with additional performances and recordings, it was now the task of other conductors to introduce and nurture Panufnik's works in the United States. Seiji Ozawa, Georg Solti, Gerard Schwarz, Panufnik, and even his Polish colleague Kazimierz Kord would carry on Stokowski's tradition.

---

[30] Theodore Strongin, '*Universal Prayer* Led by Stokowski', *The New York Times* (May 25, 1970).

Commissions and premieres in the United States (1972–1990)

In the years 1972 to 1990, Panufnik received five additional American commissions. The two most prestigious came respectively from the Boston Symphony (*Sinfonia Votiva*) and the Chicago Symphony (Symphony No. 10). Both contributed to the centennial celebrations of these distinguished orchestras. The other three were invitations from the Music Today Players (*Arbor Cosmica*), Milwaukee Chamber Orchestra (Bassoon Concerto) and the New York Chamber Symphony (*Harmony*). The significance of each of these commissions was that they were introduced to American audiences by major conductors and well-known musical organizations: Seiji Ozawa with the Boston Symphony, Georg Solti and the Chicago Symphony, Gerard Schwarz with the Music for Today Players and the New York Chamber Symphony, and the composer himself with the Milwaukee Chamber Players. The high quality of these performances proved to be a positive influence in Panufnik's reception. (See Table 3, "Panufnik Works Commissioned in the United States")

SINFONIA VOTIVA (composed 1980–81; revised 1984; first performed in America, 1982)

Panufnik's contribution to the centennial celebration of the Boston Symphony was *Sinfornia Votiva* (his 8th Symphony). Completed on August 15, 1981, four months before the imposition of martial law in Poland, the premiere took place in Boston on January 28, 1982. It was also performed at Tanglewood, the orchestra's summer home in the Berkshire Mountains, on September 1, 1982, again under Ozawa. Like many of the works that preceded it, the Symphony carried an extra-musical message: It was dedicated to the Black Madonna of Czestochowa.[31] Ironically the composer received word of the Solidarity union uprisings at the Gdańsk (Poland) shipyards just as he was beginning the piece, which only added to the emotional quality of this important commission. The musical message the composer sought to convey with this work was to pay tribute to the great orchestra and musicians for whom it was composed.[32]

Writing about *Sinfonia Votiva* at the time of its premiere, Steven Ledbetter summarized what many American writers and music critics felt about Panufnik's art in the mid-1980s.

---

[31] Andrzej Panufnik, in: *Boston Symphony Orchestra: Hundredth Birthday Season*, January 28, 1982, p. 28.
[32] *Ibid.*

His [Panufnik's] music seems always to have behind it an underlying "impulse". His works are not, at bottom mere abstract patterns, however striking may be the structural basis. They were composed with an expressive goal in mind—even a moral goal. His music responds to the ethical questions of our day and our century.[33]

ARBOR COSMICA (composed 1983; first performed in America, 1984)

One of the more intriguing works commissioned and premiered in the United States is *Arbor Cosmica*. Supported by the Koussevitzky Music Foundation, it received its first performance on November 14, 1984, under Gerard Schwarz at a Music Today concert at New York's Merkin Hall. The physical imagery for this work is identified by the composer as the tree.[34]

Scored for the somewhat unusual instrumentation of 12 solo strings (six violins, three violas, two cellos, and one contrabass), the orchestration evokes the tree's changing moods through the use of harmonics and glissandi, and by employing a variety of tempos, dynamic changes, articulations, vibrato speeds, and idiomatic bowing effects.

As the result of substantial publicity and an excellent performance the premiere was greeted with significant praise from the press. Terms and phrases like "impressive," "inspired," "quality," "worthy addition to string orchestra repertory" and "Panufnik's music has come into its own" literally jumped from the pages of New York's finest media publications. Bill Zakariasen's review in the *New York Daily News* spoke of the work's welcome addition to the repertory.

> In it [*Arbor Cosmica*] the composer expresses his great love for trees, and most of the time the string writing is evocative indeed, if mainly in an abstract manner. The slow, quiet sections (particularly movements seven and nine) are especially impressive. Altogether a worthy addition to string orchestra repertory, and it was splendidly performed.[35]

Andrew Porter, reporting for *The New Yorker* magazine, wrote of the work's paradoxical nature: It was a modern piece, but it did not sound that way.

---

[33] Steven Ledbetter, *Boston Symphony Orchestra: Hundredth Birthday Season*, January 28, 1982, p. 27.

[34] Andrzej Panufnik, quoted in: Andrew Porter, 'Arboresque', *The New Yorker*, December 10, 1984, p. 175.

[35] Bill Zakariasen, 'Another Music Today Series', *New York Daily News*, November 16, 1984.

No work of his [Panufnik's] has made a stronger first impression on me. *Arbor Cosmica* certainly fell as refreshment on ears wearied by the harmonic triteness of insistent minimalism or by the cloying reminiscences of neo-romanticism. It sounded new, and yet it is built on the traditional foundations of Western music: the twelve movements (or "Evocations") span the great circle of fifths, from C to F, that provide us with our twelve notes, and each movement ends with a tonic chord major and minor at once, with both thirds present.[36]

The British writer Nigel Osborne, who was also quoted in *The New Yorker* review, declared that the composer's music was now universally recognized.

After being rejected by the Stalinists, cast aside in the fever of modernism itself, and ignored in the flabby reaction that followed, Panufnik's music has now come into its own.[37]

And John Rockwell, writing in *The New York Times*, spoke of the work's musical quality.

The most newsworthy item on the program was a world premiere, of *Arbor Cosmica* by the 70-year-old Andrzej Panufnik... Mr. Panufnik's music was considered dangerously "formalistic" in Poland (this was before the outburst of Polish musical avant-gardism, just a few years after his departure). But in the West, he counts now as an idiosyncratic conservative, writing mostly consonant music for conventional instruments. But then again, since the tide of fashion is turning back toward accessibility, Mr. Panufnik's "conservativism" begins to look like the latest thing. Of course, in the longer run, all these trendy shifts in taste seem pretty ephemeral. What counts is quality, and Mr. Panufnik's music would seem to have that virtue; certainly *Arbor Cosmica* did.[38]

There is no question about the American reception of *Arbor Cosmica*; in all quarters it was considered an unequivocal success.

VIOLIN CONCERTO *(composed 1971; first performed in America, 1984)*

Four days after the premiere of *Arbor Cosmica* (November 18, 1984), Panufnik was in Princeton for the first American performance of his Violin Concerto. Composed originally for Yehudi Menuhin, and premiered at the 1972 City of London Music Festival, the Concerto

---

[36] Andrew Porter, 'Musical Events: Arboresque' (on *Arbor Cosmica*), *The New Yorker*, December 10, 1984, pp. 174–75.

[37] Quoted in: Andrew Porter, 'Musical Events: Arboresque', *The New Yorker*, December 10, 1984, p. 174–75.

[38] John Rockwell, 'Concert: Music Today Series at Goodman House' (on *Arbor Cosmica*), *The New York Times*, November 16, 1984.

is a work for solo violin and string orchestra. The British violinist Yfrah Neaman was the soloist with the Princeton Chamber Orchestra conducted by Portia Sonnenfeld. The review was enthusiastic, and Panufnik was present to savor the positive reception.

> The highlight of this concert was Andrzej Panufnik's Violin Concerto. Melodically, the concerto dealt largely with relationships of thirds and seconds around a definite tonal center, giving the music an almost tonal sense. His ideas were developed from a few carefully chosen motives which were molded into a clearly audible coherency, making the work both comprehensible and enjoyable. In the third movement, this melodic and harmonic matrix was fired with cross-rhythms and metric ambiguity, while in the second, it was given a contemplative, almost spiritual feeling.[39]

In the period between 1984 and 2000 the Concerto would have twelve other performances in the United States, and match the *Concertino for Timpani, Percussion and Strings* as the composer's third most performed work in America. (See Table 2).

CONCERTINO FOR TIMPANI, PERCUSSION AND STRINGS *(Composed 1980, first performed in America, 1981)*

With the exception of its American premiere on February 6, 1981, by Andre Previn and the Pittsburgh Symphony, and Panufnik's own performance on June 23, 1988 with the New York Chamber Symphony, the *Concertino for Timpani and Strings* has proven to be especially popular in America with collegiate-level groups like the Manhattan School of Music and the Peabody Conservatory percussion ensembles. This should not be surprising since the *Concertino* was commissioned by the Shell Young Musicians Scholarship and the London Symphony Orchestra as a competition piece for young percussion players. Because of its attractive musical language and its accessibility to student performers, it is anticipated that the *Concertino* will only grow in popularity with American performers and conductors in the future.

BASSOON CONCERTO (composed 1985; first performed in America, 1986)

Another of Panufnik's popular American compositions is the Bassoon Concerto (1986). Commissioned by the Polanki Polish Society of Milwaukee [The Polish Women's Cultural Club] for bassoonist Robert

---

[39] Lynn Arthur Koch, 'Contemporary Violin Concerto is the Highlight of Chamber Symphony's First '85–'86 Concert', *Princeton Town Topics* (November 21, 1984).

Thompson and the Milwaukee Chamber Orchestra, the Concerto is dedicated to and inspired by the Polish martyr Father Jerzy Popiełuszko, the Solidarity chaplain abducted and murdered in October 1984 by Polish security officers. Popiełuszko's plight is the subtext for the work's five movements.[40] But what is of special significance about this American premiere on May 18, 1986, in contrast to all others before it, is that it marked Panufnik's conducting debut in the United States. We will have more to say about Panufnik's reception as a conductor in the Epilogue of this paper.

The Concerto is scored for chamber orchestra, with flute, two clarinets and strings, and consists of five contrasting movements. The overall mood is dark and somber, focusing on the poignant fourth-movement aria, a kind of elegy featuring a long, folk-inspired melodic line that is periodically threatened by harsh interjections from the orchestra. The critic Lawrence B. Johnson described these qualities in the *Milwaukee Sentinel* review ('Bassoon Concerto is Too Demanding').

> Intense, stark, almost verbal in its dominant recitative style, the work makes equal demands on the soloist's virtuosity and dramatic skills. The concerto also taxes the listener—not so much by its harmonic language, which is fairly tame by contemporary standards, but rather by its almost relenting evocation of torment. Panufnik has painted psychological shadows nearly devoid of light, even at the close, when apparently he intends to convey hope. In purely musical terms, the result is a limited, repetitive vocabulary, rhetoric terse to a fault.[41]

While the composer insisted that the Concerto was an abstract work with no literary program, he seemed to contradict himself when he described the piece in the Milwaukee Chamber Orchestra program:

> ... in my music an echo—just an echo—of, say, the priest's patriotic sermon, his humble prayer, or even his last, fatal interrogation by the secret police before his tortured body was thrown into the reservoir by the Vistula river.[42]

It is interesting to note that both Milwaukee critics, while acknowledging the quality of the work and the fine performance, questioned the excessive technical demands the composer placed on Robert Thompson, the soloist.

---

[40] Andrzej Panufnik, quoted in the program of *The Milwaukee Chamber Orchestra*, May 18, 1986.

[41] Larwence B. Johnson, 'Bassoon Concerto is Too Demanding', *Milwaukee Sentinel*, May 19, 1986.

[42] Andrzej Panufnik, 'Concerto for Bassoon and Chamber Orchestra: Composer's Notes', [Program of the] *Milwaukee Chamber Orchestra*, May 18, 1986.

It carries a line charged with emotion through the first three movements, pathos in the fourth, and drama in the fifth. But the performance left one primary question unanswered: Is the bassoon capable of carrying the emotional weight Panufnik has given it?[43]

HARMONY—A POEM FOR CHAMBER ORCHESTRA
(composed, 1989; first performed in America, 1989)

Harmony was commissioned by New York's 92nd Street Y in honor of the composer's 75th birthday. It was completed in April and premiered on December 16, 1989 with the composer conducting the New York Chamber Symphony. The title refers partly to the geometric structure — not only to the vertical sound (harmony based on 8- and 9-note scales), but also to the horizontal sound (melodic lines constructed on two 3-note cells) as well as the use of two meters, of 4 and 3. It also relates to the "harmonious" balance of orchestral color: The composition is designed stereophonically, with dialogues between strings and woodwinds, both sections having equal significance.

The sub-title "Poem" refers to the poetic and emotional element. The work is dedicated to Camilla Panufnik, in recognition of the 25th anniversary of their marriage. Hence the composer's instructions to the performers to create a "warm, lyrical climate; all the instruments [are to]'sing' in *andante cantabile* throughout the work, as in a kind of Love Song."

This 18-minute work is scored for strings (a minimum of seventeen, a maximum of thirty-six) without double-basses and wood-winds (pairs of flutes, oboes, clarinets and bassoons). At the New York premiere the woodwinds sat as a group on the conductor's right—where the second violins or cellos might be placed in a traditional orchestral seating plan—creating an antiphonal effect as the sound emerged from the stage. Adding to the effect was the very slow tempo—the quarter-note at about MM=40, in a 4/4 and 3/4 metric structure.

In the program of the premiere, Joseph Horowitz wrote of the paradox one discovers in Panufnik's musical language which combines Romantic subject matter (titles from his catalog include *Invocation for Peace, Sinfonia Elegiaca, Tragic Overture* and *Universal Prayer*) with a penchant for spare, formal design.[44] This special kind of "Minimalism" is a fascinating aspect of this piece.

---

[43] Laurence B. Johnson, 'Bassoon Concerto is Too Demanding', *op. cit.*; James Chute, 'Entertainment', *The Milwaukee Journal*, May 19, 1986.

[44] Program of the *New York Chamber Symphony of the 92nd Street Y*, December 16, 1989, p. 4.

SYMPHONY NO. 10 *(composed, 1988; revised 1990; first performed in America, 1990)*

A tenth symphony is a great accomplishment for any composer, especially when so many of that composer's earlier works were destroyed by the ravages of war. Panufnik's "Tenth," his last American commission, was written for the Chicago Symphony Orchestra and performed as the first of eight works ordered for that Orchestra's centennial year. The Symphony received its first performance on February 1, 1990, with the composer on the podium.

Unlike Panufnik's previous works in this genre, the single-movement 10th bears no descriptive title. It is clear that the composer wishes the listener to consider it as "absolute music" and that is the spirit in which the music critics in Chicago approached the premiere.

> Thursday night, the eight composers who have yet to fulfill Chicago Symphony commissions in honor of the orchestra's centennial found themselves with a very tough act to follow. The occasion was the world premiere of Symphony No. 10 by Andrzej Panufnik, under the composer's own direction... No more auspicious means to honor a great symphony orchestra—also for that matter, a great composer—could have been imagined.

In the final paragraph of his review, John von Rhein made an interesting suggestion about a possible sub-title for this new work.

> Hearing the final section—its quietly flowing strings and harp evoking a vast stillness after the jagged rhythmic exertions of the middle pages—one cannot help but think of the recent relaxation of official controls on creative artists in Poland that is allowing Panufnik to return to his homeland for the first time since his departure in 1954. The music seems to carry a fervent (if implicit) message of reconciliation; one wonders if Panufnik had ever considered calling it "Sinfonia curativa," a symphony of healing.[45]

The National Philharmonic (formerly Warsaw Philharmonic) included Symphony No. 10 on the program of its seventeen-city tour of the United States in October and November 1993. Kazimierz Kord opened each concert with the Symphony, which was followed by the Rachmaninov's Concerto No. 1 in F-sharp minor for Piano and Orchestra (performed by Ruth Loredo) and Prokofiev's *Romeo and Juliet* (Selections from Suites Nos. 1 and 2, Op. 64). As a result of this tour the Symphony stands today as the composer's second most performed work in the United States. (See Table 2)

---

[45] John von Rhein, *Chicago Tribune*, February 2, 1990.

Panufnik's final appearance in the United States

The last of Panufnik's thirteen trips to the United States occurred at the end of April and the beginning of May, 1990, when he conducted the Seattle Symphony in his *Nocturne* and *Sinfonia Votiva*. These performances tool place on April 30 and May 1, 1990.

Epilogue

In spite of more than two hundred and fifty performances of thirty-five works, and with seven ballet productions based on his concert works to his credit, Panufnik is still not as well know to American concert-goers as he deserves to be. It is a rather curious phenomenon that the intense wave of sympathy Americans showed towards Poles in the fifty-year period of political oppression (1939–89) did not result in a greater interest in the music of Polish composers in the United States; Panufnik is the prime, but not the only, example of this neglect. In his second trip to the New World (in the fall of 1960), he sensed ambivalence on the part of Americans concerning the so-called "Eastern Europe problem." As a result he expressed deep disappointment in the understanding that Americans had of the dire political circumstances that existed in his native Poland.

> I found the political climate profoundly depressing, especially as I thought about my fellow countrymen back in Poland with their great faith in America's professed dedication to justice, liberty and full democracy; and the persistent hope of Poles that the greatest power in the Western world would one day come to their aid and free them from the Soviets, or at least give them some moral support in their pursuit of independence and freedom under the shared banner of Western civilization. This passionate longing of my countrymen was obviously not understood by Americans, who did not seem to me to have any concept that Polish people had a need for democracy as great as theirs.[46]

Gerard Schwarz, who has conducted more Panufnik works in the United States than any other conductor, including Stokowski (See Table 4), and is given credit for assuming the venerable maestro's role of championing the composer's works, picked up on this theme in a 1986 interview given to *New York Times* reporter Tim Page:

> Panufnik is a composer who should be better known in the United States. He has an uncanny ability to create a mood—a very intense, powerful mood—using the simplest musical means. It's clearly music of our time, but

---

[46] Andrzej Panufnik, *Composing Myself, op. cit.*, p. 282.

it looks back to Panifnuk's roots, the music of Poland, the music he grew up with, so it sounds old and new at the same time.[47]

To American audiences, Panufnik is viewed as a powerful symbol: an icon of persecution at the hands of the Nazis and Soviets. He is also seen as a tragic and courageous figure in the cultural life of the 20th century. This sympathetic view is reinforced by the spiritual and poetic qualities in his works. But, as Ted Libbey wrote in a 1988 review in the *New York Post*:

> His [Panufnik's] music comes with none of the labels that experts like to attach to the work of contemporary composers: it's simply well-crafted, approachable, imaginative, appealing and very polite. No wonder [American] audiences like it.[48]

A close study of American reviews will reveal that Panufnik is best understood and received by those who have taken the time and made the effort to get to know his music. The large-city music critics (New York, Chicago, Boston, Philadelphia and Seattle) have generally been the most sympathetic. They recognize the "Polish" influences in his works, they appreciate the musical craftsmanship, and they are intrigued among other things with the composer's continuous search for new formal solutions to express his original musical ideas. Panufnik's unique modernism, where intricate structure is the dominating presence, and in which form is bent to its limits in order to exact overpowering emotion, has received special praise in the American press. Critics have generally applauded his original, innovative musical language because is not drawn from common resources or from the "politically-correct" international avant-garde style.

But they also continually refer to the "Polish" influences in his music, which they see as always present, under the surface. For example, in five of the eight works commissioned and premiered in the United States, there is a "Polish" reference in each of them. The obvious exceptions are *Arbor Cosmica*, *Harmony* and Symphony No. 10, compositions that can be viewed as more abstract. As Nigel Osborne, a British writer has pointed out, these goals and intentions unite in the composer's seemingly obsessive identification with his native Poland:

---

[47] Quoted in: Tim Page, 'Music Today—More Than Just Another Series', *The New York Times* (September 28, 1986).

[48] Ted Libbey, 'Panufnik's Rhapsodic *Landscape*', *The New York Post* (June 25, 1988).

> There is a personal, almost animal bond with Poland which has never been broken: it is the umbilical chord of musical technique which binds Polish music to Panufnik both as a mother and as a child.[49]

Panufnik's conducting skills, which were first in evidence in the United States in 1986, when he was invited to conduct the premiere of his Bassoon Concerto in Milwaukee (Wisconsin),[50] have received substantial praise in the press. Four other major conducting engagements followed his Milwaukee debut in New York, Chicago and Seattle (he twice conducted the New York Chamber Symphony). *The New York Times* review of his first New York conducting assignment on June 23, 1988, which included four of his own works (*Landscape, Arbor Cosmica*, Bassoon Concerto, *Concertino for Timpani, Percussion and Strings*), was glowing.

> When Mr. Panufnik strode onto the stage and ascended the podium, he looked like a conductor. He bore himself with the requisite imperiousness; his technique was authoritative, and his flowing white hair and commanding profile bespoke a mighty maestro at work.[51]

His final conducting appearance in the United States took place on April 30, 1990 in Seattle, where he led the Seattle Symphony Orchestra in two of his own works, *Sinfonia Votiva* and *Nocturne*.

A fascinating aspect of Panufnik's reception is the connection some writers have made between *his* music and the broader context of composers who have come from Eastern Europe (Russia, Estonia and Poland) in the late-20th century and incorporated a new kind of spirituality in their music. John Rockwell, the *New York Times* critic, suggests that composers like Sophia Gubaidulina, Arvo Pärt, Henryk Górecki and Panufnik, though distinctive in musical language,

---

[49] Nigel Osborne, 'Panufnik at 70', *Tempo* 150 (September 1984), p. 10.

[50] A little known fact in America is Panufik's background as a conductor. He studied conducting in the 1930s in Vienna, Paris and London with one of the most distinguished conductors in the early years of the century, Felix Weingartner, who wrote: "Andrzej Panufnik took my course in conducting at the State Academy of Music during the winter of 1937–38. He is a very gifted conductor and will certainly make his way." [Quoted in the program of the New York Philharmonic, March 24, 1949.] He was appointed conductor of the Cracow and then the Warsaw Philharmonics in the late 1940s, also leading the Berlin and London Philharmonics, and then served as conductor of the City of Birmingham Symphony from 1957–1959.

[51] John Rockwell, 'Get Thee Behind Me, Podium', *The New York Times* (July 24, 1988).

nevertheless reflect a growing trend in Eastern European music over the last third of the 20th century.[52]

In one sense these works can be described as minimalist, referring to a reductive musical esthetic in which a sparing application of means serves larger emotional ends. This movement predated and is unrelated to the American school of Philip Glass, Steve Reich and John Adams. But it shares an understanding with later minimalists that repetition, where wisely employed, can be one of music's most direct paths to the soul. This special brand of minimalism is brooding, combining meditative contemplation with a lingering European angst. Against the pomp and rhetoric of conventional symphonic grandiosity, it operates in near-silent protest, an intense understatement which drowns out blustering optimism.

In the view of American writers, Panufnik's music also contains another fundamental characteristic of the late-20th century: It confounds musical orthodoxies because it is neither determinedly abstract and chromatic, in spite of the composer's protest to the contrary, nor always easily accessible—the two principal opposing modes of Western composition of our time. Instead, it has its roots not only in older religious traditions but also in the sound-color experiments of the music of Szymanowski and early post-World War I developments in Poland. But as Bernard Jacobson wrote in 1996:

> Panufnik's music never sounds remotely like that of any of those foreunners or colleagues, for each of these resources and methods is used in an entirely individual way, and in the furtherance of an entirely personal artistic vision.[53]

A final unifying factor in Panufnik's art is a determined opposition to Communist political and esthetic orthodoxies by insisting on musical forms and spiritual beliefs directly antagonistic to official doctrines (i.e. "Soviet Realism"). We must not forget that a mere seven years before Panufnik's defection to the West, Poles were experiencing the most repressive period of "Socialist Realism." We now know that two years after Panufnik's defection significant changes took place in Poland that opened the flood-gates to unbridled experimentation and freedom for the artist. One can only speculate

---

[52] John Rockwell, 'East Europe Rethinks Music, Too', *The New York Times* (November 25, 1990.

[53] Quoted from: Bernard Jacobson, *A Polish Renaissance* (London: Phaidon Press, 1996), p. 131–32.

what Panufnik might have accomplished had he chosen to remain and compose in this less restrictive artistic environment.

But the persistent references to "Polish subjects" in Panufnik's music suggests that political repression can encourage the very thing censors hope to discourage. And it makes one wonder, now that political circumstances in Eastern Europe have changed so dramatically, whether the continued composition of this music can endure. On the surface its future seems bright. Already this movement is a welcome alternative for composers discouraged by hyper-elitist music, and the easy pandering of neo-Romanticism. Even now, one can rest reasonably sure that these works will count for future historians as a crucially important legacy of late-20th century composition. *New York Times* critic John Rockwell picked up on this theme in 1990 when he wrote:

> Andrzej Panufnik may hardly be a household name in the United States, but his music is very likely to appeal to mainstream classical-music audiences in centuries to come.[54]

---

[54] John Rockwell, 'Panufnik Conducts His Music', *The New York Times* (June 25, 1988).

Table 1.
Andrzej Panufnik's thirteen visits to the United States

Date	Location	Purpose of the trip
February 1955	Detroit	Attended the United States premiere of *Tragic Overture* and *Symphony of Peace*
Fall 1960	New York	An extended stay in the U. S.
April 1962	Newark (New Jersey)	Attended the performance of *Polonia* with the Newark Pops
December 1966	New York	Attended the New York premiere of *Sinfonia Sacra*
May 1970	New York	Attended the world premiere of *Universal Prayer*
January 1982	Boston	Attended the world premiere of *Sinfonia Votiva*
November 1982	Chicago	Attended the performance of *Sinfonia Sacra* with the Chicago Symphony
November 1984	New York	Attended the world premiere of *Arbor Cosmica* in New York and US premiere of the Violin Concerto in Princeton
May 1986	Milwaukee	Conducted the world premiere of the Bassoon Concerto with the Milwaukee Chamber Orchestra
June 1988	New York	Made his New York conducting debut with the New York Chamber Symphony [*Landscape, Arbor Cosmica*, Bassoon Concerto, *Concertino*]
December 1989	New York	Conducted the New York Chamber Symphony in the world premiere of *Harmony* as well as the Violin Concerto
Jan/Feb 1990	Chicago	Conducted the Chicago Symphony in the world premiere Symphony No. 10 as well as the Violin Concerto
April/May 1990	Seattle	Conducted the Seattle Symphony

Table 2.
Panufnik's works most often performed
in the United States (3 or more)

Work	Times performed
Sinfonia Sacra	46
Symphony No. 10	23*
Concertino for percussion and strings	13
Violin Concerto	13
Bassoon Concerto	12
Tragic Overture	12
Nocturne	10
Autumn Music	8
Arbor Cosmica	8
Old Polish Suite	6
Heroic Overture	5
Sinfonia Votiva	7
Harmony	6
Homage à Chopin	4
Jagiellonian Triptych	3
Piano Concerto	3
Piano Trio	3
Universal Prayer	3

* Includes performances presented by the National Philharmonic (formerly Warsaw Philharmonic) on the 1993 tour of the eastern United States.

Table 3.
Panufnik Works Commissioned in the United States

Work (Year)	Commissioner	Dedication
Sinfonia Elegiaca (1957; rev. 1966)	Houston Symphony Orchestra	The Victims of World War II
Sinfonia Sacra (1963)	Kościuszko Foundation, Inc. (With the help of Leopold Stokowski)	Tribute to Poland's Millennium of Christianity and Statehood
Katyń Epitaph (1968)	American Symphony Orchestra	To the memory of 15,000 defenseless Polish prisoners of war murdered in Russia
[*Universal Prayer*] (1968–69)	Premiered by Stokowski	Not commissioned
Sinfonia Votiva (1982)	Boston Symphony Orchestra and supported in part by a generous grant from the Massachusetts Council on the Arts and Humanities	The Black Madonna of Czestochowa
Arbor Cosmica (1984)	Koussevitsky Foundation for the Music Today Players	To the memory of Serge and Natalie Koussevitzky
Bassoon Concerto (1986)	Polanki Polish Society of Milwaukee for the Milwaukee Chamber Orchestra	To the memory of the Polish martyr, Father Jerzy Popiełuszko
Harmony (1989)	92nd Street Y for the New York Chamber Orchestra	Camilla Panufnik
Symphony No. 10 (1988, rev 1990)	Sir Georg Solti and the Chicago Symphony Orchestra	The CSO's Centenary Year (1990)

Table 4.
Most influential conductors
in Panufnik's reception in the U. S.

Conductor	Number of times conducted a Panufnik work
Gerard Schwarz	25
Andrzej Panufnik	22
Kazimierz Kord*	17
Leopold Stokowski	16
William Smith	8
Stanislaw Skrowaczewski	7
Gilbert Levine	5
Seiji Ozawa	4
Georg Solti	3

* Kazimierz Kord conducted *Symphony No. 10* in a seventeen city American tour with the National Philharmonic (formerly Warsaw Philharmonic). The tour began October 27 and ended on November 21, 1993. It covered the eastern half of the country, culminating in a Carnegie Hall performance on November 19, 1993.

Index of Names

Index of Panufnik's Works

Notes on the Authors

Beata Bolesławska graduated in musicology at the University of Warsaw. She is the author of the monograph *Panufnik* (Kraków: PWM 2001). Since 1997 she has been working by the organisation of the International Festival of Contemporary Music "Warsaw Autumn". Currently she makes the post-graduated studies with Prof. Adrian Thomas at Cardiff University, preparing a doctoral thesis about the symphonies in Polish music after Second World War.

Bernard Jacobson, music critic and poet, is currently a contributing Editor of Fanfare Magazine, a member of the Board of Directors of Theodore Presser Co. music publishers, and programme annotator for the chamber Orchestra of Philadelphia. He has spent periods as music critic of the Chicago Dailly News, visiting professor of music at Roosevelt University in Chicago, director of Southern Arts in Winchester, England, promotion director of Boosey & Hawkes Music Publishers, programme annotator and musicologist for the Philadelphia Orchestra, artistic director of the Residentie Orkest in The Hague, and artistic adviser to the North Netherlands Orchestra. His publications include among others a book about Panufnik, Lutosławski, Penderecki and Górecki, entitled *A Polish Renaissance* (London: Phaidon Press 1996). His poetry has been set to music by the American composer Richard Wernick and the Englishman Wilfred Josephs.

Alicja Jarzębska is Professor at the Institute of Musicology at the Jagellonian University in Kraków and director of this Institute. In the centre of her scholarly interests are music theory of 18th–20th century, methods of analysis of a musical work and history and aesthetics of 20th-century music. She published many entries in *Encyklopedia Muzyczna PWM* and in *Encyclopedia Britannica*, articles in Polish and foreign journals and books (for example *Studies on Penderecki*, Princeton, New Jersey 2002) and 3 books: *Idee relacji serialnych w muzyce XX wieku* (Ideas of Serial Relations in 20th-Century Music) (Kraków: Musica Iagellonica 1995), *Strawiński. Myśli i muzyka* (Stravinsky. Ideas and Music) (Kraków: Musica Iagellonica 2001) and *Z dziejów myśli o muzyce* (History of Ideas in Music) (Kraków: Musica Iagellonica 2002).

Violetta Kostka is Assistant Professor at the Accademy of Music in Gdańsk. She is the author of doctoral thesis on songs by 20th-century Polish composers (unpublished) and several articles on 20th-century music.

Alina Królak graduated in music theory at the Academy of Music in Bydgoszcz. She is the author of M.A. thesis on solo concertos of Panufnik.

Niall O'Loughlin is Senior Lecturer in Music and Director of the Arts Centre of Loughborough University, in the United Kingdom. He is an English musicologist with a long-standing interest in the 20th-century music of Central Europe, especially Slovenia, Austria and Poland. He has contributed extensively to *The New Grove Dictionary of Music and Musicians*, *The New Grove Dictionary of Musical Instruments* and to the series *Slovenski glasbeni dnevi* (Slovenian Music Days). His book *Novejsa glasba w Sloveniji* (New Music in Slovenia) was published in 2000.

Jadwiga Paja-Stach is Professor at the Institute of Musicology at the Jagellonian University in Kraków. She is vice-director of this Institute and a head of the Department of New Music. Among her interests are mainly methods of analysis of a musical work and history of the 20th-century music. She is the author of 4 books: *Dzieła otwarte w twórczości kompozytorów polskich XX wieku* (Open Works in the Music of 20th-Century Composers) (Kraków: Wydawnictwo Uniwersytetu Jagiellońskiego 1992), *Lutosławski* (Kraków: Musica Iagellonica 1996), *Lutosławski i jego styl muzyczny* (Lutosławski and his Musical Style) (Kraków: Musica Iagellonica 1997), *Twórczość Willema Pijpera w kontekście muzyki XX wieku / The Work of Willem Pijper in the Context of Twentieth Century Music* (Kraków: Musica Iagellonica 2002).

Camilla Panufnik married to Sir Andrzej Panufnik 1963–91. Born 1937 in Kent, England. Educated in English boarding school, in India and at the Sorbonne, Paris. Worked in London, in the USA and with Algerian refuges in Morocco. Since 1958, photographer and writer of photo-features for leading British newspapers such as *The Times*, *Times Educational Supplement* and *Guardian*. As photographer, specialising in arts subjects and in fund-raising photography for children in need. Elected Fellow of the Royal Photographic Society (1967). Exhibitions in leading venues in London, New York, Warsaw, Paris, etc.; 27 books published in several languages, mostly psychological/educational, all with her own photographs and written text; about The Royal Ballet School, children in hospital, disabled children, etc.
Currently is member of the Rada Artystyczna Teatru Wielkiego—Opery Narodowej in Warsaw, Governor of Sadler's Wells Theatre, member of Advisory Boards of London Symphony Orchestra, LSO Education, London Musici, Park Lane Group for Young Musicians, Trustee of Richmond Music Trust (for schools); also promoting Polish music in London and assisting many other British arts and charitable causes. She is now preparing the Panufnik archive and the Panufnik website. She has two children, both composers, Roxanna (opera, Mass, harp concerto, etc.) and Jem ('breakbeat' music DJ and graphic artist).

Piotr Papla graduated in musicology at the Jagiellonian University. He wrote M.A. thesis on Stefan Kisielewski's orchestral music. His current project includes a doctoral thesis on Pendrecki's concertos.

Anna Piotrowska graduated in musicology at the Jagiellonian University. She wrote a doctoral dissertation on the idea of national music in the concepts of the 20th-century American composers (2002).

Charles Bodman Rae is a composer and pianist. He is currently Elder Professor of Music and Director of the Elder Conservatorium of Music at the University of Adelaide, Australia. He was previously Director of Studies at the Royal Northern College of Music in Manchester, and Head of School of Composition at Leeds College of Music. His monograph *The music of Lutoslawski* has been published in English (London 1994) and Polish (*Muzyka Lutosławskiego*, Warszawa: PWN 1996) and is now its third edition.

Ewa Siemdaj is Assistant Professor at the Accademy of Music in Cracow. She wrote a doctoral dissertation entitled on the symphonic works by Andrzej Panufnik (*Poetyka twórczości symfonicznej Andrzeja Panufnika*, Kraków: Akademia Muzyczna w Krakowic 2002, published as: *Andrzej Panufnik. Twórczość symfoniczna* (Andrzej Panufnik. The Symphonic Oeuvre), Kraków: Academy of Music, 2003). She published several articles on 20th-century music.

Andrzej Sitarz is Research Fellow at the Institute of Musicology, Jagiellonian University, Kraków. The most important sphere of his interest is Polish late 18th- and 19th-century music. He has edited Feliks Janiewicz's *Complete Works* (in three volumes—1st: 1996, 2nd: 1998, 3rd: in print) and is a co-editor and member of the Editorial Committee of Ignacy Jan Paderewski's *Complete Works* (8 of 12 volumes published since 1997). Since 1993 he is also a deputy manager of Musica Iagellonica publishers.

Renata Suchowiejko is Assistant Professor at the Institute of Musicology at the Jagiellonian University in Kraków. The French music of the turn of the 19th century and 19th-century Polish music is in the centre of her scientific interest. She wrote PhD thesis *Issues of Style in the Sonatas for Violin and Piano of Cesar Franck and his Pupils* (1997). She published the critical edition of the manuscript of Maria Szymanowska, entitled *Album musical Marii Szymanowskiej / Album musical de Maria Szymanowska* (Kraków: Musica Iagellonica 1999). Currently she is making a research on Henryk Wieniawski and his works in the context of violin music of the 19th century.

Zbigniew Skowron is Professor at the Institute of Musicology, University of Warsaw. He graduated in Polish philology and musicology at the University of Warsaw, and in music theory at the Academy of Music in Warsaw. In 1987–8 he studied with Leonard B. Meyer at the University of Pensylvania on an American Council of

Learned Societies fellowship. Among his scholarly interests are aesthetic and historical aspects of 20th-century music, history of musical aesthetics, and Chopin's biography. He is the author of two books: *Teoria i estetyka awangardy muzycznej* (Theory and Aesthetics of the Musical Avant-Garde) (Warszawa: Wydawnictwa Uniwersytetu Warszawskiego 1989) and *Nowa muzyka amerykańska* (Modern American Music) (Kraków: Musica Iagellonica 1995). He is also the editor of *Lutosławski Studies* (Oxford University Press 2001) and the editor-in-chief of *Przegląd Muzykologiczny* (Musicological Review)—a yearbook of the Institue of Musicology, University of Warsaw.

Adrian Thomas is Professor of Music at Cardiff University in Wales. He was educated at the University of Nottingham, Cardiff, and Belfast as well as studying composition at the Music Academy in Kraków. In 1990–3 he was Head of Music at BBC Radio 3 in London, where he initiated the 'Polska!' festival of Polish music and culture in 1993. He is the author of numerous articles on Polish music and of two monographs: *Grażyna Bacewicz: Chamber and Orchestral Music* (Los Angeles, 1985) and *Górecki* (Oxford University Press 1997, in Polish Kraków 1998). His survey of Polish music since the death of Szymanowski will be published by Cambridge University Press in 2003. He is also currently working on a monograph on Lutosławski's Cello Concerto.

Programme of the Conference
International Musicological Conference.
Andrzej Panufnik's Music and its Reception
Conference under the patronage of Teresa Starmach, Vice-President of the City of Cracow
Cracow 23–25 November 2001
Aula of Academy of Music "Florianka"
Basztowa Street, 8

23.11.2001.
10.00

Welcome speech by Director of the Institute of Musicology UJ Zofia Fabiańska

Speech by Vice-President of the City of Cracow Teresa Starmach

Session No. 1. Chair: Jadwiga Paja-Stach

Camilla Panufnik (London): Andrzej Panufnik's life style and ethos of work

Zbigniew Skowron (Warsaw): Andrzej Panufnik's artistic attitude and his aesthetics

Alicja Jarzębska (Cracow): Time organization in Panufnik's music

Beata Bolesławska (Warsaw): Symmetry in Panufnik's symphonies

***

14.30. Session No. 2. Chair: Adrian Thomas

Niall O'Loughlin (Loughborough): Feeling and intellect in Panufnik's symphonies

Charles Bodman Rae (Adelaide): The role of the major-minor chord in Panufnik's compositional technique

Martina Homma (Köln): Balancing precomposition, inspiration and rigour in the late symphonies by Panufnik

Bernard Jacobson (Philadelphia): Panufnik's music in the context of 20th-century music

24.11.2001.
10.00. Session No. 3. Chair: Zbigniew Skowron

Ewa Siemdaj (Cracow): Panufnik's symphonies. The evolution of the composer's style

Alina Królak (Inowrocław): Pitch organization in Panufnik's concertos

Renata Suchowiejko (Cracow): The role of the pitch-cells in Panufnik's String Quartet No. 3

Jadwiga Paja-Stach (Cracow): Panufnik's piano pieces. Structures and timbres

***

16.00. Concert of Panufnik's piano pieces

Reflections — Stanisław Bromboszcz (first performance in Poland)

Pentasonata — Joanna Ejsmont

Krąg kwintowy — Gabriela Szendzielorz-Jungiewicz

25.11.2001.
10.00. Session No. 4. Chair: Alicja Jarzębska

Piotr Papla (Cracow): Reception of Panufnik's early music in Poland

Violetta Kostka (Gdańsk): Reception of Panufnik's music in Great Britain

Adrian Thomas (Cardiff): In the public eye: Panufnik and his music, 1948–54

Ray Robinson (Palm Beach): Andrzej Panufnik's reception in the United States

***

14.30. Session No. 5. Chair: Martina Homma

Anna Piotrowska (Cracow): Andrzej Panufnik—national identity of the immigrant composer

Andrzej Sitarz (Cracow): Old Polish music as adapted by Andrzej Pnufnik

Participants in the International Musicological Conference "Andrzej Panufnik's Music and its Reception": Violetta Kostka, Bernard Jacobson, Martina Homma, Andrzej Sitarz, Camilla Panufnik, Piotr Papla, Jadwiga Paja-Stach, Adrian Thomas, Alicja Jarzębska, Alina Królak, Ewa Siemdaj, Niall O'Loughlin, Beata Bolesławska, Ray Robinson
Cracow, November 25, 2001, Aula of Academy of Music "Florianka"

Uniwersytet Jagielloński
Zakład Poligraficzny
31-110 Kraków, ul. Czapskich 4